Nutshell Series

of

WEST PUBLISHING COMPANY

P.O. Box 3526

St. Paul, Minnesota 55165

April, 1981

I

NUTSHELL SERIES

Constitutional Analysis, 1979, 388 pages, by Jerre S. Williams, former Professor of Law, University of Texas.

Constitutional Power—Federal and State, 1974, 411 pages, by David E. Engdahl, Adjunct Professor of Law, University of Denver.

Consumer Law, 2nd Ed., 1981, 418 pages, by David G. Epstein, Dean and Professor of Law, University of Arkansas and Steve H. Nickles, Professor of Law, University of Arkansas.

Contracts, 1975, 307 pages, by Gordon D. Schaber, Dean and Professor of Law, McGeorge School of Law and Claude D. Rohwer, Professor of Law, McGeorge School of Law.

Corporations—Law of, 1980, 379 pages, by Robert W. Hamilton, Professor of Law, University of Texas.

Corrections and Prisoners' Rights—Law of, 1976, 353 pages, by Sheldon Krantz, Professor of Law, Boston University.

Criminal Law, 1975, 302 pages, by Arnold H. Loewy, Professor of Law, University of North Carolina.

Criminal Procedure—Constitutional Limitations, 3rd Ed., 1980, 438 pages, by Jerold H. Israel, Professor of Law, University of Michigan and Wayne R. LaFave, Professor of Law, University of Illinois.

Debtor-Creditor Law, 2nd Ed., 1980, 324 pages, by David G. Epstein, Dean and Professor of Law, University of Arkansas.

Employment Discrimination—Federal Law of, 2nd Ed., 1981, 402 pages, by Mack A. Player, Professor of Law, University of Georgia.

II

NUTSHELL SERIES

Estate Planning—Introduction to, 2nd Ed., 1978, 378 pages, by Robert J. Lynn, Professor of Law, Ohio State University.

Evidence, 2nd Ed., (May, 1981), approx. 450 pages, by Paul F. Rothstein, Professor of Law, Georgetown University.

Family Law, 1977, 400 pages, by Harry D. Krause, Professor of Law, University of Illinois.

Federal Estate and Gift Taxation, 2nd Ed., 1979, 488 pages, by John K. McNulty, Professor of Law, University of California, Berkeley.

Federal Income Taxation of Individuals, 2nd Ed., 1978, 422 pages, by John K. McNulty, Professor of Law, University of California, Berkeley.

Federal Income Taxation of Corporations and Stockholders, 2nd Ed., 1981, 362 pages, by Jonathan Sobeloff, Late Professor of Law, Georgetown University and Peter P. Weidenbruch, Jr., Professor of Law, Georgetown University.

Federal Jurisdiction, 2nd Ed., 1981, approx. 258 pages, by David P. Currie, Professor of Law, University of Chicago.

Federal Rules of Evidence, 1981, 428 pages, by Michael H. Graham, Professor of Law, University of Illinois.

Future Interests, 1981, 361 pages, by Lawrence W. Waggoner, Professor of Law, University of Michigan.

Government Contracts, 1979, 423 pages, by W. Noel Keyes, Professor of Law, Pepperdine University.

Historical Introduction to Anglo-American Law, 2nd Ed., 1973, 280 pages, by Frederick G. Kempin, Jr., Professor of Business Law, Wharton School of Finance and Commerce, University of Pennsylvania.

NUTSHELL SERIES

Injunctions, 1974, 264 pages, by John F. Dobbyn, Professor of Law, Villanova University.

International Business Transactions, 1981, 393 pages, by Donald T. Wilson, Professor of Law, Loyola University, Los Angeles.

Judicial Process, 1980, 292 pages, by William L. Reynolds, Professor of Law, University of Maryland.

Jurisdiction, 4th Ed., 1980, 232 pages, by Albert A. Ehrenzweig, Late Professor of Law, University of California, Berkeley, David W. Louisell, Late Professor of Law, University of California, Berkeley and Geoffrey C. Hazard, Jr., Professor of Law, Yale Law School.

Juvenile Courts, 2nd Ed., 1977, 275 pages, by Sanford J. Fox, Professor of Law, Boston College.

Labor Arbitration Law and Practice, 1979, 358 pages, by Dennis R. Nolan, Professor of Law, University of South Carolina.

Labor Law, 1979, 403 pages, by Douglas L. Leslie, Professor of Law, University of Virginia.

Land Use, 1978, 316 pages, by Robert R. Wright, Professor of Law, University of Arkansas, Little Rock and Susan Webber, Professor of Law, University of Arkansas, Little Rock.

Landlord and Tenant Law, 1979, 319 pages, by David S. Hill, Professor of Law, University of Colorado.

Law Study and Law Examinations—Introduction to, 1971, 389 pages, by Stanley V. Kinyon, Late Professor of Law, University of Minnesota.

Legal Interviewing and Counseling, 1976, 353 pages, by Thomas L. Shaffer, Professor of Law, Washington and Lee University.

NUTSHELL SERIES

Legal Research, 3rd Ed., 1978, 415 pages, by Morris L. Cohen, Professor of Law and Law Librarian, Harvard University.

Legislative Law and Process, 1975, 279 pages, by Jack Davies, Professor of Law, William Mitchell College of Law.

Local Government Law, 1975, 386 pages, by David J. McCarthy, Jr., Dean and Professor of Law, Georgetown University.

Mass Communications Law, 1977, 431 pages, by Harvey L. Zuckman, Professor of Law, Catholic University and Martin J. Gaynes, Lecturer in Law, Temple University.

Medical Malpractice—The Law of, 1977, 340 pages, by Joseph H. King, Professor of Law, University of Tennessee.

Military Law, 1980, 378 pages, by Charles A. Shanor, Professor of Law, Emory University and Timothy P. Terrell, Professor of Law, Emory University.

Post-Conviction Remedies, 1978, 360 pages, by Robert Popper, Professor of Law, University of Missouri, Kansas City.

Presidential Power, 1977, 328 pages, by Arthur Selwyn Miller, Professor of Law Emeritus, George Washington University.

Procedure Before Trial, 1972, 258 pages, by Delmar Karlen, Professor of Law, College of William and Mary.

Products Liability, 2nd Ed., 1981, 341 pages, by Dix W. Noel, Late Professor of Law, University of Tennessee and Jerry J. Phillips, Professor of Law, University of Tennessee.

NUTSHELL SERIES

Professional Responsibility, 1980, 399 pages, by Robert H. Aronson, Professor of Law, University of Washington, and Donald T. Weckstein, Dean and Professor of Law, University of San Diego.

Real Estate Finance, 1979, 292 pages, by Jon W. Bruce, Professor of Law, Stetson University.

Real Property, 1975, 425 pages, by Roger H. Bernhardt, Professor of Law, Golden Gate University.

Remedies, 1977, 364 pages, by John F. O'Connell, Professor of Law, Western State University College of Law, Fullerton.

Res Judicata, 1976, 310 pages, by Robert C. Casad, Professor of Law, University of Kansas.

Sales, 2nd Ed., 1981, 370 pages, by John M. Stockton, Professor of Business Law, Wharton School of Finance and Commerce, University of Pennsylvania.

Secured Transactions, 2nd Ed., (July, 1981), approx. 380 pages, by Henry J. Bailey, Professor of Law, Willamette University.

Securities Regulation, 1978, 300 pages, by David L. Ratner, Professor of Law, Cornell University.

Titles—The Calculus of Interests, 1968, 277 pages, by Oval A. Phipps, Late Professor of Law, St. Louis University.

Torts—Injuries to Persons and Property, 1977, 434 pages by Edward J. Kionka, Professor of Law, Southern Illinois University.

Torts—Injuries to Family, Social and Trade Relations, 1979, 358 pages, by Wex S. Malone, Professor of Law Emeritus, Louisiana State University.

NUTSHELL SERIES

Trial Advocacy, 1979, 402 pages, by Paul B. Bergman, Adj. Professor of Law, University of California, Los Angeles.

Trial and Practice Skills, 1978, 346 pages, by Kenney F. Hegland, Professor of Law, University of Arizona.

Uniform Commercial Code, 1975, 507 pages, by Bradford Stone, Professor of Law, Detroit College of Law.

Uniform Probate Code, 1978, 425 pages, by Lawrence H. Averill, Jr., Professor of Law, University of Wyoming.

Welfare Law—Structure and Entitlement, 1979, 455 pages, by Arthur B. LaFrance, Professor of Law, University of Maine.

Wills and Trusts, 1979, 392 pages, by Robert L. Mennell, Professor of Law, Hamline University.

Hornbook Series

and

Basic Legal Texts

of

WEST PUBLISHING COMPANY

P.O. Box 3526

St. Paul, Minnesota 55165

April, 1981

———

Administrative Law, Davis' Text on, 3rd Ed., 1972, 617 pages, by Kenneth Culp Davis, Professor of Law, University of San Diego.

Agency, Seavey's Hornbook on, 1964, 329 pages, by Warren A. Seavey, Late Professor of Law, Harvard University.

Agency and Partnership, Reuschlein & Gregory's Hornbook on the Law of, 1979 with 1981 Pocket Part, 625 pages, by Harold Gill Reuschlein, Professor of Law, St. Mary's University and William A. Gregory, Professor of Law, Southern Illinois University.

Antitrust, Sullivan's Handbook of the Law of, 1977, 886 pages, by Lawrence A. Sullivan, Professor of Law, University of California, Berkeley.

Child and the Law—The, Gottesman, (June, 1981), approx. 235 pages, by Roberta Gottesman, Washington, DC.

Common Law Pleading, Koffler and Reppy's Hornbook on, 1969, 663 pages, by Joseph H. Koffler, Professor of Law, New York Law School and Alison Reppy, Late Dean and Professor of Law, New York Law School.

Common Law Pleading, Shipman's Hornbook on, 3rd Ed., 1923, 644 pages, by Henry W. Ballantine, Late Professor of Law, University of California, Berkeley.

Constitutional Law, Nowak, Rotunda and Young's Hornbook on, 1978 with 1979 Pocket Part, 974 pages, by John E. Nowak, Professor of Law, University of Illinois, Ronald D. Rotunda, Professor of Law, University of Illinois, and J. Nelson Young, Professor of Law, University of Illinois.

Contracts, Calamari and Perillo's Hornbook on, 2nd Ed., 1977, 878 pages, by John D. Calamari, Professor of Law, Fordham University and Joseph M. Perillo, Professor of Law, Fordham University.

Contracts, Corbin's One Volume Student Ed., 1952, 1224 pages, by Arthur L. Corbin, Late Professor of Law, Yale University.

Contracts, Simpson's Hornbook on, 2nd Ed., 1965, 510 pages, by Laurence P. Simpson, Professor of Law Emeritus, New York University.

Corporate Taxation, Kahn's Hornbook on Basic, 3rd Ed., 1981, 614 pages, by Douglas A. Kahn, Professor of Law, University of Michigan.

Corporations, Henn's Hornbook on, 2nd Ed., 1970, 956 pages, by Harry G. Henn, Professor of Law, Cornell University.

Criminal Law, LaFave and Scott's Hornbook on, 1972, 763 pages, by Wayne R. LaFave, Professor of Law, University of Illinois, and Austin Scott, Jr., Late Professor of Law, University of Colorado.

HORNBOOKS & BASIC TEXTS

Damages, McCormick's Hornbook on, 1935, 811 pages, by Charles T. McCormick, Late Dean and Professor of Law, University of Texas.

Domestic Relations, Clark's Hornbook on, 1968, 754 pages, by Homer H. Clark, Jr., Professor of Law, University of Colorado.

Environmental Law, Rodgers' Hornbook on, 1977, 956 pages, by William H. Rodgers, Jr., Professor of Law, University of Washington.

Equity, McClintock's Hornbook on, 2nd Ed., 1948, 643 pages, by Henry L. McClintock, Late Professor of Law, University of Minnesota.

Estate and Gift Taxes, Lowndes, Kramer and McCord's Hornbook on, 3rd Ed., 1974, 1099 pages, by Charles L. B. Lowndes, Late Professor of Law, Duke University, Robert Kramer, Professor of Law Emeritus, George Washington University, and John H. McCord, Professor of Law, University of Illinois.

Evidence, Lilly's Introduction to, 1978, 486 pages, by Graham C. Lilly, Professor of Law, University of Virginia.

Evidence, McCormick's Hornbook on, 2nd Ed., 1972 with 1978 Pocket Part, 938 pages, General Editor, Edward W. Cleary, Professor of Law Emeritus, Arizona State University.

Federal Courts, Wright's Hornbook on, 3rd Ed., 1976, 818 pages, including Federal Rules Appendix, by Charles Alan Wright, Professor of Law, University of Texas.

Future Interest, Simes' Hornbook on, 2nd Ed., 1966, 355 pages, by Lewis M. Simes, Late Professor of Law, University of Michigan.

HORNBOOKS & BASIC TEXTS

Income Taxation, Chommie's Hornbook on, 2nd Ed., 1973, 1051 pages, by John C. Chommie, Late Professor of Law, University of Miami.

Insurance, Keeton's Basic Text on, 1971, 712 pages, by Robert E. Keeton, former Professor of Law, Harvard University.

Insurance, Keeton's Case Supplement to Basic Text, 1978, 334 pages, by Robert E. Keeton, former Professor of Law, Harvard University.

Labor Law, Gorman's Basic Text on, 1976, 914 pages, by Robert A. Gorman, Professor of Law, University of Pennsylvania.

Law of the Poor, LaFrance, Schroeder, Bennett and Boyd's Hornbook on, 1973, 558 pages, by Arthur B. LaFrance, Professor of Law, University of Maine, Milton R. Schroeder, Professor of Law, Arizona State University, Robert W. Bennett, Professor of Law, Northwestern University and William E. Boyd, Professor of Law, University of Arizona.

Law Problems, Ballentine's, 5th Ed., 1975, 767 pages, General Editor, William E. Burby, Professor of Law Emeritus, University of Southern California.

Legal Writing Style, Weihofen's, 2nd Ed., 1980, 332 pages, by Henry Weihofen, Professor of Law Emeritus, University of New Mexico.

New York Practice, Siegel's Hornbook on, 1978, with 1979–80 Pocket Part, 1011 pages, by David D. Siegel, Professor of Law, Albany Law School of Union University.

Oil and Gas, Hemingway's Hornbook on, 1971 with 1979 Pocket Part, 486 pages, by Richard W. Hemingway, Professor of Law, Texas Tech University.

HORNBOOKS & BASIC TEXTS

Partnership, Crane and Bromberg's Hornbook on, 1968, 695 pages, by Alan R. Bromberg, Professor of Law, Southern Methodist University.

Property, Boyer's Survey of, 3rd Ed., 1981, 766 pages, by Ralph E. Boyer, Professor of Law, University of Miami.

Real Estate Finance Law, Osborne, Nelson and Whitman's Hornbook on, (successor to Hornbook on Mortgages), 1979, 885 pages, by George E. Osborne, Late Professor of Law, Stanford University, Grant S. Nelson, Professor of Law, University of Missouri, Columbia and Dale A. Whitman, Professor of Law, University of Washington.

Real Property, Burby's Hornbook on, 3rd Ed., 1965, 490 pages, by William E. Burby, Professor of Law Emeritus, University of Southern California.

Real Property, Moynihan's Introduction to, 1962, 254 pages, by Cornelius J. Moynihan, Professor of Law, Suffolk University.

Remedies, Dobbs' Hornbook on, 1973, 1067 pages, by Dan B. Dobbs, Professor of Law, University of Arizona.

Sales, Nordstrom's Hornbook on, 1970, 600 pages, by Robert J. Nordstrom, former Professor of Law, Ohio State University.

Secured Transactions under the U.C.C., Henson's Hornbook on, 2nd Ed., 1979, with 1979 Pocket Part, 504 pages, by Ray D. Henson, Professor of Law, University of California, Hastings College of the Law.

Torts, Prosser's Hornbook on, 4th Ed., 1971, 1208 pages, by William L. Prosser, Late Dean and Professor of Law, University of California, Berkeley.

Trusts, Bogert's Hornbook on, 5th Ed., 1973, 726 pages, by George G. Bogert, Late Professor of Law, University of Chicago and George T. Bogert, Attorney, Chicago, Illinois.

Urban Planning and Land Development Control, Hagman's Hornbook on, 1971, 706 pages, by Donald G. Hagman, Professor of Law, University of California, Los Angeles.

Uniform Commercial Code, White and Summers' Hornbook on, 2nd Ed., 1980, 1250 pages, by James J. White, Professor of Law, University of Michigan and Robert S. Summers, Professor of Law, Cornell University.

Wills, Atkinson's Hornbook on, 2nd Ed., 1953, 975 pages, by Thomas E. Atkinson, Late Professor of Law, New York University.

Advisory Board

FEDERAL
INCOME TAXATION
OF
CORPORATIONS
AND
STOCKHOLDERS
IN A NUTSHELL

By

JONATHAN SOBELOFF
Late Professor of Law
Georgetown University Law Center

and

PETER P. WEIDENBRUCH, JR.
Dwan Professor of Taxation
Georgetown University Law Center

SECOND EDITION

ST. PAUL, MINN.
WEST PUBLISHING CO.
1981

Library of Congress Cataloging in Publication Data

Sobeloff, Jonathan.
    Federal income taxation.

    (Nutshell series)
    Bibliography: p.
    Includes index.
    1. Corporations—Taxation—United States.
I. Weidenbruch, Peter P., Jr., 1929–   joint author.
II. Title.
KF6465.S58   1981   343.7305'267   80-39834

ISBN 0-8299-2122-2

S. & W. Fed.Inc.Tax Corp. & Stock
1st Reprint—1981

PREFACE TO THE SECOND EDITION

Jonathan Sobeloff should have written this preface, for this book is almost totally his work product. Tragically stricken by illness in the very prime of his life, Jon left us this work as a continuing testimonial to his remarkable mastery of the law and his enviable clarity of thought and expression. His was a seldom encountered talent for piercing through the complexities and subtleties of highly technical material, distilling its essence, and presenting it to his reader in lucid, logical form. Subchapter C was ideal grist for Jon's mill.

My contribution to Jon's work was simply to update it to reflect pertinent legislative, administrative and judicial developments occurring subsequent to the publication of the first edition. It has been truly a privilege to have played even this small part in carrying forward the torch of enlightenment that Jon was prematurely called upon to lay aside.

PETER P. WEIDENBRUCH, JR.

Washington, D. C.
December, 1980

*

SUMMARY OF CONTENTS

*

OUTLINE

OUTLINE

OUTLINE

OUTLINE

TABLE OF AUTHORITIES CITED

CASES

(References are to Pages)

TABLE OF AUTHORITIES CITED

TABLE OF AUTHORITIES CITED

TABLE OF AUTHORITIES CITED

TABLE OF AUTHORITIES CITED

INTERNAL REVENUE CODE

(26 U.S.C.A.)

XXXV

TABLE OF AUTHORITIES CITED

XXXVI

TABLE OF AUTHORITIES CITED

TABLE OF AUTHORITIES CITED

TABLE OF AUTHORITIES CITED

TABLE OF AUTHORITIES CITED

TABLE OF AUTHORITIES CITED

TABLE OF AUTHORITIES CITED

TABLE OF AUTHORITIES CITED

TABLE OF AUTHORITIES CITED

XLV

TABLE OF AUTHORITIES CITED

TABLE OF AUTHORITIES CITED

TABLE OF AUTHORITIES CITED

TABLE OF AUTHORITIES CITED

TABLE OF AUTHORITIES CITED

L

TABLE OF AUTHORITIES CITED

PROPOSED REGULATIONS

REVENUE PROCEDURES

TABLE OF AUTHORITIES CITED

REVENUE RULINGS

TABLE OF AUTHORITIES CITED

TABLE OF AUTHORITIES CITED

FEDERAL INCOME TAXATION
of CORPORATIONS and
STOCKHOLDERS

CHAPTER 1

INTRODUCTION

Table of Sections

§ 1. Scope

This book is designed to help the law student taking a course in federal corporate income taxation. It may be used as a supplement to an assigned casebook or text, or as a course text itself. It could be read during the course and also or instead in preparation for the final exam. It is hoped that the book will also be useful to practitioners, especially newer or general practitioners of law or accounting, but also experienced and specialized practitioners, who want a general text on the various parts of this complex area.

The reader should have available a current Internal Revenue Code of 1954 ("Code") and Income Tax Regulations ("Regs") to refer to in connection with the text. Looking at Code and Regs as cited is recommended.

Citations with only a section number (e. g., § 11) are Code sections; Regs are cited, e. g., "Regs. § 1.11–1(a)".

As background, the reader should have some familiarity with the material covered in a basic federal income tax course.

§ 2. Organization of the Book

The organization of this book (and of many courses in the same subject) follows generally the life cycle of a corporation. Thus we consider the rate structures and other tax planning matters involved in a decision to incorporate in the latter part of this chapter and the capital structure of the corporation and the tax consequences of incorporation transactions in Chapters 2 and 3. The tax treatment of distributions in cash or kind by an operating corporation is next considered in Chapter 4 on Non-Liquidating Distributions. The special situation where a stockholder surrenders part or all of his stock in order to receive a distribution is considered in Chapter 5 on Redemptions and Partial Liquidations. End of the life cycle in which the corporation is completely liquidated by distribution of all of its assets to its stockholders in exchange for their stock is considered in Chapter 6 on Liquidations. The special issues raised when a corporate distribution is in the form of the corporation's own stock are considered in Chapter 7 on Stock Dividends. Where the stock dividend or similar distribution is of preferred stock, Congress has blocked the possibility of certain schemes for "bailing out" corporate earnings at capital gain instead of ordinary income rates on dividends, by "tainting the stock" under Code § 306, discussed in Chapter 8. The last-mentioned two chapters involve transactions that are generally tax-free to the stockholders involved. They lead therefore to the next four chapters dealing with tax-free reorganizations, Chapter 9, Reorganizations: In General; Chapter 10, Recapitalizations: E Reorganizations; Chapter 11, Corporate Divisions: § 355, Divisive D Reorganizations; and Chapter 12, Integrating Reorganizations. The carryover from one corporation to another in a combining tax-free reorganization, particularly the carryover of net operating loss carryovers, and limitations on such carryovers, is discussed in Chapter 13. Chapter 14 concludes the work with a discussion of the rules under Subchapter S.

The contents of the book thus are largely a succession of independent topics. With the exception of the first two chapters, and the last chapter on Subchapter S, they each cover particular transactions or groups of transactions that are covered separately under Subchapter C of the Code. The authors believe that the sequence of topics in the book is conducive to understanding the material; other sequences, however, are also practical.

Subchapter C of the Code on "Corporate Distributions and Adjustments", §§ 301–385, is divided into six Parts. All but Part IV on insolvency reorganizations are considered in this book. As organized by Subchapter C, the covered topics are I. Distributions by corporations, §§ 301–318; II. Corporate liquidations, §§ 331–346; III. Corporate organizations and reorganizations, §§ 351–368; V. Carryovers, §§ 381–383 and VI. Treatment of certain corporate interests as stock or indebtedness, § 385.

[4]

There are two extremely important issues that run through the subject matter. First, when a stockholder receives a distribution of money or other property from his corporation, and also surrenders stock in the corporation, under what circumstances will he be treated as having received a non-liquidating distribution, taxable as a dividend to the extent it is treated as coming out of corporate earnings, and under what circumstances will he instead be treated as having sold or exchanged stock for the amount of the distribution, with the result that he is treated as having a capital gain or loss on disposition of his shares? This issue is discussed in detail in Chapter 5 on Redemptions; it is also a significant part of the analysis in Chapter 8 on § 306 Stock and in Chapters 9–12 which discuss tax-free reorganizations. A second major issue is the extent to which stockholders (or bondholders) can participate in exchanges without recognition of gain on their investment; a corollary issue is the tax treatment of exchanges by corporations participating in the same transactions. Thus, as discussed in Chapter 3, individuals forming a corporation can transfer appreciated inventory or other property to it in exchange for stock (or bonds) of the corporation without recognizing the gain (excess of amount realized over adjusted basis) on their investment. Again, this issue is central to the dis-

[5]

cussion of tax-free reorganizations in Chapters 9–12.

§ 3.   Areas Not Covered

The book is limited to the consideration of corporations in general. It does not consider the special tax rules dealing with tax-exempt organizations, Subchapter F; banking institutions, Subchapter H; insurance companies, Subchapter L; regulated investment companies and real estate investment trusts, Subchapter M; or the special rules affecting railroads and public utility companies. Similarly, it does not consider the special rules applicable to foreign corporations included in Subchapter N. Only brief consideration in general terms is given in Chapter 2 to corporations classified as subject to the accumulated earnings tax or the personal holding company tax, covered in Subchapter G on corporations used to avoid income tax on shareholders.

§ 4.   Definition and Classification Issues

Under § 7701, a corporation is defined to include an association. The Regulations under this definition section list six attributes that corporations typically possess. Two of the attributes, associates and an objective to carry on business for joint profit, are held in common with partnerships and thus are disregarded in distinguishing a corporation from a partnership for tax purposes.

The current Regulations under § 7701 generally take a factor-counting approach and provide that if the business possesses a majority of the other four corporate factors (limited liability, free transferability of interests, continuity of life and centralized management), the organization will be a corporation; otherwise it will be a partnership. Regs. § 301.7701–2(a)(3) (first sentence).

§ 5. Corporate Tax Rates

(a) *In General.* In general, large corporations are taxed at a flat 46 percent rate on their taxable income. § 11. Every corporation, however, pays tax at lower rates on the first $100,000 of its taxable income. Since 1979, the rate structure for corporations under § 11 has been: 17 percent on the first $25,000 of taxable income, 20 percent on the second $25,000, 30 percent on the third $25,000, 40 percent on the fourth $25,000, and 46 percent on all income above $100,000.

For any corporation with taxable income above $100,000, the tax is simply 46 percent of that income minus $19,250. The $19,250 represents the tax benefit resulting from the lower rates applied to the first $100,000 of taxable income.

Before 1979, the corporate tax structure consisted of a normal tax rate and a surtax that was applied to income over the amount protected by the surtax exemption. The normal tax rate was 20 percent on the first $25,000 and 22 percent on any income above $25,000. All income over $50,000 was subject to the 26 percent surtax. For corporations with income above $50,000, this resulted in a 48 percent tax rate minus a tax benefit of $13,500 on the first $50,000.

(b) *Capital Gains.* If a corporation has long term capital gains, it does not enjoy the deduction of 60% of the net capital gain that individual taxpayers may claim under § 1202. Under § 1201 (a)(2), the corporation pays a flat 28 percent on its net capital gain. There is a minor exception for situations of low corporate taxable income in which the tax on the corporation's total taxable income including the net capital gain would be less if the regular corporate tax rates were applied; in that case § 1201(a) applies the regular § 11 rates. See § 1201(a) (matter in parentheses).

(c) *Subchapter S.* An important exception to the regular corporate tax rates described above is the tax treatment of corporations electing under Subchapter S of the Code, discussed in Chapter 14. These corporations, which must in general have few stockholders, no corporations or trusts as stockholders, only one class of stock and limited "passive" income, ordinarily are not taxed at all. Instead, their taxable income is in general taxed directly to their stockholders; similarly, any operating losses generally pass through to the stockholders. Capital gains of Subchapter S corporations pass through specially as capital gains to the stockholders, except that certain large capital gains, under § 1378, are taxed at the § 1201 (a) 28 percent rate to the corporation itself.

(d) *Multiple Corporations and Consolidated Returns.* To prevent abuse of the graduated tax rate structure by conducting business through several corporations with similar ownership, §§ 1561 and 1563 establish complex rules applying the lower rates of § 11(b) as if the multiple corporations were only one corporation. Each member of the group gets a pro-rata portion of the tax benefit unless the group decides upon a different allocation. The limitations on the use of the graduated tax rate apply to corporations with related beneficial ownership in a small group of people (brother-sister corporations) or with a common 80 percent-or-more parent corporation (parent-subsidiary controlled group).

A group of corporations related through one common 80 percent "parent" corporation, termed an "affiliated group" by § 1504, may elect to file a consolidated return computing taxable income on a group basis. Among other things, this allows current losses of one corporation to be offset against the current income of another. The lengthy Regulations under § 1502 provide detailed rules governing such consolidations, which are beyond the scope of this work.

§ 6. Tax Comparison of Corporate vs. Noncorporate Form

(a) *Current Tax Rates.* The tax rate differentials between corporate and noncorporate business are a major factor in the choice of business form. Compared with individual rates on the same taxable income, corporate rates offer two advantages. First, the 17–40 percent rates on the first $100,000 of taxable income will normally be lower than the individual rates applicable to a sole proprietor or partner. Second, high-income individuals with top rates in excess of 46 percent may save current taxes even on the portion of their business income taxable at the full 46 percent corporate rate. This latter point remains important notwithstanding the effect of the § 1348 50 percent maximum tax on an individual's personal service income; many high-income individuals will continue to be taxed on business income at top rates of more than 50 percent, either because such income is largely not "personal service income" or because the individuals have items of tax preference that reduce the amount of personal service income eligible for the 50 percent maximum. See § 1348(b)(2)(B).

In choosing between proprietorship or partnership operation and corporate operation of a business, the effect of non-federal income tax factors is also of large importance. Corporate operation will require larger legal and accounting fees;

there will usually be state and local taxes specially imposed on corporations. These taxes and expenses, however, are deductible for federal income tax purposes.

Limited liability is another factor that influences the choice of corporate form for the larger public corporation and also for the closely-held corporation. Large corporations with many public stockholders are generally forced by custom, the financial need for readily marketable shares and other non-tax factors to be corporations. Corporations that have accumulated a substantial amount of earnings generally are forced to continue as corporations for the additional reason that changing to the noncorporate (e. g., limited partnership) form would involve heavy taxation on stockholders, as discussed in Chapter 6 on Liquidations.

By comparison, under Subchapter K of the Code, §§ 701–761, a partnership is not taxed at all. It merely files an information return reporting the shares of income of each partner. Each partner is taxed on his share, whether actually distributed to him or not. Any losses similarly pass through to the partners according to their shares, subject to the limitation that losses reduce the partner's basis in his interest in the partnership and cannot result in deduction if the partner does not have basis left. Special items of income and deduction retain their character as they pass through to the partners so that, for example, a tax-exempt bond held by a partnership will result in each partner receiving a tax-exempt share of the bond interest.

(b) *Double Taxation.* The "double taxation" of dividends is a significant unfavorable tax aspect of corporate form. The corporation is taxed as a separate entity on its taxable income, and the stockholders are taxed on the distribution of all or part of the corporation's after-tax income. In a sense, this results in taxing the same income twice.

Example: X Corp. pays federal income tax of $49,750 on its 1980 taxable income of $150,000. X distributes its entire after-tax income of $100,250 as a dividend to its sole stockholder, A, an individual. A is taxed on the entire amount as ordinary income (ignoring the $200 per taxpayer dividend exclusion under § 116). If A's effective tax rate on this distribution is 50 percent, his tax on the dividend is $50,125 and he has $50,125 left after tax. Thus the $150,000 corporate taxable income is reduced by federal income taxes of $99,875 ($49,750 corporate and $50,125 individual), a total effective rate of 66.58 percent, leaving 33.42 percent after tax for stockholder A.

For the close corporation, the response to this double taxation is generally to avoid payment of dividends insofar as feasible. Some necessary withdrawals of money by stockholders for personal use may be recast into the form of reasonable salaries for their services to the corporation, reasonable rents or interest on property leased or loaned to the corporation, or other forms of payments which are deductible in computing corporate income tax. This approach results in accumulation of savings of after-tax corporate income in the form of retained earnings of the corporation. So long as the corporation is in active business and finds active business uses for investment of these accumulations, there generally will be no problem with the dividend-forcing taxes discussed in Chapter 2; moreover, the first $150,000 of accumulated earnings is free of accumulated earnings tax even if accumulated solely to save tax on the stockholders. Close corporations eligible to elect under Subchapter S have the alternative of avoiding double taxation on corporate earnings by submitting the stockholders to tax on their full share of corporate taxable income.

Publicly held corporations are, at least generally, immune from the dividend-forcing taxes, but may be forced by such considerations as stock market investor expectations to pay at least some dividends.

If the stockholders choose accumulation of earnings in the corporation rather than payment of dividends, the value of their stock will increase as a result, but the basis of the stock in their hands will not change. Therefore they will face a tax on selling their stock when they realize increased gain representing their interest in the retained earnings. Thus, through non-payment of dividends, the stockholder-level tax is deferred and not totally avoided; the gain, however, is eventually taxed as long-term capital gain, rather than as an ordinary income dividend.

Example: As in the previous example, X Corp. has 1980 taxable income of $150,000 and pays federal income tax of $49,750. X accumulates its $100,250 of after-tax earnings, paying no dividend to sole stockholder A. If X uses these funds profitably in its business, A benefits by having the use on his behalf of the entire $100,250, rather than just the $50,125 that would have been left if he had received a dividend of the after-tax earnings, taxable to him at 50 percent. If A sells his stock and recognizes a capital gain of at least the $100,250 retained earnings, with his § 1202 deduction he will pay regular tax on only 40 percent of the $100,250 gain at his 50 percent rate, or $20,050 tax, for an effective rate of 20 percent of the gain. Under such circumstances, the total federal income taxes will equal only $69,800 ($49,750 corporate and $20,050 individual), or 46.53 percent of the corporation's taxable income of $150,000, thus leaving 53.47 percent after tax for stockholder A. (In the interest of simplicity, the example ignores the possible additional tax that could result under § 55, imposing an alternative minimum tax upon a portion of an individual's net capital gains in some cases.)

(c) *Other Factors.* Corporate form has a number of miscellaneous tax advantages as well as some disadvantages. Principal advantages include:

—more liberal §§ 401–09 qualified employee benefit plan rules than the Keogh plan limitations applicable to proprietors and partners;

—corporate deductions under § 162 for specifically Code-blessed fringe benefits for employees, such as medical insurance plans, excluded from stockholder-employee income by §§ 105 and 106; at least $50,000 of group-term life insurance coverage, § 79; meals and lodging provided for the convenience of the employer, § 119; and qualified group legal service plans, § 120. (Note that in several of these cases, the full benefit of the exclusion at the stockholder-employee level is available only if the corporation does not discriminate under the plan in favor of stockholder-employees.)

—other fringe benefits and perquisites for stockholder-employees such as incidental personal use of corporate facilities may be more freely available in corporate form under current IRS practices;

—free initial choice of taxable year, and new election of accounting methods.

Principal disadvantages include:

—inability to pass through current losses to stockholders for use against their other income (except under Subchapter S); this is in a sense a corollary of the double taxation of income, discussed above.

CHAPTER 2

CAPITAL STRUCTURE

Table of Sections

§ 1. Debt vs. Equity

A number of tax and non-tax factors generally favor the inclusion of a substantial amount of debt in the capital structure of the corporation. Current return paid to the holder of the corporation's debt is deductible as interest expense by the corporation, but dividends paid on preferred or common stock are not deductible. From the investor's standpoint, debt is also generally preferable to stock because a creditor is not taxable on the withdrawal of his investment when the corporation repays the debt, to the extent that he has basis in his investment. In a close corporation, however, the stock investor is likely to find difficulty in selling his stock to any one but the corporation itself, and if he does that he is likely to be taxed on a dividend, as discussed in Chapter 5, dealing with redemptions of stock.

[17]

In general, under the tax law, the parties are free to use stock or debt financing as they see fit. However, if the corporation is "too thin", that is, if the proportion of debt to equity (i. e., stock) in its capital structure appears unreasonably high in the light of normal business considerations, IRS may treat purported debt instruments as actually being stock for tax purposes. This results in disallowing any deduction for interest expense claimed by the corporation.

In the Tax Reform Act of 1969, Congress added § 385 to the Code, authorizing regulations which would determine classification of instruments as debt or stock based on factors (some listed in § 385) to be spelled out in regulations. Under § 385, the factors for distinguishing debt from equity may include five listed factors which generally have been prominent in previous decided cases on this issue: (1) the amount is due on demand or at a specified date, is for a sum certain, and bears a fixed rate of interest; (2) subordination to or preference over any other corporate debt; (3) the ratio of corporate debt to equity; (4) existence of a privilege of converting the instrument into stock; and (5) the relationship between holdings of stock and holdings of the interest in question. On the last point, if purported debt is held in the same proportions as the holders hold stock, (e. g., two-thirds of the debt by the two-thirds stockholders and one-third by the one-third stockholder), it is more likely to be considered as an equity investment. Although the Treasury Department has published proposed regulations under § 385, these have not yet been issued in final form.

In general, the cases raising the debt-or-equity issue have referred not only to the intention of the parties, but also to whether an outside lender would have loaned money to the corporation on a similar basis. Judicial resolutions of debt or equity controversies have taken an all-or-nothing approach: thus, for example, in the extreme case of a corporation with $1,000 of stock and $499,000 of indebtedness, the entire $499,000 debt is likely to be treated as equity, even assuming that a capital structure of $250,000 stock and $250,000 debt would have been treated as such for tax purposes. This suggests that the parties seeking to form a corporation with a substantial amount of debt may wish to do so boldly (a debt ratio of three times the amount of stock is generally thought to be safe, although the cases warn that there are no rules of thumb) but not recklessly since the penalty for going too far may be loss of debt treatment on the total amount of purported debt, including the otherwise safe portion.

An exception to the tax planning rule that debt is generally preferable to equity arises when the holder of the investment is itself a corporation.

Under § 243, all or at least 85 percent of the dividends received on a stock investment are deductible and hence tax-free to the corporate recipient, as discussed in Chapter 4 on Nonliquidating Distributions. Accordingly, a corporation choosing an investment vehicle may favor preferred stock over debt.

§ 2. Tax Treatment of Losses on Investments

In general, an investor in either stock or debt of a corporation receives some form of capital loss treatment if he either sells for less than basis or suffers total worthlessness of his investment. See §§ 165, 166. The major exceptions to this general rule which may permit ordinary loss treatment are: (1) an individual investor who is also in a trade or business, e. g., as a corporate employee, and makes a further loan for the *dominant* purpose of protecting his business position, Generes (U.S.1972), avoids the non-business debt rule of § 166(d). However, as in *Generes*, protecting a business position as a corporate employee will rarely be a major stockholder's *dominant* motive for advancing money to a shaky corporation because he has more at stake as an investor; Whipple (U.S.1963) holds that his original stockholder-creditor activities, even if he spends all his time with the activities of a wholly-owned corporation, are those of an investor and do not constitute a business. The alternative procedure of obtaining corporate financing from a third party creditor with a guarantee by the stockholder likewise produces a non-business bad debt loss when, after corporate reverses, the stockholder is called upon to pay the debt. Putnam (U.S.1956); Regs. § 1.166–8(b). (2) a corporate investor holding debt obligations will receive ordinary loss treatment under § 166(a) so long as the debt is not represented by a "security", § 165(g). However, if the security is in an affiliated corporation which meets the test of § 165(g)(3), ordinary loss treatment is available.

§ 3. Section 1244 Stock

A corporation which meets the requirements of § 1244 permits its investors to have ordinary loss rather than capital loss treatment on losses sustained on investment in its common stock to the extent of $50,000 a year per investor ($100,000 on a joint return). The requirements of § 1244 are complex and have led to litigation, but since there is nothing to lose by trying, it is normal practice to include in the corporate documents connected with the issuance of stock for any small corporation the necessary language to constitute a § 1244 plan, available in most form books.

§ 4. Accumulated Earnings Tax

The accumulated earnings tax under § 531 and following is a substantial limitation on the ability of the corporation to postpone or avoid double taxation on corporate profits by accumulating earnings in the corporation rather than paying them out as dividends. This penalty tax is based on both objective and subjective elements. It is intended not to apply as a revenue-raising measure, but rather to force corporations to pay dividends of money not needed in the business.

The tax is imposed by § 531 at the rate of 27½ percent of "accumulated taxable income" of up to $100,000 for the taxable year plus 38½ percent of accumulated taxable income above $100,000. The tax is imposed only on a corporation described in § 532, that is, a corporation "formed or availed of for the purpose of avoiding the income tax with respect to its shareholders * * * by permitting earnings and profits to accumulate instead of being divided or distributed." § 532(a). Thus one key element in the imposition of this penalty tax is a subjective finding as to the purpose of the corporation, generally equated by the cases with the purpose of its dominant stockholders. The Supreme Court has interpreted this language to mean that the issue is whether avoidance of tax on stockholders was "one of the purposes" of accumulating earnings in the corporation. Donruss Co. (U.S.1969).

The objective factors are contained in § 535(c), which provides a "credit" (here really like a deduction) generally for an amount equal to the part of the current year's earnings and profits "retained for the reasonable needs of the business," with a minimum credit of an amount sufficient to bring the accumulated earnings and profits of the corporation up to $150,000. Thus any corporation may freely accumulate the first $150,000 of its earnings and profits, even for the purpose of avoiding tax on its stockholders, without being subject to the accumulated earnings tax. After the accumulated earnings and profits reach $150,000 the principal practical issue becomes whether further earnings need to be retained for business purposes. If business needs for the accumulations exist and are one of the reasons for the accumulation, then even though the corporation has as one of its purposes the prohibited one of avoiding tax on stockholders, the credit under § 535(c) will prevent the imposition of the accumulated earnings tax for that year. John P. Scripps Newspapers (T.C.1965).

A corporation should have and should document plans for the business use of liquid assets which are not obviously used in the business operations, so as to be able to prove that its accumulated earnings beyond $150,000 are "retained for the reasonable needs of the business." Regs. § 1.537–2(b) lists situations which if sufficiently supported by the facts will justify accumulation of earnings; Regs. § 1.537–2(c) gives examples of situations indicative of the prohibited purpose. The approach of the courts has been to permit a corporation to totally finance its operations from retained earnings without borrowing from outside sources. Thus, funds required for working capital are needed in the business, as are funds saved pursuant to definite plans to use them for building a factory, or otherwise expanding the business in existing or new areas. Funds for which there is no definite business purpose, invested in passive "nonbusiness" investments such as marketable stocks and bonds are generally considered investment rather than business uses of funds.

Details of the operation of the tax are beyond the scope of this work but a general idea of its purpose and operation should be kept in mind for brief consideration in connection with exam questions primarily on other subjects.

§ 5. Personal Holding Company Tax

The personal holding company tax is imposed upon certain closely held "incorporated pocketbooks". Because the tax is at a flat rate of 70 percent on personal holding company income and there is a provision for the payment of a deficiency dividend after the corporation is caught which eliminates the liability for the tax (but not penalties or interest thereon), the tax is rarely actually paid. The tax is imposed by § 541 on the undistributed personal holding company income for the taxable year of every personal holding company, defined in § 542 to be generally a corporation more than half of whose stock is owned, constructively or actually, by five or fewer individuals and which has more than specified minimum percentages of passive types of income. The undistributed personal holding company income, defined in § 545, is the taxable income for the year with certain adjustments minus the dividends paid deduction as defined in § 561. As in the case of the accumulated earnings tax, adjustments allow for such items as regular federal income taxes and capital gains. Also as in the case of the accumulated earnings tax, special deductions provided for a corporation such as the deduction of 85 or 100 percent of dividends received from another corporation, are not allowed in computing taxable income for this purpose. Thus if a corporation which is sufficiently closely held has as its sole income $30,000 of fully deductible dividends per year, it will generally be a personal holding company subject to 70 percent tax on the $30,000 unless it pays out $30,000 a year in dividends to its stockholders.

A special type of personal holding company income is income from certain personal service contracts. This arises if a 25 percent or more stockholder is designated or can be designated by someone other than the corporation as the person who is to perform services under a contract in which the corporation must furnish personal services. § 543(a)(7). This provision would classify as a personal holding company a corporation designed simply to market the services of a movie actor or other highly compensated person. However, the typical professional service corporation which normally furnishes the services of a particular doctor but is not contractually bound to do so would not generally be covered by this provision.

CHAPTER 3

INCORPORATIONS

Table of Sections

[*27*]

§ 1. Introduction

Without a special Code provision, § 351, the transfer of business assets by entrepreneurs to a newly formed corporation in exchange for its stock or securities would be a taxable event. A businessman would recognize a gain (or loss) if the fair market value of the stock or securities he receives for any asset is greater (or less) than the basis of the asset. Section 351 reflects a longstanding Congressional policy to prevent any income tax impact which might impede this type

[*28*]

of simple business transaction. Conceptually, under this policy such transactions are not taxable because, in a sense, the businessman merely changes his form of ownership of the same assets from direct ownership to ownership through the vehicle of a controlled corporation. Section 357 preserves this nonrecognition treatment for typical transactions in which the transferred assets are subject to liabilities. To the extent that § 351 (or § 357) prevents recognition of gain or loss to the businessman, referred to in the Code as the "transferor" (of assets), it is logically accompanied by § 358 which prescribes a substituted basis for the stock or securities he receives in the exchange, and § 362 which prescribes a carryover basis for the assets in the hands of the corporation. Partial recognition of gain occurs under § 351(b) if the transferor receives "boot" in addition to stock or securities and results in an equivalent increase in his and the corporation's basis.

The student may be expected to understand the circumstances under which and the extent to which § 351 (and its companion sections) applies and does not apply to typical transactions and the mechanics of application.

§ 2. Requirements to Qualify for a Tax-Free Exchange

Section 351 requires a transfer to a corporation of (1) property by (2) (a group of) one or more persons (transferors) (3) solely in exchange for (4) stock or securities in the corporation which is (5) controlled immediately after the transfer by the (group of) transferors. Each of these numbered concepts raises issues.

(a) *Definition of Property*. Services are not property, Regs. § 1.351–1(a)(1)(i); if someone simply receives stock as payment for services, § 351 does not apply to him. He is taxable on the value of the stock under §§ 61 and 83, and the corporation may have a § 162 business expense deduction in the same amount.

Cash is property. This feature makes no difference directly to someone who simply transfers cash for stock, since he would not recognize any gain or loss regardless of § 351. But because he is a transferor of "property", his stock counts in determining "control" (see e below).

(b) *By One or More Persons*. The greater the number of transferors, the less each one seems likely to have a continuing interest, merely changed in form, in the assets he himself transfers. Yet there is no specified limit on the number of transferors. The Regulations require

[*30*]

merely that they act in concert under a prearranged plan. Regs. § 1.351–1(a)(1).

(c) *"Solely"*. As with other tax-free exchange
provisions in the Code (e. g. §§ 354, 1031), the
statement in § 351(a) that the exchange must be
"solely" for the permitted consideration (here
stock or securities in the transferee) is false and
misleading unless it is read with the accompanying boot provisions, § 351(b), discussed below.

(d) *For "Stock or Securities" of Such Corporation*. The concept of "stock" representing a
continuing investment poses little difficulty. "Securities" here means relatively long term debt of
the corporation, i. e. "bonds", including debentures. If the transferor exchanges his assets entirely for bonds in forming the corporation,
(while others transfer assets for stock, and he
owns no stock), he has transformed his interest
to that of a creditor and the Service has ruled
that § 351 does not apply to him, for lack of a
"continuity of interest". Rev.Rul. 73–472. (In
a transfer to an existing corporation, however,
any transferor who is part of a group of transferors which is in control immediately after the
transfers could receive only securities and still
qualify under § 351 if he already owned stock,
under companion Rev.Rul. 73–473). If a transferor obtains (or already owns) some stock, thus
maintaining a continuing interest, the rule of

[*31*]

§ 351 is extremely liberal in its treatment of securities (compare § 356 which treats bonds received for stock in a reorganization as "boot").

However, mere short term (generally less than five years) debt (a "note") or an account payable of the corporation is usually not thought to qualify as a security because of its close resemblance to cash (as opposed to an ongoing interest in the corporation). See Pinellas Ice and Cold Storage Co. (U.S.1933). To the extent that length of maturity is a factor in determining whether a given instrument is a security, case law generally indicates a dividing point at five years, see generally George Nye (T.C.1968) and authorities cited therein; I.R.S. usually will agree that a more than five year instrument is a security. (I.R.S. ordinarily will refuse to give an advance ruling on the tax consequences of a § 351 transfer in which debt is received. Rev.Proc. 80–22. In the reorganization area, I.R.S. will leave open for audit the question of whether a more than five year instrument is a security, but will not rule at all on a less than 5 year instrument.) The "thin corporation" security should pose no special problem here—if not a security, it should be stock.

(e) *Control.* The transferor group must be in control of the corporation immediately after the transfer. The "control" test is taken from the reorganization area definition in § 368(c): at least 80% of the total combined voting power of all classes of voting stock, and at least 80% of the total number of shares of each class of the outstanding nonvoting stock. Rev.Rul. 59–259. Note that stock ownership must be actual under § 351; there are no applicable attribution rules. See § 318(a) (attribution rules apply only where expressly made applicable). **Example:** Husband, Wife and Son each own ⅓ of the stock of X Corp. Husband and Son transfer property to X in exchange for securities. The transaction is not within § 351 because the transferors (Husband and Son) are not in control immediately after the transfer.

(i) Incorporations: No problem of control normally arises in a typical incorporation, i. e., the formation of a new corporation. The transferors of property (including cash) will receive 100 percent of the stock of the new corporation. Note that § 351 also covers transfers to an existing corporation by shareholder(s) who after the exchange have at least 80 percent control, regardless of whether they had control before the transfer.

(ii) Group of transferors: To be treated as a group, the transferors must have agreed among themselves on their rights and must make their transfers at a reasonable pace. Regs. § 1.351–1(a)(1).

(iii) Transfer of services, etc: One who transfers some property (including cash) for stock or

[*33*]

securities normally counts as part of the group, even though he also contributes services in return for stock or securities. All stock owned (immediately after the transfer) by a person who transfers property (except for a nominal transfer made for avoidance purposes) is counted for control purposes, including any stock he already owned or obtained for services. It is not necessary that 80 percent of the stock be received for transfers of property but merely that the transferors own 80 percent immediately after, however and whenever acquired. Thus, if A transfers property worth $50,000 and B transfers property worth $15,000 and services worth $35,000, each for 50 percent of the stock of Newcorp, total fair market value (FMV) $100,000, then A and B are both property transferors who own 100 percent of the stock issued after the transfer and both of their property transfers are governed by § 351, even though B has $35,000 of ordinary income from his services. Regs. § 1.351–1(a)(2), *Example (3)*.

(iv) Avoidance transactions: The Regulations, § 1.351–1(a)(1), provide that attempts to qualify a transfer under § 351 by having someone transfer a nominal amount of property will fail. **Example:** Upon incorporation, 78 percent of the stock in Newcorp is issued to A for property worth $78,000 and 22 percent to B for services worth $22,000. The transaction fails to qualify under § 351, because A, the only transferor of property, does not have 80 percent control, so A will recognize gain, if any. Having B transfer $100 in cash in addition to his services in an attempt to qualify A's exchange will not succeed. However, if B transfers $10,000, A will clearly succeed. The Service has created a "safe harbor" rule for issuing advance rulings on intermediate situations: transferred property will not be considered of nominal value if its fair market value equals or exceeds 10 percent of the fair market value of the stock already owned or to be received in exchange for the services. Rev.Proc. 77–37. Thus in the above example if B exchanges $2,200 or more in property in addition to $22,000 in services, A will be able to qualify under § 351.

The 10 percent safe harbor rule also applies to situations where a minority stockholder wishes to make a tax-free transfer of property to a corporation. If the other stockholders are willing to transfer an amount equal to or exceeding 10 percent of their stock's fair market value, the transfer by the minority stockholder will qualify. If the majority of stock is owned by one stockholder this safe harbor rule may be of little use since it focuses on percentage values rather than the amount of the transfer. Thus, in the case of an existing corporation X in which A owns 78 percent and B owns 22 percent of the stock, total FMV $100,000, if B wishes to make a tax-free transfer of an additional $2,200 of property to the corporation, A would have to transfer an additional $7,800 to X to bring the transactions within the safe harbor rule.

(v) Dispositions of stock: If a transferor, pursuant to a pre-arrangement, promptly sells shares received in the exchange, he does not own the shares "immediately after" the transfer for purposes of the control test. Regs. § 1.351–1(a)(1).

In American Bantam Car Co. (T.C.1948), the transferors to a newly-formed corporation transferred, within a more or less short time after the incorporation, an amount of voting stock greater than 20 percent of the outstanding total to underwriters, as compensation for selling stock issued by the new corporation. In determining whether the exchange of assets for stock and the subsequent transfer of a portion of that stock should be considered steps in the same transaction for purposes of the "control immediately after" requirement, the courts have considered numerous factors, such as the parties' intent and the time element involved. In *American Bantam Car*, for example, the Tax Court, holding that the initial exchange was a completed independently viable incorporation, relied upon the facts that the businessmen and the underwriters did not enter into a written contract until after the incorporating exchange and that the underwriters' rights to the stock were contingent upon their sales success.

Consequently, the steps were not found to be so mutually interdependent that they could be considered units of a single transaction. A "control" problem may also arise if the corporation issues additional shares to outside investors soon after the initial incorporation, thus reducing the interest of the original transferors below 80 percent. In that case it may well be argued either that the subsequent transfer is independent, or, if it must be integrated, that the outside investors are in fact part of the original control group of transferors to the corporation. (See further discussion in answer to review question (e), infra.)

(vi) Distributions of a corporate transferor: Section 351(c) prescribes a special rule in determining "control" under § 351 in the case of a transferor which is itself a corporation. The fact that it distributes stock which it receives in the exchange to its shareholders is ignored.

(f) *Disproportionate Issuance of Stock and Securities.* Assume that two individuals, A and B, transfer property of equal value to a newly formed corporation in return for all of its stock. Must A and B each receive stock of equal value for the transaction to receive tax-free treatment under § 351? The Senate Report on the 1954 Code indicates that in deleting the pre-'54 express statutory provision requiring such proportionality as a condition to a tax-free exchange, Congress intended that the requirement be eliminated. This view is reflected in Regs. § 1.351–1(b) and the cross references of § 351(e)(3) and (4) which indicate that it is not necessary that the distribution of stock and securities be substantially proportionate to the transferors' respective interests in the property transferred but warn that the Service will scrutinize the entire transaction and in appropriate cases will treat the disproportionate element as a gift subject to tax under § 2501 and following, or as payment of compensation taxable to the recipient under § 61(a)(1) (and perhaps involving recognition of gain on the constructively transferred stock, and/or a business expense deduction for the deemed payer), or as satisfaction of an obligation of one transferor to the other. For example, in the transfer of equal value property by A and B mentioned above, if A received 60 shares of common stock and B received only 40, the difference of 20 shares could be attributable to A's having rendered services to the corporation, with the value of the 20 shares being taxable to A as compensation under § 61(a)(1); or A could have rendered services to B (unrelated to the assets transferred or the corporate business), with A and B each being treated as having received 50 shares for property, with 10 shares then being transferred by B to A as compensation. Similarly, if A had rendered no services but A and B were related, A and B might each be treated as having received 50 shares for property, of which

B made a gift of 10 shares to A. Compare Regs. § 1.351–1(b)(2), *Examples (1) and (2)*.

§ 3. Treatment of Boot

The transferor may receive, in addition to the permitted tax-free consideration of stock or securities, cash or other property. This other consideration, especially short-term notes, or cash, is called "boot", a term which presumably originally was applied because the other property represents something extra or "to boot" in the exchange. As in other tax-free exchange provisions (§§ 356, 1031(b)) the transferor must recognize realized gain, if any, to the extent of the boot received, i. e., the amount of money and the fair market value of other property such as notes. Loss, if any, is not recognized. **Example:** In a transaction which otherwise would qualify under § 351(a), A transfers land with adjusted basis of $10,000 and receives in exchange total consideration of $50,000: common stock, fair market value (FMV) $20,000, securities FMV $10,000, short-term notes FMV $15,000 and $5,000 cash. Of his realized gain of $40,000 ("amount realized" $50,-000, in the terminology of § 1001, less adjusted basis $10,000) he recognizes $20,000 (the total of the boot, cash $5,000, and other property FMV $15,000, which he receives). (His basis in the properties received and that of the corporation in the assets transferred are increased to reflect the recognition of gain. See below §§ 5 and 7.)

Example: If the facts were the same, except that A's adjusted basis in the land was $90,000, his realized loss of $40,000 would not be recognized. § 351(b)(2). (His unrecognized loss would be preserved through his substituted basis in his stock and securities and the corporation's carryover basis in the land; see below §§ 5 and 7.)

If one transferor transfers several assets, the Service has ruled that the boot he receives must be allocated to the transferred assets on an asset-by-asset basis in proportion to their relative fair market values in order to determine both the amount and character (i. e., capital, ordinary) of the gain to be recognized. Rev.Rul. 68–55. On analogy to a sale by each transferor, the first step is to determine the sale price (amount realized) separately for each asset which he transfers. Thus an asset which represents 10 percent of the total asset value he transfers for stock and boot is treated as exchanged for 10 percent of the stock and 10 percent of the boot received. Also under this ruling, loss produced on one asset goes unrecognized under § 351 and cannot be netted against gains recognized on other assets.

Example: A, one of several unrelated transferors in a transaction which otherwise would

[*40*]

qualify under § 351(a), transfers inventory, machinery (§ 1245 property) and capital assets with a fair market value of $100 in exchange for stock worth $50, securities worth $30 and $20 in cash, which is boot. If the fair market values (FMV) and adjusted bases of the items are as given below, then the boot would be allocated and gain recognized in the following manner.

	Total	Inventory	Machinery	Capital Assets
Fair Market Value	$100	$ 70	$ 20	$ 10
% of Total FMV	—	70%	20%	10%
FMV of stocks	$ 50	$ 35	$ 10	$ 5
FMV of securities	30	21	6	3
Cash received (boot)	20	14	4	2
Amount realized	$100	$ 70	$ 20	$ 10
Adjusted Basis	—	40	10	30
Gain (loss) realized	—	$ 30	$ 10	($ 20)
Gain recognized	$ 18	$ 14	$ 4	0

The gain recognized for any asset is the gain realized to the extent of the boot allocated to that asset. Thus, for example, on the inventory a gain of $30 is realized. Only $14 of that amount, representing the inventory's portion of the boot, is recognized. Note also that since the loss on any asset is not recognized (e. g. the capital assets here), it is entirely possible that a transferor may be required to recognize a gain even though in the aggregate he realizes a loss. For example, even if A had an adjusted basis of $60 in the capital assets here and thus realized a $50 loss on those assets, he still would have been required to recognize $18 of gain, although overall he actually lost $10. This unfavorable loss position may be a factor leading a transferor to attempt to avoid falling within the mandatory provisions of § 351 (see § 10 below).

The character of any gain recognized on an asset is determined by reference to the particular asset transferred. Accordingly, if in the above example the capital assets had been held for the length of time required by § 1222(3) and had been transferred at a time when their value exceeded their adjusted basis the gain would have been long-term capital gain. With the machinery, § 1245 property, the character of the $4 recognized gain depends upon the amount of previous depreciation deductions subject to recapture. If, for example, the amount of previous depreciation deducted ("depreciation") totals $3, then $3 of the § 351(b) gain recognized on the § 1245 property would be ordinary income and $1 would be capital gain. If, as most likely would be the case, depreciation was $4 or more, then the entire $4 gain recognized would be ordinary income.

It should also be noted that in permitting securities to be received tax-free rather than as boot, § 351 differs from the reorganization provisions. In these latter sections (§§ 354 and 356), securities received in exchange for stock are treated as boot.

§ 4. Liabilities Relieved

(a) *In General.* In any exchange, if a transferor is relieved of liabilities, because they are assumed or the transferred property is subject to them, the amount realized, and thus the gain realized, includes the amount of these relieved liabilities. § 1001. Relief from liabilities is not treated as boot for purposes of § 351, and will not disqualify a transfer under § 351. See § 357(a). Liabilities do not cause recognition of gain in a § 351 transaction unless the special rules of § 357 (b) (avoidance transactions) or § 357(c) (liabilities in excess of basis) apply.

(b) *Avoidance Transactions.* Section 357(b) threatens boot treatment to a transferor if the principal purpose for which a liability is taken over by the corporation is either a "tax avoidance" or not a "bona fide business purpose". The latter situation would arise if the transferor borrows against his business assets for reasons such as a vacation, a personal stock market investment, or a down payment on a home, and shortly thereafter transfers the assets subject to the liability to a new corporation for its stock. This arrangement is considered too close to that where the corporation pays cash boot to the transferor, which it might obtain by borrowing against the business assets. If any of the transferor's liabilities are relieved for either forbidden purpose, *all* of his liabilities relieved in the exchange (even normal business liabilities), count as boot. Regs. § 1.357–1(c). Any boot that does result is then allocated among the assets transferred in proportion to their relative fair market values. See Regs. § 1.357–2(b), *Examples (1) and (2)*.

(c) *Liabilities in Excess of Basis.* The amount by which liabilities relieved (other than certain trade accounts payable of a cash basis taxpayer) exceed the transferor's aggregate basis in the assets transferred will be treated as gain. § 357 (c). This rule applies to each transferor individually and not to the group as a whole. Rev.Rul. 66–142. Theoretically, the rule applies mechanically regardless of the amount of gain realized. Since liabilities assumed (or to which the property is subject, in the usual case) are an amount realized, overall gain realized would exist.

More significantly, since § 357(c) applies to the aggregate liabilities of which a transferor is relieved in excess of the aggregate basis of assets transferred, it can normally be avoided by his transferring additional assets with basis, including cash which doesn't technically have a basis but is treated as if it did. See Raich (T.C.1966).

Although the entire excess is gain, the Regulations for § 357(c), in a manner similar to the treatment of boot under § 357(b), provide for the allocation of the excess among all the transferred assets in proportion to their relative fair market value for the purpose of characterizing the gain as ordinary or capital and long or short-term. Regs. § 1.357–2(b). This is questionable in that it allocates, for purposes of characterization, gain to assets regardless of the amount of realized gain on such assets. The rationale for allocating § 357 (c) recognized gain as if it were boot would be that since the aggregate basis of all the transferred assets is compared with the amount of liabilities under § 357(c), the gain is recognized regarding all assets (in proportion to value) rather than those with realized gains. According to the *Raich* decision, although transferred cash also counts as basis against liabilities, the allocation of gain is confined to non-cash assets.

Example: In a transaction which otherwise qualifies under § 351, A transfers a building with an adjusted basis of $10,000 subject to a mortgage liability of $25,000, for stock in Newcorp, FMV $50,000. A must recognize a $15,000 gain on transfer of the building. (Note that apparently the building itself should be worth $75,000 on these facts, so that the gain realized of $65,000 would more than cover the $15,000 recognized gain). The character of the gain is determined by the character of the transferred asset; here, because of the building, the gain would be treated under § 1250, and (if A owns actually or constructively 80 percent of the stock by value, e. g., if he is the only transferor in this example) under § 1239 to the extent not covered by § 1250.

[45]

Rev.Rul. 75–514. Regs. § 1.1250–1(c)(4). If A also transfers other assets, FMV and adjusted basis $15,000, for additional stock or securities, however, the aggregate basis will no longer be exceeded by the liabilities, § 357(c) will not apply, and under the general rule of § 357(a) he will recognize no gain despite the relieved liabilities. Section 357(c) cannot, though, be avoided by the giving of the taxpayer's own note, in contrast to cash, to the corporation for the amount of excess liabilities over basis, because the taxpayer has no basis in his own note. Rev.Rul. 68–629.

Section 357(c) is also not applicable if the motivation behind the assumption of the liability is either tax avoidance or a non-business purpose. In such cases, § 357(b) takes precedence over § 357(c) and the entire amount of the transferor's liabilities assumed is considered boot. See § 357 (c)(2). The distinction between the two provisions may be important in determining the gain to be recognized in a transaction.

Example: In a § 351 transaction A transfers two assets, each with an adjusted basis of $2,500 and a fair market value of $7,500. In return he receives stock and securities worth $8,000 and has his liabilities on the assets assumed. The assets together are subject to total liabilities of $7,000, $3,000 of which is not for a bona fide business purpose. If § 357(c) were applicable, the excess of total liabilities over aggregate basis, here $2,000, would be considered *gain*. Because of the lack of a bona fide business purpose, however, all of the liabilities ($7,000) are considered *boot*. The boot would be allocated between the two assets on the basis of fair market value, with each asset receiving $3,500 of the boot. As the gain realized on each asset ($5,000) is higher than the allocated boot, the total $7,000 amount of the boot produces recognized gain.

§ 5. Basis and Holding Period to Transferor

(a) *Basis*. As in other nonrecognition transactions (e. g., § 1031), the transferor's realized but unrecognized gain is preserved by transferring his adjusted basis in the transferred property to the nonrecognition property (i. e. stock and securities) received. § 358(a)(1). The transferor's basis in any boot received will be fair market value, § 358(a)(2); any cash received is in effect given a basis equal to its fair market value by the decrease in basis in the nonrecognition property provided by § 358(a)(1)(A)(ii). The transferor's substituted basis in the nonrecognition property is allocated among the stock and securities received by the transferor in proportion to their relative fair market values. Regs. § 1.358–2(b)(2).

Example: In the first example in 3 above, A realized $40,000 gain but recognized $20,000 gain in a § 351 transaction when he exchanged property with an adjusted basis of $10,000 for $50,000 consideration of which $20,000 was boot. His basis would be determined as follows:

Property Received	FMV	Adjusted Basis
cash	$ 5,000	not applicable (like $5,000)
boot (short term notes)	$15,000	$15,000
nonrecognition property:		
securities	10,000	3,333
stock	20,000	6,667
Total	$50,000	$25,000 (like $30,000)

Following the language of § 358(a), the transferor's adjusted basis in the nonrecognition property (i. e., the stock and securities) is his basis in the property exchanged ($10,000) decreased by the value of the boot and money received ($20,000) and increased by the amount of recognized gain ($20,000) to give an adjusted basis in the stock and securities of $10,000, which is then allocated between the two types of nonrecognition property in proportion to their relative fair market values: $10,000/$30,000, or ⅓, to the securities and $20,000/$30,000, or ⅔, to the stock. The transferor's basis in the short-term notes will be their fair market value.

(b) *Holding Period.* In determining the holding period of the stock or securities received in a § 351 exchange, the transferor uses, or "tacks," the holding period derived from the assets transferred to the corporation. See § 1223(1).

This rule applies only to capital and § 1231 assets; otherwise the holding period begins from the date of the exchange. If there is a combination of different kinds of property being transferred, the different holding periods must be allocated among the stock and securities received; in proportion to the bases of the transferred assets, according to Runkle (B.T.A.1939). Thus, for example, if A exchanges long term capital assets (FMV $60 and adjusted basis of $40) and inventory (FMV $20 and adjusted basis of $20) and $20 cash for stock in Newcorp FMV $100 in a transaction otherwise qualifying under § 351 and then sells his Newcorp stock three months later for $110, $15 (i. e., 40/80—basis in long term capital assets over total basis) of his $30 gain will be treated as long term capital gain and $15 (i. e., 40/80—basis in cash and inventory over total basis) will be treated as short term capital gain.

(c) *Effect of Liabilities.* Solely for the purpose of determining the transferor's basis, relieved liabilities (other than certain trade accounts payable of a cash basis taxpayer; see further discussion in § 9(b), infra) are treated like money received and thus will reduce the transferor's basis in the stock and securities he receives. See § 358(d). This reduction for liabilities relieved occurs regardless of whether or not the liabilities result in recognition of any gain to the transferor; to the extent that under § 357(b) or (c) the transferor must report gain, he will of course have an offsetting increase in basis. Understanding and recall of this rule may be aided by noting that liabilities relieved are payment to the transferor which, though not taxable, do represent a partial recovery of his capital or basis. Also the value of the consideration received other than relieved liabilities, (that is stock, securities, cash and other property) will normally be equal to the value of the property transferred less the amount of liabilities relieved; an equivalent reduction in basis must be made in order to preserve the correct amount of potential gain.

Example: A transfers property with fair market value (FMV) $55, adjusted basis (AB) $40, subject to a liability of $30, for all of the stock of Newcorp, fair market value $25. (Note that the stock value, in an exchange of equal values, is equal to the net value of the transfer, $55–$30). No gain is recognized under §§ 351 and 357(a). A's basis in the stock is $10 ($40–$30). His potential gain on a sale of the stock is $15 ($25 FMV–$10 AB), the same as was his potential gain on the sale of the original property ($55 FMV–$40 AB).

§ 6. The Transferee Corporation: The Issuance of Stock or Debt

(a) *Issuance of Stock:* § *1032.* The transferee corporation recognizes no gain (or loss) on the issuance or sale or exchange of its own stock (even treasury shares which it has purchased for less [or more] than their present fair market value). § 1032. Payments made in its own stock for services, supplies, etc., are treated as expenditures to the extent of the fair market value of the stock, to be deducted by the corporation under § 162 or capitalized as appropriate.

(b) *Issuance of Securities or Other Debt.* The transferee corporation has no immediate tax consequences from the borrowing represented by the issuance of debt instruments for cash or in exchange for property. There is no "exchange" in principle; rather the corporation is agreeing to make a future cash payment for property or to repay a cash loan.

If the debt is issued for money in an amount less than the principal amount of the debt, the corporation can normally deduct the difference as amortization of "original issue discount" over the life of the debt. § 1232; Regs. § 1.163–4. If debt is issued for property other than money, normally under § 1232 it is considered to have been issued for its full principal amount, with no original issue discount. Exceptions are provided if either the property transferred consists of stock or securities traded in an established market, or the debt issued is part of an issue traded on an established market. § 1232(b)(2) (last two sentences). These exceptions are inapplicable if the debt is issued pursuant to a tax-free reorganization, discussed in Chapters 9–12.

§ 7.   Basis and Holding Period of the Transferee Corporation

(a) *Transferee Corporation's Basis in Assets— In General.* The corporation takes the transferred assets at the same basis they had in the hands of the transferor, but increased by the amount of any gain recognized by the transferor. § 362(a)(1).

Note that relieved liabilities or cash or other boot paid as such have no effect on the corporation except indirectly to the extent that they may cause the transferor to recognize gain. The transferor's potential gain in a transferred asset is thus preserved in the hands of the corporation, except to the extent that it has already been recognized to the transferor in the § 351 transfer.

(b) *Allocation of Transferee Corporation's Basis in Assets.* In a tax-free § 351 transfer each transferred asset retains the same basis it had in the hands of the transferor. There is no need for determination of fair market values of assets for FMV basis allocations. See P. A. Birren & Son (7th Cir. 1940). If gain is recognized by the

[*52*]

transferor, there is a question, not answered by the Code or the Regulations, whether the resulting increase in asset basis to the corporation should be allocated to all assets (or to all potential gain assets) in proportion to basis, potential gain, or fair market value. Since boot is allocated asset-by-asset in determining the transferor's recognized gain (under Rev.Rul. 68–55), the *Birren* approach suggests that the corporation should add to the basis of each asset the gain recognized on its transfer. For example, if the transferor has already been taxed on $5,000 of ordinary income under § 1245 (recapture of depreciation) because of boot allocation to machinery transferred, it seems proper to allocate the $5,000 of increased basis to this asset to prevent the corporation being taxed on the same gain under § 1245 upon a future sale of the machinery.

(c) *Holding Period.* The corporation can tack the transferor's holding period (in determining whether an asset has been held for the required period under § 1222 or § 1231) of the transferor because its basis is determined by reference to the transferor's basis. § 1223(2). There is no restriction here, as there is in § 1223(1), limiting tacking to assets that were either capital or § 1231 assets in the hands of the transferor.

§ 8.   Other Tax Attributes Acquired by Transferee Corporation

Although the general theory of § 351 has the corporation stepping into the transferor's shoes with regard to the basis of the transferred assets, there is no provision which provides for this result in regard to other important tax attributes.

If the assets acquired in a § 351 transfer are § 453 installment contracts, Regs. § 1.453–9(c) provides that the transferor need not pick up the unreported profit, but the corporation must continue to report profit (with reference to its basis) as each installment is collected. However, the corporation as a new owner of depreciable property elects its own methods of depreciation and makes a new determination of useful life; it is also a second user of the property and therefore ineligible to continue using those accelerated methods of depreciation (i. e., other than straight line) mentioned in § 167(b), which are limited under § 167(c) to first users of property. Sections 1245 and 1250, (relating to recapture of depreciation) cause no recognition of gain upon a § 351(a) transfer, but do characterize some gain as ordinary income when recognition occurs under §§ 351(b) or 357(b) or (c) with respect to property on which depreciation deductions have been taken, §§ 1245(b)(3), 1250(d)(3). To the extent that a corporation acquires § 1245 or § 1250 property with recapture potential still unrecognized, it inherits that potential with the property. Regs. §§ 1.1245–2(c)(2) and 1.1250–3(c)(3). Also in a § 351 transaction there will normally be no recapture of investment credit since the transfer is usually a "mere change in the form of conducting the trade or business" and the requirements for avoiding recapture under § 47(b) will be met. Accounting methods of a business transferred by an individual under § 351 generally need not be continued. Even if the transferor in a § 351 transaction is itself a corporation, as in the formation of a subsidiary corporation, the Code provision for carryover of attributes in some tax-free acquisitions of one corporation's assets by another corporation does not apply. See § 381(a). Thus the corporation cannot acquire net operating loss carryovers, accounting methods or other attributes under § 381 in a § 351 transaction. (There may be some allocation of the corporate transferor's earnings and profits to the transferee in a § 351 transfer if the transferor redeems a substantial part of its stock, etc., under Regs. § 1.312–11(a), e. g., if the transferor distributes stock of the transferee in redemption of some of its stock, in a transaction not covered by § 355.)

§ 9. Midstream Income Problems

If an existing business incorporates, in a § 351 transaction, there may be several hidden difficulties present for the unwary taxpayer.

(a) *The Tax Benefit Rule and Bad Debt Reserves.* The tax benefit rule is a judicial doctrine (codified to some extent in § 111) reflecting the view that if the taxpayer received an income tax benefit by deducting an item in a prior year, the subsequent recovery of the item is income in the year of recovery. In the § 351 area the Service had used this rule prior to 1970 to argue that transferors should include in income the bad debt reserve associated with any transferred accounts receivable. The theory was that since the reserve was no longer needed by the transferor, he should include in income the amount of the reserve which had already been used as deduction. In the Nash decision (1970), however, the Supreme Court held that if the receivables were transferred for consideration equal only to their book value net of the reserve, there was no "recovery" and hence no includible income. By implication, however, *Nash* seemed to require income inclusion to the extent that the transferor receives stock and other consideration worth more than the net book value of the receivables. Normally, however, there will be no income because assuming that the amount of the reserve is reasonable, the stock received in an equal exchange for the receivables will only be worth as much as the net value of the receivables.

(b) *Accounts Receivable and Payable of a Cash Method Taxpayer.* For a cash method taxpayer accounts receivable have a zero basis in a § 351 transfer. Rev.Rul. 69–442. A problem arose if the transferred assets consisted mainly of accounts receivable, and there was a relatively large amount of accounts payable and other liabilities included in the transaction, in that the taxpayer could be required to recognize as gain an unexpected amount of excess liabilities under § 357(c). The Tax Court originally took such a position (with disastrous results for the taxpayer) in cases such as Raich (T.C.1966). After contrary decisions on different theories in two Courts of Appeals, Bongiovanni (2d Cir. 1972) (payables of a cash method taxpayer are not "liabilities" under § 357(c) until they are paid) and Thatcher (9th Cir. 1976) (undeducted liabilities are "liabilities" under § 357(c) but transferor, not transferee, takes expense deduction when liability is paid by transferee), the Tax Court reconsidered its position in Focht (T.C.1977) and held that for § 357(c) purposes the term "liabilities" does not include accounts payable which would be deductible expenses if paid by the transferor. The court reasoned that the assumption of a deductible obligation of a cash method taxpayer is a non-realization event since it is improper to treat the assumed liability as income to the transferor and yet at the same time deny him the tax benefit (i. e. deduction) for its satisfaction. This position was subsequently adopted by Congress, with respect to § 351 transfers occurring after November 6, 1978, through the enactment of § 357(c)(3). This new Code provision applies to trade accounts payable if payment by the transferor would have entitled him to a deduction; it is inapplicable, however, to any case where the incurrence of the liability resulted in the creation of, or an increase in, the basis of any property.

Where no offsetting payables exist, other difficulties with receivables may arise for a cash method taxpayer. The Service (or sometimes the corporate transferee) has on occasion asserted that the transferor(s) of accounts receivable should be taxed thereon, basing its arguments on any of several theories:

(1) assignment of income (the Commissioner seeking to assign income to the party actually earning it under Lucas v. Earl (U.S.1930));

(2) requirement that the taxpayer's method of accounting clearly reflect income under § 446(b) (e. g., Palmer (9th Cir. 1959), in which an incorporating taxpayer in the construction business was required to change to the percentage of completion method from the completed contract method, and thus to report income from pre-transfer work); or

(3) allocation of income and deductions among businesses controlled by the same in-

terests to clearly reflect income under § 482 (e. g., Rooney (9th Cir. 1962) where a farmer who had deducted the expenses of raising crops and then transferred his assets to a corporation which harvested and sold the corps was denied the expense deductions, which were instead allocated to the corporation).

§ 10. Avoiding § 351

Section 351 is not elective. It requires nonrecognition of gain or loss whenever its requirements are met. Normally a transferor will want to take advantage of the tax-free provisions of § 351. In some cases, however, he may seek to avoid § 351 in order to recognize a loss on a transferred asset, or to recognize a gain in order to obtain a stepped-up corporate basis for an asset. If § 351 is avoided, the corporation will have a § 1012 cost basis (See Regs. § 1.1032–1(d)), in the face amount of its short-term notes, for example, rather than a carryover basis under § 362. A loss asset if sold may produce ordinary loss, e. g., under § 1231 whereas a transferor's stock or securities might, if received tax-free with carryover basis, not be saleable and if sold would produce only capital loss. A gain asset may be land which he seeks to sell to the corporation for installment payments for long term capital gain, whereas the land if transferred to the corporation under § 351 with a low substituted basis, would produce ordinary income upon sale because the corporation will have dealer status. Although the use of boot such as short-term notes in a § 351 transaction will suffice to cause a transferor to recognize gain (which will result in an increase in the corporation's basis in the transferred assets), it will not cause recognition of a transferor's loss. This boot route offers safe gain recognition but it is useful only if the corporation will have available cash for payment of the short-term notes.

Transferors seeking total avoidance of § 351 have sometimes formed the corporation with an initial modest transfer of cash for some stock, and shortly thereafter made a purported sale of major assets (e. g., land) to the corporation for a cash down-payment and at least one additional future installment. In cases such as Nye (T.C. 1968) the substance of such a transaction has been combined into a § 351 transfer despite its form; moreover, the installment note has sometimes been held to be a security because of its long term (or in other cases such as Burr Oaks Corp. (7th Cir. 1966), stock because the corporation was thinly capitalized) rather than boot.

Another method of avoiding § 351 in some cases may be to dislodge control "immediately after" the transfer by a pre-arranged sale of stock by the transferors to outsiders.

If a transferor transfers several assets of different types and does avoid § 351, he must allocate the total consideration received to each type of asset, either under an arms-length sales agreement, or in proportion to relative fair market values.

Several sections of the Code limit the benefits to be derived from using the sales method over that of § 351. Through full (§ 1245) or partial (§ 1250) ordinary income treatment of gain attributable to previous depreciation, the recapture sections discourage the sale of depreciated machinery or buildings in order to obtain a stepped-up basis. Section 1239 provides ordinary income treatment for *all* gain on sales of depreciable property between an individual and his 80 percent owned (by value of stock, with attribution rules) corporation, and (as amended in 1976) between two corporations, if more than 80 percent of each is owned (with attribution) by the same individual. Section 267 prevents deduction of loss upon sale between a stockholder and his more than 50 percent owned (by value of stock, with attribution rules) corporation.

If a corporation, particularly one already established, distributes securities, notes or money to stockholders upon their transfer of property, one must also be wary of a possible dividend. Such a disguised dividend could be found to the extent that the distributed consideration clearly exceeds the value of the transferred property. This dividend consequence could apply whether or not the property transfer portion of the transaction qualifies under § 351(a), involves boot under § 351 (b) or constitutes a non-§ 351 sale. (As discussed in the next chapter a "dividend" occurs only if the corporation has sufficient earnings and profits; the consequences under § 301(c) of a distribution without sufficient earnings and profits are also discussed in the next chapter.)

§ 11. Review Question

As an example of some of the points raised in this chapter, the following problem may be studied.

Review Question

On January 1, 1980, Mr. A transfers $10,000 in cash and two items of business equipment to newly-formed Vault Corporation ("Vault") in exchange for 2 shares of Vault common stock (all of the stock) and a Vault debenture, due December 31, 1989, bearing 7% per annum interest and having a principal amount and fair market value of $20,000. At the time, Vault has no other assets or liabilities. One of the two items of business equipment has a fair market value of $45,000 and an adjusted basis of $50,000 in A's hands at the time of transfer; the other has a fair market value of $45,000 and adjusted basis in A's hands of $30,000, and is transferred to Vault subject to a liability of $35,000. In answering each of the following, explain your answer briefly.

(a) Does A realize or recognize any gain or loss from this transaction, and if so, of what character?

(b) Does Vault?

(c) What is A's basis in his Vault stock?

(d) What is Vault's basis in each item of equipment?

(e) How would your answers to the preceding questions be affected if all of the facts were the same except that Vault, at A's direction, issues one of the two shares of stock to A's wife?

Answers

(a) Realization upon item 1 is a $5,000 loss. Upon item 2 it is a $15,000 gain. § 1001. There would be no recognition of gain or loss as § 351 is applicable to this sole stockholder with control. The ten year debenture seems a security; there does not appear to be a problem of a "thin" corporation. The liability relieved does not exceed A's aggregate basis of $90,000 (counting cash), so § 357(c) does not apply.

(b) No. Concerning the stock, see § 1032. The bond is a mere agreement to pay.

(c) A's total basis in the consideration received is $55,000, i. e. $90,000 (basis of transferred property plus invested cash) less $35,000 (liability relieved). § 358. This total basis must then be allocated between the stock and securities in the proportion which the particular stock's (or security's) fair market value bears to the total received consideration's fair market value (FMV). In the absence of other information, the total fair market value of the consideration received is determined by the sum of the fair market value of the assets transferred, $100,000 ($45,000 + $45,000 + $10,000) less the liability relieved ($35,000) equals $65,000. Thus, the basis allocated to the stock would be the fraction

$45,000 ($65,000 FMV of stock and securities received − $20,000 FMV of security)

_____

$65,000 (total FMV of stock and securities received) multiplied by the total basis of $55,000.

= $38,076.92. (Basis of debt = 20/65 × $55,000 = $16,923.08.)

(d) Vault's basis in the equipment is the same as that held by A, $50,000 in item 1 and $30,000 in item 2. § 362(a) and *Birren.*

(e) The issue is whether the transferor husband is in control immediately after the transfer, since there are no attribution rules under § 351 by which he could be considered to own his wife's stock. Probably § 351 does apply, see Stanton

(3d Cir. 1975) (where the transferor husband received 51 percent and his wife received 49 percent of the stock of the newly formed corporation), since the transferor husband had at all times the absolute right to designate the recipient of all the stock of the transferee corporation and the gift of the stock to the wife does not seem to be an integral part of the business transaction under *American Bantam Car Co.* If § 351 is not applicable, the result would be that A would recognize a gain of $15,000. The gain would be ordinary income under § 1239, because A transferred depreciable property and more than 80 percent of the corporation's stock is owned by A and his spouse. The loss is disallowed under § 267. A's basis in the stock would be his cost under § 1012. A's total cost in the two shares plus the debenture would be $65,000, the net amount (FMV of equipment plus cash, less liability) that he paid, of which $20,000 (FMV) would be allocable to the debenture and $45,000 (FMV) to the two shares of stock. A's cost basis in one retained share would be $22,500 (FMV). (His wife's basis under § 1015 in the other gift share would be A's basis of $22,500.) Vault's basis for each item, also cost under § 1012, would be $45,000 for each item, the fair market value (in an equal exchange), or a total of $90,000.

CHAPTER 4

NONLIQUIDATING DISTRIBUTIONS

Table of Sections

§ 1. Introduction

This chapter covers corporate distributions of cash or other property to stockholders of the type termed "section 301 distributions" by the Code. This is the area generally of "dividends" in the corporate law sense, i. e., property distributions by a corporation to its stockholders. For tax purposes, however, such § 301 distributions are "dividends," as defined in § 316, only to the extent that they are out of the current or accumulated earnings and profits of the distributing corporation. Under § 61 the stockholder includes a "dividend" as gross income, with the minor exception that $200 per year of dividends (and interest) or $400 on a joint return, can be excluded by individual stockholders under § 116. If the

[*66*]

stockholder is itself a corporation, it can deduct 85 or 100 percent of the dividend under § 243; thus to a corporate recipient, dividends are more attractive taxwise than even capital gains. A distribution is treated under § 301(c)(1) as coming out of earnings and profits ("e & p"), that is, it is a "dividend", to the extent that e & p exists; to the extent that a distribution is not fully covered by e & p, it is a return of the stockholder's basis under § 301(c)(2) and then results in gain under § 301(c)(3). The painful complexity of this area is fortunately offset by its irrelevance in most situations; usually it will be clear that there are plenty of e & p to cover a cash distribution or that there are no e & p, and non-liquidating distributions in kind are relatively rare. Unfortunately, the student must nevertheless master the outlines of the complex rules for several reasons: general understanding of the area, a start toward working on those harder questions which actually arise, and the relevance of these concepts in such later chapters as redemptions, stock dividends and reorganizations.

A number of types of distributions to stockholders are not covered by § 301 and are treated in other chapters. If a stockholder turns in some of his shares in order to receive a distribution of property, the transaction, termed a "redemption", may qualify as a sale of the shares under § 302 (a), or the sale aspect may be ignored and the

transaction treated as simply a § 301 distribution
on his remaining shares. See § 302(d). Such redemption transactions are the subject of Chapter
5.   Also treated separately are distributions to
stockholders of the corporation's own stock,
whether as a mere distribution or "stock dividend" under § 305, or as part of a "recapitalization" in which the recipient must exchange other
stock or securities to receive the new stock.   Distributions (or exchanges) to stockholders of stock
not in the corporation itself, but in a subsidiary
corporation, are covered separately in the chapter
on "Corporate Divisions."   In all of these cases,
if Code requirements for tax-free treatment of
the distribution are not met, the result may be
treatment as a § 301 distribution under the rules
discussed in this chapter.

Also put to one side is the area of distributions
to stockholders in the complete liquidation of the
corporation.   If a complete liquidation is treated
under the general rule of § 331, the earnings and
profits of the corporation are ignored and the
stockholder treats the transaction as a sale or
exchange of his shares for whatever liquidation
distribution he receives.   See Chapter 6. It should
also be noted that § 301 applies only to amounts
paid to the stockholder in his capacity as such
and therefore does not apply to payments made
to a stockholder in his capacity as a lessor, employee, creditor, etc. (unless such payments are

excessive and therefore held to be disguised dividends). Regs. § 1.301–1(c).

§ 2. Dividends

Under the two-part definition of § 316, a distribution to stockholders is a dividend if it is out of either (1) earnings and profits of the current taxable year, computed at the end of the year without reduction for distributions during the year ("current e & p") or (2) post-1913 accumulated earnings and profits as of the date of the distribution ("accumulated e & p").

The current earnings source of dividends is applied first. A distribution is "out of" e & p if e & p exist. If there are sufficient current e & p to cover the distributions of the taxable year, they are dividends; it is unnecessary then to consider the status of the accumulated e & p account. Thus, a corporation, such as the typical corporation with publicly traded stock, which only pays dividends in the corporate sense that are well covered by the current year's earnings, will be paying dividends for tax purposes (assuming a reasonably close equivalence between its corporate earnings and e & p as computed for tax purposes).

If current e & p are insufficient to cover all the distributions of the taxable year, they are allocated among the distributions. Normally, the allocation will be pro rata to all distributions. If one class of stock has priority over another in distributions, however, its owners will be considered to receive all available e & p ahead of the other classes. See Rev.Rul. 69–440.

Example: M Corp. distributes $4,000 to stockholders in the taxable year. Accumulated e & p at the beginning of the year are zero or a deficit; the current e & p (i. e., computed at the end of the year without reduction for distributions) are $2,500. Distributions on Common stock: January 1, $1,000; April 1, $1,000. Distributions on Preferred stock: June 30, $1,000; December 30, $1,000. The $2,000 preferred distributions are dividends out of the $2,500 current e & p. One-quarter ($500/$2,000) of the January and April common stock distributions is a dividend, $250 in January and $250 in April. Three-quarters of these common stock distributions are returns of capital or taxable gain under § 301(c)(2) and (3).

If there are insufficient current e & p to cover the year's distributions, accumulated e & p become relevant. If accumulated e & p are insufficient to cover all distributions, allocation is simply by date of distribution, in chronological order. Allocation of accumulated e & p becomes significant if there are no current e & p and there is a transfer of shares during the year. For example, in the case of a corporation with no current e & p if pro rata distributions of $1,000 are received by one stockholder in May and by his successor in December, and accumulated e & p are exhausted by the May distribution, the May stockholder will have a taxable dividend, but the December stockholder will have a return of capital or a taxable gain.

If e & p for the current year exist, then the accumulated e & p are calculated up to the beginning of the present taxable year, and the current year's e & p are determined separately at the end of the year. If, however, current e & p are in deficit, so that only accumulated e & p can be a source of dividends, then the effect of the year's loss on accumulated e & p must be calculated as of the date of the distribution. Although the Regulations suggest that losses which can be shown to have taken place during a specific period of the year can be used to reduce accumulated e & p during that particular period, Regs. § 1.316–2(b) (last sentence), the Service has not followed this approach. In Rev.Rul. 74–164 it stated that losses were to be prorated over the entire year; the ruling appears to treat this proration as mandatory even if, as in the Ruling's own fact pattern, the losses were clearly assignable to a definite period of the year.

Example: M Corp. distributed $25,000 to its stockholders on July 1, 1979. The company had $50,000 in accumulated e & p at the beginning of

1979. During the first half of the year, M Corp. lost $70,000, but for the year it made a $5,000 profit. In this case the entire $25,000 would be a dividend under § 301. $5,000 of the distribution would come from current e & p, while the other $20,000 would come from accumulated e & p.

If, slightly altering the above facts, M Corp. had instead ended 1979 with a $10,000 loss, the entire $25,000 would still be a dividend, although the analysis would be somewhat different. The $10,000 loss would be prorated over the entire year so that by the July 1 distribution accumulated e & p would have been reduced by half of the loss, or $5,000. There would still be sufficient e & p, however, to cover the distribution.

This analysis follows the Service's reasoning in Rev.Rul. 74–164, but under the Regulations an alternative analysis might be possible so that the distribution would not be a dividend. Under this latter approach accumulated e & p would be reduced by $70,000 during the first half of the year, since the large loss could be shown to have occurred during this period; the $60,000 gain in the last half of 1979 would increase accumulated e & p by that amount for that period. The difference in these two possible approaches is important, since if the loss for the year is prorated, the distribution is a dividend. If, on the other hand, the entire $70,000 loss is allowed to reduce accumulated e & p for the months before July, the distribution is a return of capital.

§ 3. Nondividend Distributions

Nonliquidating distributions to stockholders which are not dividends because they are not covered by either current or accumulated e & p are treated by each stockholder under § 301(c)(2) as a reduction of basis in shares, and after basis is reduced to zero, under § 301(c)(3) as gain on the shares. To the extent that his stock has available basis to absorb such a nondividend distribution, a stockholder has no gross income but is treated as receiving a return of his capital investment. The character (ordinary or capital, long or short term) of the gain received by a stockholder after recovery of his basis is the same as he would have received on a sale of the shares at a gain. Note that the Code provides no possibility of reporting a loss upon receipt of a nonliquidating distribution under § 301 of less than the stockholder's basis since the stockholder has not yet disposed of his shares. If a stockholder recovers his entire basis, his zero basis will result in capital gain if he sells the shares and will prevent any loss deduction if the shares subsequently become worthless. § 165(b).

To a stockholder who is an individual, nondividend treatment is not painful if tax-free, and even if involving capital gain (if long term) is preferable to the ordinary income treatment of a dividend distribution. To a stockholder which is itself a corporation, however, with § 243 available to offset 85 percent or all of a dividend, nondividend treatment with perhaps a 28 percent tax if there is capital gain will normally be less attractive than dividend treatment.

If a stockholder has some shares with a low basis and others acquired at a different time with a higher basis he must allocate the nondividend distribution pro rata to all of his shares. In the case of a large (yet nonliquidating) nondividend distribution, this can result in a substantial capital gain on the low basis shares while there is no gain (but no loss) in the high basis shares, whose remaining basis cannot be used to absorb the gain on the low basis shares. See Johnson (4th Cir. 1971).

Example: M Corp. has $100,000 of accumulated e & p at the start of 1979, and zero current e & p for 1979. On June 5, 1979 M Corp. distributes $300,000 in cash pro rata to its stockholders. As owners of 10 percent of the shares each, stockholders A, B, and C each receive $30,000. A's adjusted basis in his shares is $16,000; B's adjusted basis is $44,000; and C has two equal blocks of stock, one with adjusted basis of $8,000 and the other with adjusted basis of $22,000. Each of the three stockholders has a dividend of $10,000, representing the proportion ($100,000/300,000) of his $30,000 distribution which is covered by e & p. A applies $16,000 of his remaining $20,000 distribution to reduce his $16,000 stock basis to zero and reports capital gain of $4,000; B applies the remaining $20,000 distribution to reduce his $44,000 basis to $24,000; C allocates $10,000 of the remaining $20,000 to reduce his basis in one block from $8,000 to zero and reports $2,000 capital gain on that block, and allocates the other $10,000 to reduce his basis in the other block from $22,000 to $12,000.

§ 4. Earnings and Profits

Section 312 of the Code provides no definition of "earnings and profits," but it does provide for the effect on e & p of many specified corporate transactions. The e & p for any taxable year can be computed by starting with taxable income, subtracting items such as federal income taxes, and adding tax-free income items. Unlike taxable income, the accumulated earnings and profits account of the corporation is decreased by dividend distributions to stockholders; thus the same earnings will not serve more than once as the source of dividend treatment for a distribution. See § 312(a). Similarly, taxes paid reduce e & p, and this is true even for nondeductible taxes like the federal income tax itself. See Ferguson (T.C. 1966). The Regulations answer many of the major questions untouched by the Code itself, and make clear the general pattern that receipts and disbursements which affect dividend-paying capacity in the corporate sense generally affect e & p even though they do not enter into the computation of taxable income, see, generally, Regs. § 1.-312–6(b); however, as to matters of accounting, i. e., timing, the methods followed in computing the corporation's taxable income generally govern its e & p computation also. For example, as to receipts, § 103 tax-exempt interest on municipal bonds and the § 101 tax-free excess life insurance proceeds received over premiums paid are included in the corporate recipient's e & p; similarly the full amount of dividends received from other corporations is included in e & p even though 85 or 100 percent is deducted under § 243 in computing taxable income. As to disbursements, in addition to dividends, taxes paid, and deductible business expenses, the excessive portion of salary paid, disallowed as a deduction, also decreases e & p. Examples of the effect of accounting or timing rules include capitalization and depreciation of capital outlays, application of the taxpayer's general accrual or cash method, and application of special tax methods like installment reporting under § 453. Thus installment profits will be reported and included in e & p as payments are received. Depletion deductions are limited to "cost depletion", Regs. § 1.312–6(c), inasmuch as percentage depletion is an artificial deduction not related to the actual depletion of the mineral. The Tax Reform Act of 1969 added a special rule for accelerated depreciation to correct a situation in which certain corporations, particularly owners of rental real estate and public utilities, were able to regularly pay dividends in the corporate sense because they had earnings using straight-line depreciation, but the dividends were at least partially tax-free as a return of capital because of the effect of accelerated depreciation on the e & p as computed for tax purposes. Section 312(k), fully effective in 1973, provides generally that only straight-line depreciation is deductible in computing e & p. There is also no "statute of limitations" as to earnings and profits, so that a newly discovered large income item or improper deduction or incorrect reduction in earnings and profits in a previous year, as to which a tax deficiency would be barred by statutory time limitations, could result in increased or decreased accumulated e & p, thereby changing the nature of a current distribution (e. g., from a return of capital into a dividend).

Example: X Corp. distributes $100,000 to stockholders in 1978, when it apparently has neither current nor accumulated e & p. The stockholders treat the distribution as a § 301(c)(2) return of capital. In 1980, however, it is discovered that in 1966 X Corp. had distributed to its stockholders appreciated property with a fair market value of

$100,000 and an adjusted basis in its hands of $10,000 and had incorrectly purported to reduce e & p by the fair market value instead of by the adjusted basis of the distributed property, see § 312(a)(3). There are no other corrections to the e & p account. X's accumulated e & p thus were $90,000 at the time of the 1976 $100,000 distribution, and 9/10 of the distribution to each stockholder was taxable as a dividend.

When the e & p reductions exceed the e & p increases, the existing accumulated e & p is reduced, and may reach zero or even be reduced below zero to a deficit position. Once accumulated e & p is reduced to zero or below, distributions to stockholders which are not out of current e & p cease to reduce accumulated e & p. That is, if there is no current e & p, the distribution will reduce the recipient's basis or cause gain under §§ 301(c)(2) and (3), and consistent with this return-of-capital treatment at the stockholder level, it will not reduce e & p at the corporate level. Thus operating losses, in general, may produce or increase deficits in e & p, but distributions to stockholders cannot. A deficit in accumulated e & p is reduced by current operations which produce e & p until eventually the accumulated e & p may be brought above zero and become again a potential source of dividends.

Example: Cyclical Corporation had after-tax earnings of 10 one year, followed by losses of 10 the next year, as determined for purposes of e & p computations, in a recurring pattern for its first five years of operation. As permitted under local law, it distributed 5 to stockholders each year. On these facts at the end of year 1, after dividends of 5 from current e & p of 10, its accumulated e & p account stands at 5. In year 2 there is no current e & p and the distribution of 5 will be a dividend to the extent that it is covered by accumulated e & p on the date of distribution. Using the approach of Rev.Rul. 74–164, the losses of 10 are considered to occur ratably throughout the year. A midyear distribution of 5 would occur just as the accumulated e & p account has reached zero and would thus not be a dividend and would not reduce e & p. E & p at the end of year 2 would be reduced by 10 to a deficit of 5. Year 3 would bring a dividend of 5 from current e & p, with the remaining 5 of e & p restoring the accumulated e & p account to zero. In year 4, the distribution would have no effect on e & p, and losses would reduce the e & p account by 10 to a deficit of 10. In year 5, current e & p of 10 would be applied 5 to a dividend and 5 to reduce the deficit in accumulated e & p as of the end of year 5, to 5. If operations continued in this fashion, accumulated e & p would continue to increase (reduce the deficit) by 5 every odd year and decrease (increase the deficit) by 10 every even year.

§ 5. Distributions in Kind

Under § 301(b) if distributions by a corporation to its stockholders are property other than
money, the "amount" of the distribution is determined differently for corporate and noncorporate
stockholders. To a noncorporate stockholder the
"amount" of a distribution in kind is the fair market value of the property received, § 301(b)(1)
(A), and accordingly the stockholder takes fair
market value as his basis in the distributed property, § 301(d)(1). If the stockholder is a corporation, however, the "amount" of the distribution is the lower of the fair market value of the
property received or its adjusted basis in the
hands of the distributing corporation immediately
before the distribution (increased in the amount
of any gain recognized to the distributing corporation under sections such as 311, 1245, or 1250),
§ 301(b)(1)(B), and the stockholder corporation
takes this same amount as its basis in the distributed property. (Caution: In considering a hoped-
for dividend in kind, note that I.R.S. might claim
that the transaction is a partial liquidation as
in Fowler Hosiery (T.C.1961), aff'd (7th Cir.
1962), as discussed infra, Chapter 6, § 11(d).)
The special treatment of corporate distributees is
due to the facts that intercorporate dividends are
taxed little or nothing because of the § 243 deduction, and that the distributing corporation
generally, under § 311(a), does not recognize

gain when it distributes property with a fair market value in excess of basis. Consequently, without the special rule, there would exist the possibility that a corporation, without recognizing any gain, could distribute greatly appreciated property to an affiliated corporation, which in turn could take a 100 percent dividend deduction and also receive the property with a step-up in basis. Therefore this favorable treatment is restricted to the lower of basis or fair market value, the corporate distributees must report dividends in the more limited amount, and they must take the same approach as to basis, i. e., generally a carry-over basis for the property received rather than a step-up of basis to a higher fair market value. In applying the "lesser of fair market value or adjusted basis" rule, the adjusted basis of the property in the hands of the distributing corporation immediately before the distribution is increased for any gain recognized to the distributing corporation (under the exceptions and overrides to § 311(a) discussed below). See Regs. § 1.301–1 (d), first sentence. The amount of the distribution computed under the foregoing rules is reduced (but not below zero) under § 301(b)(2) by the amount of any liabilities of the corporation either assumed by the stockholder or to which the distributed property is subject.

The distributing corporation generally recognizes no gain (or loss) upon a § 301 distribution

of appreciated (or depreciated) property to its
stockholders under § 311(a). This rule would apply, for example, if a corporation distributes vacant land with a basis of $50,000 and a fair mar-
ket value of $300,000, as a nonliquidating distri-
bution to its stockholders. This general rule is
subject to a number of significant exceptions stated in § 311 itself, plus the effect of other sections
of the Code, such as §§ 1245 and 1250 on depreciation recapture, which override § 311.

The exceptions are:

Section 453(d). As indicated in § 311(a),
if receivables representing the right to uncollected installments being reported under
§ 453 are distributed, the distribution constitutes a "disposition" for the fair market
value of the receivables under § 453(d), so
that the distributing corporation must report
as much uncollected profit (if any) as it
would have had if it had sold the receivables.
The Service is particularly strict in this area
and interprets the Code sections literally.
Notwithstanding the fact that the corporation must recognize gain upon distributing
installment obligations, no adjustment to the
bases of the obligations distributed can be
made either for applying the "lesser of fair
market value or adjusted basis" rule for corporate stockholders or for making proper ad-

justments in the distributor's e & p. See Rev.Rul. 74–337.

Section 311(b). If LIFO inventory (which tends to have a low basis representing price levels prevailing when the corporation adopted LIFO) is distributed, the difference between its basis and the higher basis which would have applied if the more usual FIFO rules were used, must be recognized as gain by the distributing corporation.

Section 311(c). If a stockholder assumes or takes subject to a liability which exceeds the distributing corporation's basis in the property, gain is recognized in the amount of such excess as if the property had been sold by the corporation.

Section 311(d). If the distribution is in redemption of stock (and thus outside the scope of this chapter) all gain (but no loss) is recognized on property distributed, with a number of exceptions, as discussed in the chapter on Redemptions.

Besides these situations described in § 311(a)–(d), other sections of the Code may take precedence over the normal nonrecognition rule of § 311(a). Included among these are:

Sections 1245, 1250, 1251–1254. A distribution of property of a type subject to depreciation recapture is treated under these sections like a sale of the property at its fair market value. This can cause a significant amount of ordinary income in some cases. It prevents avoidance of § 1245, for example, by distributing machinery with a low basis reflecting depreciation deductions to its individual stockholders, who could then use their stepped-up fair market value basis to sell the property with no further gain. Note that recapture occurs even if the distributee is a corporation which (but for the recapture) would have taken the property without a step-up in basis.

Section 341. If various types of assets are disposed of by a collapsible corporation which had filed a consent under § 341(f), gain will be recognized to the corporate distributor in certain circumstances despite the general rule of § 311(a).

Section 617(d). The disposition of property as to which mining exploration expenditures have been claimed as deductions may lead to the recapture of such expenditures if the conditions of § 617(d) are met.

Section 47(a)(1). If the distribution is an early disposition of property for which the § 38 investment tax credit was taken, an additional tax will be imposed to recoup the unearned credit.

Notwithstanding the general principle of non-recognition of gain for the company distributing property as a dividend, the judicially-created assignment of income doctrine may also take precedence over § 311(a). A leading example of the use of this doctrine is First State Bank of Stratford (5th Cir. 1948). In this case a bank distributed to its stockholders as a dividend notes, previously deducted as bad debts but later found to have some value, with a bank employee acting as agent in collecting on the notes. Only the notes on which it was expected that collections would be made were declared as dividends. The Court of Appeals held that these notes represented corporate income which could not be avoided by anticipatory assignment; thus the bank was taxable on the bad debt recovery and the stockholders were taxable on a cash dividend.

Another example of this principle is the *Lynch* decision (9th Cir. 1951). There the closely-held corporation declared as a dividend apples grown in the company's orchards. The corporation also acted as agent in selling the fruit for the stockholders. The appellate court stated that the corporation should be required to recognize gain from the sale of the apples. Not only was there a distribution of corporate inventory with the expectation of immediate sale by the stockholders, but an even stronger case was made because the

[*85*]

sale was to be made by utilizing the corporation's facilities.

In passing the present provision § 311, the Senate Finance Committee stated that the law on the assignment of income doctrine in property distributions, as shown for example in *First State Bank of Stratford*, was not to be changed. Additionally, the Regulations state that "where property is distributed by a corporation, which distribution is in effect an anticipatory assignment of income, such income may be taxable to the corporation", § 1.311–1(a).

The effect of a distribution in kind on the distributing corporation's earnings and profits is to reduce e & p by the adjusted basis of the property distributed. See § 312(a)(3). If the property is distributed with liabilities, or if gain is recognized to the distributing corporation, § 312(c) provides cryptically for "proper adjustment". "Proper adjustment" in general requires that any gain recognized to the corporation (for example because of liabilities in excess of basis or recapture of depreciation) increases e & p; any income tax that eventually results will of course reduce e & p. Regs. § 1.312–3 allows an increase in the reduction of e & p for gain recognized under §§ 311, 1245, etc. (which gain increased the e & p) and Regs. § 1.312–4 provides examples. Under § 312(b), if "inventory assets" (defined to include inventory, property held for sale to customers by a dealer, and unrealized receivables from the sale of such property or for services) are distributed, e & p are increased by the excess of the fair market value of such items over their basis and then reduced by fair market value (or total e & p, if less). The result is that distributions of inventory create enough e & p (if the corporation does not otherwise have a deficit in current e & p) to cause their full appreciation in value to be treated as a dividend; otherwise, a corporation with zero e & p could step up the basis of appreciated land as to which it is a dealer or similar ordinary income property, to fair market value in the hands of individual stockholders, who would be free to sell without reporting any income, at the cost of merely reducing the basis of their stock. Note that distributions of LIFO inventory result in gain under § 311(b) (to bring its basis up to FIFO) and e & p, whereas distributions of other inventory-type assets produce merely e & p under § 312(b) but not gain to the distributing corporation.

The proper adjustment for the fact that the distributing corporation is relieved of liabilities along with the distributed property is to reduce the amount treated as distributed by the amount of the liabilities.

Example: Distribution of property with adjusted basis of 3, subject to a liability of 2, and with fair market value of 5, reduces e & p by 1, the adjusted basis less the liability. If the facts are the same except that the liability is 4, the distribution does not reduce e & p (basis is more than covered by the liability, or, in other words, basis is increased to reflect gain recognized and then is just offset by the liability), and the gain of 1 recognized to the distributing corporation under § 311 (c) causes an increase in e & p of 1. The tax on the gain will eventually reduce e & p. Note that the "amount" received by an individual sole stockholder in the above examples would be 3 (fair market value of 5 less liability of 2) or 1 (FMV of 5 less liability of 4).

Example: Taxi Corporation has accumulated earnings and profits of $10,000; for the current taxable year it has neither profits nor losses. On March 5, the Corporation distributes to its sole stockholder, A, a taxicab which cost $4,000 originally but, because of depreciation deductions, has an adjusted basis of $100 immediately before the distribution. The taxicab has a fair market value of $900 and is subject to a liability of $700. The "amount" received by A under § 301(b)(1)(A) and (2)(B) is $200 (fair market value $900 less liability $700) all of which under § 301(c)(1) is a dividend because it is well covered by the $10,000 accumulated e & p. The corporation recognizes $800 gain as ordinary income from recapture of depreciation under § 1245 (previous depreciation

of $3,900 on this personal property, limited how-
ever to the excess of fair market value, $900,
over adjusted basis, $100). If the distributed
property had not been subject to recapture, the
corporation would have recognized $600 gain,
capital or ordinary depending on the nature of
the property, under § 311(c) ($700 liability less
$100 adjusted basis); since the same gain cannot
be recognized twice, the recapture section (providing for the recognition of the larger gain)
takes precedence and § 311(c) does not operate
in the example. The § 1245 gain recognized of
$800 increases e & p $800; eventual tax on this
gain will reduce e & p. Under Regs. §§ 1.312–3
and 1.312–4, reduction of e & p from the distribution is:

$$+100 \quad \text{(basis)}$$
$$-700 \quad \text{(liability)}$$
$$\underline{+800} \quad \text{(§ 1245 gain)}$$
$$+200 \quad \text{reduction of e \& p.}$$

The $800 recapture gain, less the $200 reduction,
gives a net increase of $600, less eventual tax on
the gain.

Note that if the sole stockholder in this example were itself a corporation, it would also include
an amount of $200 under § 301(b)(1)(B)(ii):
the basic amount of $900, (representing lesser of
fair market value of $900 or adjusted basis of

$900 after the increase from $100 by $800 for gain recognized under § 1245, under Regs. § 1.-301–1(d), first sentence), reduced by $700 of liabilities, the same as in the case of an individual stockholder. This $200 would be included in gross income as a dividend, but the corporate stockholder would have an offsetting deduction under § 243, generally for the full $200 in the case of a sole stockholder (a member of an affiliated group, which would file the necessary election), or else $170 (85 percent). Note also that if the facts were that Taxi Corporation for the current taxable year has neither profits nor losses (apart from the transaction in this example), the $800 (minus eventual tax) current e & p generated by this transaction because of § 1245 gain would cause the $200 received by the sole stockholder (individual or corporate) to be a dividend even if accumulated e & p at the start of the year were zero or a deficit, instead of $10,000.

§ 6.   Distribution of Corporation's Own Obligations

Some special considerations apply if a corporation makes a § 301 distribution of its bond or note to a stockholder. The Code, defining "property" in § 317(a), excludes the distributing corporation's own stock (or rights to receive its stock) but makes no mention of its obligations; the Regulations treat such obligations as property.

Thus an individual stockholder receives a § 301 (b)(1)(A) "amount" equal to the fair market value of the distributed obligation. The Regulations (§ 1.301–1(d)) on distributions of property to stockholders which are corporations provide that the "amount" of a distribution of obligations of the distributing corporation is fair market value; this eliminates the usual rule for corporate distributees of using adjusted basis, if lower. The reason for this procedure is that a distributing corporation could not have basis in its own promise to pay; even if it reacquired its note or bond, that should close the transaction so that a reissue of the debt would be regarded as a new transaction. (The same Regulation likewise treats stock or stock rights of the distributing corporation as received by a corporation at fair market value, with no possibility of applying a lower adjusted basis, if such stock or rights is not distributed tax-free but is treated as property under § 305). A corporation distributing its own obligation reduces its earnings and profits by the *principal amount*, which the corporation is promising to pay; for this special type of property any conceivable "adjusted basis" is irrelevant. See Regs. § 1.312–1(a)(2).

If the corporation does not distribute its own debt obligation, but assumes the debt of a stockholder to a third party, it has been held that no distribution of property occurs while the stock-

holder remains liable (after the corporation) on
the debt until the corporation actually makes
payment to the third party. See Maher (8th Cir.
1972); I.R.S. announced in Rev.Rul. 77–360 that
it will follow *Maher* on this point.

§ 7. Disguised Dividends

Stockholders, particularly of a closely held corporation with substantial e & p, normally would
like to draw economic benefits out of the corporation in ways that are tax-free to themselves,
and/or deductible by the corporation. Because
dividends are taxable and not deductible, substi-
tutes designed for more favorable tax treatment
are a common issue, with litigated examples reflected in many weekly issues of the looseleaf tax
services. A partial list of transactions which
may represent disguised dividends includes:
loans by the corporation to stockholders under
circumstances suggesting that there is no intention of repayment; sales of property to stockholders at abnormally low prices; excess payments to
stockholders purportedly for goods or services
supplied by them to the corporation in their capacity as employees (the perennial problem of
"unreasonable compensation"), lessors, contrac-
tors, or suppliers; and free use of corporate property such as yachts and automobiles, for personal
rather than business purposes.

Classification of a payment under state law, which may require each share to receive a pro rata share of any property distribution, is of course not determinative of whether a transaction constitutes a § 301 distribution for tax purposes. The fact that an economic benefit goes to persons who are stockholders in proportion to their shareholdings suggests a dividend; but many payments that were not pro rata have been held to be disguised dividends. As long as the benefit seems to be available because of the recipient's share ownership, the fact that other stockholders are less able to secure such benefits, less demanding, or merely willing to permit others, perhaps relatives, to so benefit, does not prevent dividend treatment. Moreover, if the stockholder obtains an economic benefit, for example by purchasing a hotel from the corporation for $170,000 less than its fair market value, there is a dividend in that amount even assuming that there was no corporate intention to distribute a dividend. See Honigman (6th Cir. 1972). Occasionally a constructive dividend to a controlling stockholder may be found if the corporation makes a payment to a third party under circumstances indicating that it merely serves the controlling stockholder's personal wishes. See Rev.Rul. 79–9 (contribution to charitable foundation formed and supported by the stockholders of a closely held corporation,

[*93*]

with the stockholders or their families receiving an economic benefit as a result of the contribution); Montgomery Engineering Co. (3rd Cir. 1965) (payment to widow of corporate employee because controlling stockholder wanted to right a wrong done to the widow by her husband).

CHAPTER 5

REDEMPTIONS, INCLUDING PARTIAL LIQUIDATIONS

Table of Sections

[*95*]

§ 1. Introduction

A "redemption" of stock occurs if the corporation which issued the stock acquires it from a stockholder for money or other property (other than the acquiring corporation's stock or warrants). § 317, Regs. § 1.302–1(a). (A transaction in which a stockholder transfers stock to the corporation for purported corporate debt instruments may not be a "redemption" at all if the purported debt is held to be stock (compare discussion in Chapter 2 on Capital Structure), § 317, Regs. § 1.302–4(d)). The problem addressed by the Code is to distinguish redemptions which should be treated like a sale of stock by the stockholders (ignoring the fact that a distribution is

[*96*]

made by the corporation) from those which should be treated like the receipt of a distribution (a dividend to the extent of e & p) by a stockholder (ignoring the sale of shares). The Code allows no blended treatment: a particular dollar received by a redeeming stockholder is either all sale proceeds, or all a § 301 distribution. There are two basic tests underlying the rules for determining eligibility for sale treatment; if the redemption fails both of these tests, § 302(d) provides that it receives § 301 distribution treatment. Sale treatment applies if:

(1) Tested at the stockholder level, the redemption significantly reduces the proportionate interest of the stockholder in the corporation under § 302(a) (or qualifies under § 303 relating to certain death taxes and expenses where the stock was part of a decedent stockholder's gross estate); or

(2) Tested at the corporate level, the redemption represents a contraction of corporate business, resulting in partial liquidation treatment under §§ 346 and 331(a)(2).

The polar cases at the stockholder level are illustrated by the following two examples:

(1) A corporation owned equally by six unrelated individuals redeems all of the stock owned by one of them in order to settle a policy dispute. The stockholder whose inter-

est is terminated is in the same position as if he had sold his stock.

(2) If the same corporation were to accumulate earnings and then redeem an equal amount of stock from each stockholder, the stockholders' proportionate interests in the corporation would remain unchanged and the transaction would have the same practical effect as if a § 301 distribution had been made without the surrender of stock.

The principal stockholder-level tests are contained in § 302(b); § 302(a) provides that if a corporation redeems its stock and if § 302(b)(1) ("not essentially equivalent to a dividend"), a vague holdover from the 1939 Code, or the more mechanical "safe harbor" rules of § 302(b)(2) (substantially disproportionate redemptions) or § 302(b)(3) (complete termination of a stockholder's interest) apply, the redemption will be treated as a sale.

Attribution rules are provided in § 318 to prevent taxpayers from using one of the sale treatment exceptions of § 302 for redemption of their actually owned shares while maintaining their interest in the corporation indirectly through a close relative or an entity such as a trust or corporation.

The possibility that a taxpayer may bail out earnings at capital gain rates through the sale of his stock in one corporation to a related corporation is limited by § 304, which applies the redemption principles of §§ 302 and 303 to such transactions.

Gain or loss on a redemption which qualifies for sale treatment (normally capital in nature) is determined as it would be in any sale under § 1001 by comparing the adjusted basis in the shares redeemed with the "amount realized". On a redemption that does not qualify, the entire "amount realized" is, under § 302(d), treated as a § 301 distribution and produces dividend income to the extent of earnings and profits. In determining the amount of dividend income the stockholder's basis in the redeemed shares is not subtracted from the amount realized; instead the stockholder's basis in the redeemed shares is allocated to his remaining shares.

Example: B Corp., which has substantial e & p, redeems 2 of stockholder S's 10 shares of B Corp. stock (in which S has an adjusted basis of $10 per share) for $15 per share in a nonqualifying redemption. The entire amount received ($30) will be treated as a § 301 distribution and since B Corp. has sufficient e & p to cover the $30 amount, S has a dividend of $30 and the $20 adjusted basis of the 2 redeemed shares will be spread over the remaining 8 shares, giving S a new adjusted basis of $12.50 ($10 $+ \dfrac{\$20}{8}$) per share.

The tax consequences of a redemption to the acquiring corporation if it distributes property other than cash are governed primarily by § 311 (taxability of corporations on nonliquidating distributions), or § 336 (taxability of corporations on liquidating distributions). Adjustments to the corporation's earnings and profits account are made under § 312.

Partial liquidations (other than as part of a plan of complete liquidation) will be considered together with nonliquidating redemptions in this chapter. Distributions in complete liquidation are covered in Chapter 6. The special consequences of redemptions of "section 306 stock" are covered in Chapter 8.

§ 2. Substantially Disproportionate Redemptions: § 302(b)(2)

Sale treatment of a redemption is assured if the stockholder meets the tests for reduction of his percentage interest in the corporation provided in § 302(b)(2). There is a three part test: first, the stockholder must reduce his percentage of *voting* stock; and second, his percentage of common stock, voting or nonvoting, to less than 80 percent of what it was before the redemption; and third, immediately after the redemption, he must own less than 50 percent of the total combined voting power of the stock in the corporation. The Regulations interpret the § 302(b)(2) redemption by the stockholder as including all the stock he redeems in the transaction; thus nonvoting preferred shares redeemed by a stockholder along with qualifying voting common qualify as part of a disproportionate redemption. Regs. § 1.302–3(a). In applying these tests, the redeemed stockholder is considered to own, both before and after the redemption, stock attributed to him under § 318 as well as his actually owned shares. § 302(c)(1). Note that the stockholder's percentage interest is affected both by changes in the number of his shares and by changes in the total number of shares outstanding caused by the redemption and any other simultaneous redemptions from other stockholders.

Example: A and B, unrelated individuals, each own 60 of the 120 outstanding shares of common stock of M Corp., the only class of stock outstanding. M redeems 20 of A's shares. The redemption is not substantially disproportionate under § 302(b)(2): before the redemption A's interest in the voting (and common) stock is 50% (60/120); after the redemption his interest is 40% (40/100); the 20 redeemed shares reduced A's holding from 60 to 40 but also reduced the total shares outstanding from 120 to 100; 40% is *exactly* 80% of 50% and thus does not meet the requirement that his interest be reduced to *less than* 80% of his former interest. If 21 of A's shares had been redeemed, instead of 20, his percentage of voting and common stock would have been reduced to 39.39 percent (39/99) which is just under 80 percent (i. e., 78.78 percent) of his former 50 percent interest; the redemption would qualify because it meets both the less than 80 percent (substantially disproportionate) test and the less than 50 percent of the total voting power test. However, if when 21 of A's shares are redeemed, 5 of B's shares are also redeemed, neither stockholder's redemption would qualify under § 302(b)(2).

Where more than one event occurs as part of a plan, such as a redemption from one or more stockholders, plus a sale of some stock, or issuance of new stock, the before and after tests of § 302(b)(2) are applied before and after the entire planned transaction. Rev.Rul. 75–447. Section 302(b)(2) does not apply if the plan involves a series of redemptions having the purpose or effect of a redemption that is not substantially disproportionate. § 302(b)(2)(D). Thus, if there are three equal stockholders, one has half his stock redeemed (33⅓ percent to 20 percent), 4 months later another has half *his* stock redeemed (40 percent to 25 percent), and 4 months later the third has half his stock redeemed (50 percent to 33⅓ percent), the overall effect is that there are again three equal stockholders; and the three pro rata redemptions would fail to qualify if made pursuant to a plan. Similarly, if a redemption to one stockholder, viewed in isolation, is substantially disproportionate but the other stockholders agree to sell shares to the redeemed stockholder thereby making the total transaction not substantially disproportionate, then the redemption will presumably not satisfy § 302(b)(2).

§ 3. Termination of Interest: § 302(b)(3) and Waiver of Family Attribution by § 302(c)

(a) *In General.* Sale treatment is provided by § 302(b)(3) if the redemption is of all of the stock in the corporation owned by the redeemed stockholder. From a broad theoretical standpoint, such a "complete termination of interest" carries the general idea of a substantially disproportionate redemption to its ultimate limits; if a stockholder is no longer a stockholder after the redemption, logically he has no stock on which he can be considered to receive a dividend. Note, however, that if a stockholder takes at least partly purported debt instruments for his stock, his claim of termination of interest may be challenged if his rights are significantly greater, or less, than usual creditor's rights, Regs. § 1.302–4(d) and (e), and if the instrument is stock, the transaction may not be a redemption at all, but a recapitalization as discussed in Chapter 10.

It might seem that § 302(b)(3) adds little to what is already provided by § 302(b)(2), since a

[*103*]

reduction of stock ownership to zero obviously is a reduction to less than 80 percent of the former stock interest. The principal technical significance of § 302(b)(3), however, is that upon filing the appropriate agreement under § 302(c), the stockholder who surrenders all of his actually owned stock, and retains no prohibited interest, is not subject to the family attribution rules of § 318(a)(1).

Example: A father owns 60 percent, and each of his two sons owns 20 percent, of the stock of a corporation. Under the attribution rules, the father is considered to own 100 percent of the stock because stock of his children is attributed to him. He is still considered to own 100 percent no matter how many of his shares are redeemed because any stock not actually owned by him is owned by his children. Similarly, each son is considered to own his father's stock (but not his brother's) as well as his own; even if a son has all of his actually owned shares redeemed, reducing his interest from $^{80}/_{100}$ to $^{60}/_{80}$, or from 80 percent to 75 percent, he meets neither the less than 80 percent test (which requires that his interest be less than 64 percent, i. e., 80 percent of his former 80 percent interest), nor the less than 50 percent of the total voting power test. However, if any of the three surrenders for redemption all of his actually owned stock, retains no prohibited interest, and files the necessary agreement under § 302(c),

[*104*]

thereby "waiving" the family attribution rules for purposes of § 302(b)(3), he qualifies for sale treatment.

Another minor mechanical effect of § 302(b)(3) is that it covers complete redemptions from a stockholder who owns only nonvoting stock, (or voting preferred) and who thus cannot reduce his percentage interest in the voting (or common) stock (since it is already at zero) to less than 80 percent of what it was, as is required by by § 302(b)(2). See Regs. § 1.302–3(a).

(b) *Waiver of Family Attribution.* Section 302(c)(2)(A) provides that the family attribution rules shall not apply, i. e., it grants a "waiver" of the rules, in determining whether a redeemed stockholder has completely terminated his stock interest as required under § 302(b)(3). Family attribution, § 318(a)(1), as discussed below otherwise treats the redeemed stockholder as owning stock owned by his spouse, children, grandchildren and parents. Section 302(c)(2)(A) establishes three conditions for waiving family attribution in applying § 302(b)(3):

(1) Immediately after the distribution, the distributee (the redeemed stockholder) has no interest in the corporation other than as a creditor; specifically listed as prohibited interests are serving as an officer, director or employee. Traditionally IRS has taken the

[*105*]

position that the performance of services for the corporation, with or without compensation, is prohibited. This position was reaffirmed in 1978 with the publication of IRS' non-acquiescence in the holding of Lennard (T.C.1974) that the performance of accounting services, as an independent contractor, does not constitute an "interest" in the corporation. The Service has, however, ruled that a landlord-tenant relationship is not a prohibited interest. Rev.Rul. 70–639.

(2) The distributee must not acquire a prohibited interest within a 10 year (forward) period (except stock acquired by bequest or inheritance, but including stock reacquired due to the corporation's default on credit terms of the sale agreement). The reacquired interest must be an actual one. The acquisition of stock by other family members will not be attributed to the redeemed stockholder. Rev.Rul. 71–562.

(3) The distributee must file with his tax return for the year of the redemption an agreement to notify IRS if he does acquire a prohibited interest within the 10 year period. Regs. § 1.302–4(a)(1). An inadvertent delay will not disqualify the stockholder, Regs. § 1.302–4(a)(2), and the courts generally require substantial, not strict, compliance with the time limitation. If the dis-

tributee does acquire a prohibited interest within the 10 year period, the waiver of attribution is lost retroactively, with the probable result that his redemption transaction retroactively loses its character as a sale and becomes a § 301 distribution. Section 302(c)(2) specifically extends the statute of limitations on the taxable year of the redemption to one year after the distributee notifies IRS of his acquisition of a prohibited interest.

There is an exception, § 302(c)(2)(B), to the waiver of attribution if either (1) any of the stock redeemed was acquired by the redeemed stockholder within the 10 year (backward) period preceding the redemption from a person whose stock is attributable to the redeemed stockholder or (2) any such related person acquired stock from the redeemed stockholder in the preceding 10 year period. The purpose of this exception is to foreclose the possibility of, say, a father owning a substantial block of stock in a corporation making a gift of a portion of the stock to his son who might have it redeemed, terminating his interest and thereby receive sale treatment, whereas if the stock had been redeemed from the father himself, the proceeds would have been treated as a § 301 distribution. An exception to this exception is provided if the transfer of stock between the distributee and the related party did not have tax avoidance as one of its principal purposes. See § 302(c)(2)(B) (last sentence).

Example: All of a son's actually owned stock, constituting 7 percent of the outstanding stock, is redeemed. The son had acquired the stock 5 years earlier from his father, who at the time of the redemption owns 75 percent of the outstanding stock. Under the "exception," the son generally cannot obtain waiver of the attribution rules, and thus cannot qualify for sale treatment, because there was a transfer from a related party to him within the previous 10 year period; however, suppose that the father had given his son the stock to encourage his son's interest in the business and the redemption occurred as the son left the business because of lack of opportunity; on these facts, the Service, finding that the gift was made for bona-fide business reasons with no plan for the future redemption, has ruled that under the "exception to the exception", attribution is waived if the son files the necessary agreement and stays out of the business for 10 years after the redemption. Rev.Rul. 56–584.

§ 4. Redemptions "Not Essentially Equivalent to Dividends": § 302(b)(1)

A redemption that fails to meet the mechanical "safe harbor" rules of § 302(b)(2) or (b)(3) may nevertheless qualify for sale treatment under § 302(b)(1) if it is "not essentially equivalent to

a dividend." This general test was made somewhat more precise in 1970 by the Supreme Court
in the *Davis* case. The test depends strictly upon the "net effect" of the redemption; a "business
purpose" will not result in sale treatment for an
essentially pro rata distribution. There must be
a meaningful reduction in the stockholder's proportionate interest in the corporation, and the attribution rules of § 318 apply in determining
whether such a reduction has occurred.

In *Davis*, originally the taxpayer and his wife
each owned 250 shares of a corporation and an
unrelated individual 500. The corporation issued
to the taxpayer 1000 shares of nonvoting preferred stock for $25,000, thus increasing the cor-
poration's working capital (and the taxpayer's
proportionate stock interest) temporarily so as to
qualify for a loan, with the understanding that
the corporation would redeem the preferred stock
(presumably with sale treatment) when the loan
had been repaid. Later the taxpayer purchased
the unrelated stockholder's 500 shares and gave
them to his children; still later, after the loan
was repaid, the corporation redeemed the taxpayer's preferred stock for $25,000, his cost basis.
Since the "net effect" of the redemption was to
leave the distributee's ownership interest unchanged at 100 percent (25 percent directly and
75 percent by family attribution) the redemption
could not be accorded sale treatment despite the

existence of a business purpose for the issuance and later redemption of the preferred stock.

Where there are two or more classes of stock, the Service, following Himmel (2d Cir. 1964), has indicated that it will consider the effect of a redemption on the stockholder's proportionate interest in: (1) voting power, (2) corporate earnings, and (3) net assets on liquidation. Rev.Rul. 75–502.

Because the § 302(b)(1) test "depends upon the facts and circumstances of each case," Regs. § 1.302–2(b), it is of limited use for planning purposes. Nevertheless, published rulings or cases indicate at least 5 situations in which § 302(b)(1) might be relied on:

(1) A redemption from a noncontrolling minority stockholder which fails to qualify under § 302(b)(2) because it does not quite meet the requirement that the distributee's percentage stock interest be reduced to less than 80% of his former interest. For example, a redemption which reduces a stockholder's interest from 30 percent to 24.3 percent (81 percent of the former interest instead of less than 80 percent) Rev.Rul. 75–512, or from 11 percent to 9 percent (81.8 percent of of the former interest) Rev.Rul. 56–183, or from 27 percent to 22.27 percent (82.5 percent of the former interest) Rev.Rul. 76–364.

(2) Various redemptions of only preferred stock (which is not § 306 stock): a redemption from a minority common stockholder of all of his preferred shares, compare Rev.Rul. 74–515; a redemption of all of the outstanding preferred stock where it is not held in proportion to common, Rev.Rul. 68–547; or a redemption of half of his preferred stock from an owner of only preferred stock, Regs. § 1.302–2(a). This does not meet the requirements of § 302(b)(2) for reduction of both voting stock and common stock interests but qualifies under § 302(b)(1).

(3) With only one class of stock outstanding a redemption which reduces the taxpayer's stock interest from 57 percent to 50 percent is a meaningful reduction because it ends majority control (where the other 50% was held by an unrelated stockholder); a reduction to 51 percent would not be meaningful. Rev.Rul. 75–502. A reduction from 85 percent to 62 percent is meaningful where it ends the stockholder's possession of a ⅔ majority required by the applicable state corporate law for certain major actions such as a merger or amendment of the corporate articles. Wright (8th Cir. 1973).

(4) A redemption from a minority stockholder whose relative stock interest in the corporation is minimal and who exercises no

[*111*]

control over the corporation. For example, a redemption which reduces a stockholder's interest from .0001118 percent to .0001081 percent (96.7 percent of the former interest). Rev.Rul. 76–385.

(5) A redemption which fails under § 302 (b)(2) because of family attribution may qualify under § 302(b)(1) if the attribution is considered merely as one of the relevant facts and circumstances and is outweighed by the reduction in actually owned shares in light of other circumstances such as intra-family disaffection. In Robin Haft Trust (1973) the Tax Court held that the attribution rules are determinative irrespective of the personal relationships which exist among the members of a family. The First Circuit (1975) reversed, holding that although attribution rules apply, family hostility could also be weighed under § 302(b)(1), citing Regs. § 1.302–2(b) (constructive ownership is "one of the facts to be considered"). The IRS has announced that it will not follow the First Circuit's decision; accordingly, reliance upon intra-family disaffection to support capital gain treatment under § 302(b)(1) will invite litigation. Rev.Rul. 80–26.

In the phrase "essentially equivalent to a dividend" in § 302(b)(1), the word dividend is not used in its Code sense of a distribution out of earnings and profits. Regs. § 1.302–2(a) states that the absence of corporate earnings and profits does not prevent a redemption distribution from having dividend equivalence, "that is, having the same effect as a distribution without any redemption of stock." If there are no earnings and profits the dividend equivalent redemption is still treated by § 302(d) as a § 301 distribution, first reducing the stockholder's basis in his remaining stock (to which the basis of his redeemed stock has been transferred) under § 301(c)(2) and the excess resulting in capital gain under § 301(c)(3).

§ 5. Operation of Attribution Rules: § 318

(a) *Introduction.* Specific rules for constructive ownership of stock ("attribution"), provided in § 318, are made applicable by § 302(c)(1) to the redemption rules. (There are several other, somewhat different sets of attribution rules in the Code, such as those in § 544 relating to personal holding companies. Attribution rules are applied only under Code sections to which they are specifically made applicable. For example, there are no attribution rules under § 351, so issuance of stock to a transferor's wife or son may raise a problem as to the necessary "control" under that section.)

At the outset it is important to note that attribution as to redemptions applies only for purposes of determining the tax effect to a redeemed stockholder of an actual distribution to him; there are no constructive distributions. Whether the actual dstribution has the effect of a sale or a dividend to its actual recipient is thus determined in light of whether the redeemed stockholder has achieved a meaningful reduction in his actual and constructive proportionate interest in the corporation.

(b) *Family Attribution.* The distributee is deemed to own the stock owned by his spouse, parents, children and grandchildren. Note that there is no attribution between brothers and sisters (compare the § 544 rules).

(c) *Attribution from an Entity to Its Owners or Beneficiaries.* A proportionate part of the stock owned by a corporation is deemed to be owned by a stockholder who owns 50 percent or more in value of the stock of the owning corporation. Similarly, stock owned by a partnership or estate is attributed proportionately to its partners or beneficiaries, and stock owned by a trust to its beneficiaries in proportion to their actuarial interest (or to the owner of a grantor trust).

Example: A actually owns 50 shares of the stock of Wig Corp. The other 50 shares of Wig Corp. are owned by M Corp. The stock of M Corp. is owned 60 percent by A and 40 percent by B, who is unrelated. If A sells 30 of his 50 Wig shares to Wig Corp., reducing his actual owner-

[*114*]

ship from $\frac{5}{100}$ to $\frac{2}{70}$, the redemption fails to qualify under § 302(b)(2). As a 60 percent owner of
M Corp., A is considered to own 30 (60 percent)
of M Corp.'s 50 Wig shares before and after the
redemption. His ownership of Wig shares drops
from $\frac{80}{100}$ to $\frac{5}{70}$; or from 80 percent to 71.4 percent, which is more than 50% and therefore fails
under § 302(b)(2)(B).

(d) *Attribution to an Entity from Its Owners
or Beneficiaries.* Stock owned by a partner, estate beneficiary, or more than 5 percent trust beneficiary is attributed to the partnership, estate
or trust; stock owned by a 50 percent or more
stockholder is attributed to his corporation. Attribution in this direction (beneficiary to entity)
is of all stock owned by the beneficiary as con-
trasted with entity to beneficiary attribution,
which is of only a proportionate part.

Example: The facts as to stock ownership are
the same as in the preceding example, but A does
not sell any of his stock; M Corp. sells 30 of its
50 Wig Corp. shares for cash to Wig Corp.; Wig
Corp. has sufficient e & p to cover the cash distribution and the transaction is not a partial liquidation. In testing this redemption to determine its treatment by M Corp., M Corp. is considered to own 100 percent of Wig Corp.'s shares
before the redemption (50 actual and 50 owned by
its 50 percent-or-more stockholder A) and $\frac{7}{70}$ or

100 percent after the redemption (20 actual and 50 by attribution) so the distribution receives dividend treatment (and thus is eligible for the 85 percent intercorporate dividends received deduction under § 243).

(e) *Option Attribution.* The holder of an option to acquire stock is considered to own such stock.

(f) *Reattribution of Stock.* Important operating rules are provided in § 318(a)(5). Generally, stock is reattributed from one constructive owner to another until it reaches the redeemed taxpayer. There are two important exceptions. First, stock of one family member constructively owned by a second family member by family attribution is not attributed again to a third family member by family attribution. For example, if a father and two sons own all the stock of a corporation, and one son's stock is redeemed, he is considered to own by attribution his father's actual shares, but not his brother's shares even though they are considered owned by his father. Second, under paragraph (5)(C) of § 318(a), added in 1964, stock attributed once by beneficiary-to-entity attribution is not reattributed by entity-to-beneficiary attribution; this ends a type of so-called sidewise attribution among beneficiaries. A corporation is not, of course, considered to own its own stock nor can the same share

count as more than one share. Regs. § 1.318–1
(b).

(g) *Waiver of Family Attribution by an Estate
or Trust.* A common problem involving attribution between an entity and beneficiary arises in
planning for post-death redemptions when the decedent's estate and perhaps a trust under his will
as well as the beneficiaries and their family members may own stock. The Service has ruled that
waiver of family attribution by filing the necessary agreement under § 302(c)(2) prevents only
family attribution which is the last step in a
chain of attribution; if a redemption is actually
from an estate or a trust, a waiver cannot stop
family attribution of stock to a beneficiary so as
to prevent beneficiary-entity reattribution of the
stock to the estate or trust. Rev.Rul. 59–233.
Thus a redemption of all the stock actually owned
by an estate of which the beneficiaries owned no
actual stock was doomed by attribution of stock
from the father of the beneficiaries to the beneficiaries and thence to the estate; if the children
had owned the redeemed stock outright instead of
through the estate, they could have waived attribution from their father and qualified under §
302(b)(3). The Tax Court disagreed with this
position in Crawford, (1973), (Nonacq.), and the
Fifth Circuit, in Rickey (1979), likewise has indicated that the IRS' reading of the waiver of
attribution rules is insufficiently flexible. Clear-

ly, considerable further litigation can be expected in this area.

§ 6.   Redemptions to Pay Death Taxes: § 303

The death of a stockholder whose estate consists largely of stock in a closely held corporation may require redemption of at least part of his stock to obtain funds for payment of estate taxes and administrative expenses. In 1950, Congress responded to the politically compelling problem that such redemptions would frequently be essentially equivalent to a dividend, resulting possibly in a heavy tax burden or a sale of controlling stock to some large corporation. The Congressional response, which was further refined in 1954 as § 303 of the Code, provides generally that if stock in a corporation is a specified large part of the estate, an amount of stock which would be sufficient to pay death taxes and administration expenses can be redeemed with sale rather than dividend treatment. Because stock basis is stepped up to fair market value under § 1014, sale treatment of redemptions permits money to be withdrawn from the corporation essentially tax-free. A considerable number of changes in § 303 were made by the Tax Reform Act of 1976. Since the changes are effective only for estates of decedents dying after December 31, 1976, old § 303 will have some importance for a number of years.

Section 303(a) provides sale treatment for a redemption of stock which has been included in the federal estate tax gross estate of a decedent, to the extent that the amount distributed by the redeeming corporation does not exceed the total federal and state death taxes, plus the funeral and administration expenses deductible for federal estate tax purposes. Section 303(b) prescribes limitations as to time for the redemption and as to the required relationship of the amount of stock owned by the decedent to the total value of his estate. If the death occurred before 1977, the normal time limit for § 303 stock redemptions is generally 4 years after the date of death. § 303 (b)(1)(A). For stock of post-1976 decedents, the maximum time for redemption is extended to the due date of the last installment (a maximum of 15 years from the date on which payment would ordinarily be due) if the estate elects to pay estate taxes in installments under § 6166 or § 6166A. § 303(b)(1)(C). The value of the stock in the decedent's federal estate tax gross estate, for pre-1977 decedents, must be more than 35 percent of the gross estate or more than 50 percent of the taxable estate. As amended, § 303(b) (2) is more restrictive: it requires for post-1976 decedents that the value of the stock in the decedent's gross estate must be more than 50 percent of the adjusted gross estate, i. e., the value of the gross estate after deductions specified in § 2053 or § 2054 (losses, debts and administration expenses). For purposes of meeting the old 35/50 or the new 50 percent test, stock of two or more corporations is treated as stock of one corporation if the gross estate includes more than 75 percent in value of the outstanding stock of each corporation.

Section 303(c) provides that if stock eligible for a § 303 redemption is exchanged for new stock the basis of which is determined with reference to the basis of the old stock, the new stock is equally eligible for § 303 redemption.

Redemptions need not be made by the probate estate of the decedent to qualify. Thus stock which the decedent transferred during his life under conditions which avoid probate but leave the property in his gross estate for estate tax purposes can be redeemed from its owner. Similarly, if the executor has distributed the stock as directed by the will, the beneficiary can use § 303. These interpretations are provided by Regs. § 1.-303–2(f) which also states that § 303 is not available to one who acquired the stock by gift or purchase from someone to whom the stock passed from the decedent, nor to one receiving stock in satisfaction of a specific bequest of a sum of money, who in effect purchased the stock from the executor.

Since the amount of stock which may be redeemed under § 303 is limited by the amount of death taxes and administration expenses, an important issue arises as to which redemptions will qualify if there is more than one redemption. The Service has adopted a simple rule by 1975 amendment to the Regulations that distributions in redemption of eligible stock shall be applied against the total amount which qualifies in the order in which distributions are made. Regs. § 1.303–2(g). This late interpretation is questionable in permitting a redemption which is earlier in time to exhaust the benefits of § 303 thereby dooming a later redemption to dividend treatment, even though the earlier redemption would have qualified for sale treatment under § 302.

The actual mechanics of § 303 are strikingly favorable to the taxpayer in permitting redemptions to qualify to the full extent of all death taxes and expenses even though there is plenty of cash in the estate from other sources and the proceeds of the redemption are not used for that purpose. In fact, in estates of pre-1977 decedents, a stockholder whose bequest is free of any obligation to pay death taxes or expenses can nevertheless use § 303. For stock passing from post-1976 decedents, new § 303(b)(3) limits § 303 sale treatment to an amount equal to the redeemed stockholder's share of death taxes and expenses.

§ 7. Redemptions Through Related Corporations: § 304

A stockholder might withdraw funds from a corporation without being subject to the possibility of dividend treatment under § 302 if he sold to the corporation not its own stock but stock of a related corporation. Because the effect of this might be essentially the same as a redemption by the related corporation, § 304 provides rules for applying §§ 302 and 303 to such transactions. There are separate rules for acquisitions in parent-subsidiary and in all other related corporation situations. If the stock of one of two corporations under common control, such as brother-sister corporations, is sold to the other, § 304(a) (1), the general related corporation rule, treats the stock as a contribution to the capital of the acquiring corporation, and treats the payment as a distribution in redemption of stock of the acquiring corporation. If stock of the parent is sold to a 50 percent owned subsidiary, § 304(a) (2) treats the payment as a distribution in redemption of stock of the parent. However, in both situations, determination as to whether § 302(b) provides sale treatment are made by reference to stock of the issuing corporation. § 304 (b)(1). In the general related corporation situation, dividend amounts are determined with reference to the earnings and profits of the acquiring corporation; but if a subsidiary acquires a parent's stock, the payment is treated as going first from the subsidiary to the parent (thus creating earnings and profits) and then to the redeemed stockholder. § 304(b)(2). Under § 304 (c), control is defined as 50 percent by vote or value, with slightly broadened § 318 attribution (shares attributed between a corporation and its stockholders regardless of whether the stockholder owns 50 percent). Examples illustrating both situations are in Regs. § 1.304–2 and –3.

Example: A owns actually 50 of the 100 shares of M Corp.'s stock and 50 of the 100 shares of N Corp. The other stockholders are unrelated. If A sold half his M Corp. shares to M Corp. he would reduce his interest from $^{50}/_{100}$ to $^{25}/_{75}$, or from 50 percent to 33⅓ percent and would have sale treatment under § 302(b)(2) (he has reduced to less than 40 percent which is 80 percent of 50 percent). If he sells half his M Corp. shares to related N Corp., the "redeemed" shares are still outstanding and after the redemption he owns 37.5 percent (actual 25 and constructive 12.5 [50 percent of the 25 shares owned by N Corp.]). This is still under 40 percent and sufficient for sale treatment under §§ 302(b)(2) and 304(a) (1). If he had sold fewer M Corp. shares to N Corp. so that the transaction did not qualify under the tests of §§ 302(b)(2) or (b)(1), the entire payment he received would be treated under § 302(d) as a § 301 distribution from N Corp.

and thus be a dividend to the extent of N Corp.'s earnings and profits. N Corp.'s basis in the M Corp. shares would be the same as A's basis; A would add the basis of these M Corp. shares to his N Corp. shares. Regs. § 1.304–2(c), *Example (1)*.

The detailed application of § 304 is probably outside the scope of a basic corporate income tax course. Two practical points seem worth noting, however.

(1) Section 304 may overlap with § 351, for example if an individual who owns all of the stock of two active corporations with e & p, transfers all of the stock of one corporation to the other in exchange for its stock and cash or securities. The Service contends that § 351 applies to the stock for stock exchange, but § 304 governs the exchange of stock for cash or securities, causing § 301 treatment of the amount realized. This seems the proper rule, and is supported by Coates Trust (9th Cir. 1973), but Haserot (6th Cir. 1968) is contra. The IRS has announced that it will not follow *Haserot*. Rev.Rul. 73–2.

(2) If the distributing corporation is newly formed or otherwise has no earnings and profits, return of basis and capital gain rather than a dividend may result under § 301. However, e & p may be created later in the distributing corporation's taxable year and retroactively cause dividend treatment.

§ 8. Redemptions Treated as § 301 Distributions: § 302(d)

If a redemption does not qualify for sale or exchange treatment, the stockholder's surrender of shares is ignored and he is treated as receiving a § 301 distribution. This has two important current tax consequences (assuming that the corporation has earnings and profits to cover the distribution): (1) he has an ordinary income dividend rather than capital gain and (2) the amount he receives is entirely included in gross income, rather than being offset by his basis in the redeemed shares. The difference in treatment depending upon whether the redemption qualifies is thus most extreme where the stock has a high basis, for example because basis has been stepped up by reason of the recent death of a predecessor stockholder. If the redemption qualifies for sale treatment, there will be little or no capital gain or loss and thus no tax; if the redemption fails to qualify, and there are sufficient earnings and profits, the entire distribution will be taxable as a dividend.

Example: R Corp. redeems 100 shares of its stock from Joe Franklin for their fair market value, $25,000. Joe's adjusted basis in the redeemed shares is $26,000; he retains another 100 shares which also have an adjusted basis of $26,-000 before the redemption. If the redemption qualifies as a sale (under §§ 302(a), 303 or 346 and 331(a)(2)), Joe reports a $1,000 capital loss. If the redemption fails to qualify, the entire $25,-000 "amount realized" is treated as a § 301 distribution. If the distribution is covered by earnings and profits, Joe reports a $25,000 dividend.

Moreover, a problem of "disappearing basis" of the redeemed shares arises when the redemption is treated as a dividend. This results from the Code's approach of ignoring the redeemed shares and their basis which would be relevant in a sale of the shares, to focus solely on the corporate distribution aspect of the transaction. The problem is generally solved by Regs. § 1.302–2(c), which provides examples of appropriate adjustments to basis. The basis of the redeemed shares is added to the basis of any retained shares; if no shares are retained but the stockholder still has dividend treatment because of constructive ownership of other shares, his lost basis is awarded to the relative's shares by the example in the regulation. Thus in the Joe Franklin example above, if Joe reports a dividend of $25,000, his basis in the retained shares is $52,000 under Regs. § 1.302–2(c) *Example (1)*, reflecting the basis in both the retained and the redeemed shares; this $52,000 basis would be reduced by any part of the $25,000 § 301 distribution not treated as a dividend because not covered by earnings and profits; Joe would report no gain or loss. However, Regs. § 1.302–2(c) does not answer all the potential questions in this area. An example of the remaining problems can be found in Rev.Rul. 70–496, where the Service held on the particular facts of that transaction that the basis was "lost" in a § 304–§ 301 dividend redemption.

If there are not sufficient e & p to cover a non-sale redemption, the usual § 301 rules apply: the distribution applies first to reduce basis under § 301(c)(2) and then results in a gain on the stockholder's investment (normally capital gain) under § 301(c)(3).

Dividend treatment of a redemption would normally be a good result for a stockholder that is itself a corporation because of the 85 percent or 100 percent dividends received deduction under § 243. In Rev.Rul. 77–226, however, I.R.S. disallowed hoped-for dividend treatment to a corporation which purchased $1,000,000 of a publicly-traded nonvoting preferred stock, had $200,000 worth redeemed and then sold the remainder on the market for a hoped-for capital loss measured from its $1,000,000 basis. The Service treated the entire transaction as a § 302(b)(3) complete termination of interest under *Zenz* principles, as discussed in § 9.

§ 9. Redemptions in Connection with the Sale of a Corporation

Redemptions are commonly useful in connection with sale of the stock of a closely held corporation to a new owner. A redemption takes non-essential liquid assets out of the corporation and reduces the price which the purchasers must pay. Such plans are referred to as "bootstrap" sales; the buyer doesn't have the needed cash but "pulls himself up by his bootstraps" by using the cash in the corporation to help pay for acquisition of the corporation. A similar situation is the use of a redemption to take out one stockholder or group, leaving the other stockholder or group as sole owners.

One bootstrap plan is for the selling stockholders to sell part of their stock to the corporation and the rest to the new owners in one simultaneous transaction. After losing in Zenz v. Quinlivan (6th Cir. 1954) on the similar point under the 1939 Code, the Service stopped contending that this should be treated as first a pro rata dividend redemption from the seller and then a sale of the rest of his stock, and ruled that the redemption with the related sale could qualify under § 302(b)(3) as a termination of interest.

The *Zenz* principle that the sequence of the events is irrelevant as long as both redemption and sale are part of an overall plan applies to reduction as well as complete termination of interest. Thus § 302(b)(2) applies to two stockholders who reduce their ownership from 50 percent to 33⅓ percent each under an integrated plan by selling some of their stock to a third party and then having enough of their shares redeemed to make all three equal one-third stockholders. Rev. Rul. 75–447.

The Service also has ruled that the buyer does not have a dividend, Rev.Rul. 69–608, although the simultaneous redemption has the same economic effect as if the buyer had purchased all the shares, partly on credit, and then, as new 100 percent owner, caused the redemption of some shares to get the cash to pay his debt for them. If a stockholder first enters into a contract to buy another stockholder's stock, and then in a separate later transaction assigns the contract to the corporation which buys the stock, the use of corporate funds to discharge the buyer's obligation was held in Wall (4th Cir. 1947) and Sullivan (8th Cir. 1966) to be a dividend to the buyer. Thus the form or sequence of the events is important unless the events occur as part of one overall plan. In Holsey, (3d Cir. 1958) a buyer who held only an option to buy, rather than being unconditionally bound by contract, was held not to have a dividend when he assigned the option to the corporation, which purchased the stock. The principal caution in this area appears to be to think through the transaction sufficiently in advance so that before anything is agreed upon, any redemption will be foreseen and made part of the overall plan and agreement. Otherwise, if a stockholder enters a binding unconditional agreement to buy stock, a later decision to use corporate funds to redeem the stock will result in the discharge of his obligation being treated as a dividend.

§ 10.　Partial Liquidations:　§§ 331(a)(2) and 346(a)(2) and (b)

(a) *In General.*　A redemption, pro rata or disproportionate, may not resemble a § 301 distribution because it is in connection with a partial liquidation.　In a partial liquidation the stockholders no longer retain a continuing interest in the same business, but in a materially reduced one, a result quite different from an ordinary § 301 distribution.　As a result the Code provides, in § 331 (a)(2), that amounts distributed in partial liquidation of a corporation are to be treated as received in exchange for the redeemed stock, thus normally resulting in capital gain or loss.　Section 346 defines two pertinent types of partial liquidations.　The general one, under § 346(a)(2) is redemption distributions "not essentially equivalent to a dividend", a phrase interpreted in this context to require a corporate level business contraction. The other, under § 346(b), is a safe-harbor provision for a specifically defined case of corporate contraction, where the corporation has two active businesses, each with a five year history, and distributes the assets or proceeds of one of them while continuing to conduct the other.　(A third type of "partial liquidation", under § 346(a)(1) is one of a series of distributions pursuant to a plan of complete liquidation and thus discussed in Chapter 6 on Complete Liquidations.)

If a liquidating redemption is not pro rata, a stockholder may qualify for sale treatment under both § 302(a) and § 346, see § 346(c); this overlap has little practical significance, but Regs. § 1.-346–2 provides that only § 346 applies so that any limitation of § 302, such as the 10 year prohibited interest rule of § 302(c)(2)(A), does not apply. In the event that the amount distributed is in excess of that permitted under § 346, Regs. § 1.302–1(b) provides that amounts which qualify under both § 302(a) and § 346 will be considered as qualifying under § 302(a) for purposes of determining the amount available for distribution in partial liquidation to the other stockholders. (Rev.Rul. 74–465, however, limits this rule to cash distributions and holds that a property distribution comes under § 346 even if it would also have qualified under § 302(a).) Section 267, disallowing losses on sales between an individual and his more than 50 percent owned corporation, is specifically inapplicable to "losses in cases of distributions in corporate liquidations" and its application to redemptions is therefore limited to those qualifying for sale treatment only under § 302(a) or § 303.

If property is distributed in kind, the stockholder takes it with a fair market value basis under § 334(a), the general liquidation basis provision; this is generally the same as the § 1012 cost basis the stockholder takes in property distributed in a nonliquidating sale-treated redemption.

(b) *Section 346(b): Termination of One of Two Active Businesses.* As in the case of analyzing § 302, we consider first the specific safe-harbor tests and then the vague general concept. Section 346(b) provides that a distribution shall be treated as a qualifying corporate contraction if the following requirements are met:

—the corporation is engaged in at least two active businesses and the distribution consists of the assets (meaning all the assets, Gordon (2d Cir. 1970)) of one trade or business, or is attributable to the corporation's ceasing to conduct one trade or business (meaning usually that the business assets have been sold and all the proceeds are distributed). Or, some assets can be distributed in kind and the rest sold and the proceeds distributed. Regs. § 1.346–1(b)(2) (second sentence).

—the trade or business has a five year history: it has been actively conducted for the past five years (by the corporation or a predecessor) and was not acquired within that period in a transaction in which gain or loss was recognized in whole or in part (that is, generally, recognized to someone who sold the business, so that the business cannot have been acquired in the past five years by purchase or in a corporate reorganization where "boot" was paid. See Chapter 12 on Acquisitive Reorganizations.)

—immediately after the distribution, the corporation is still engaged in another business which also meets the five year history test.

The active business requirements are intended to insure a significant contraction in business activity of the corporation, as opposed to a mere bail-out of liquid assets which could occur if a passive business, such as holding stocks and bonds for investment, is terminated. These requirements are the same as several of those incorporated into § 355 which provides for tax-free corporate division, i. e., a distribution tax-free to stockholders of a five year active parent corporation of all of the stock of a five year active subsidiary. See Chapter 11, Corporate Divisions, for more detailed discussion of the active business tests. The requirement that the business be conducted for five years, and not be purchased within that period, prevents a corporation with liquid assets from using them to purchase business assets or a going business and after an insignificant period of operation distributing them or their proceeds in a purported contraction of business activity. (Picking up an old active business by a tax-free merger and then selling it and distributing its proceeds within one taxable year meets the active business requirement because the corporation is considered a continuation of the previous corporate owner of the business; the stockholders of that corporation largely continue as stockholders in the merged corporation.)

(c) *Section 346(a)(2): Corporate Contraction "Not Essentially Equivalent to a Dividend."* The key to this provision is not revealed in the Code itself. Prior to the 1954 Code, redemptions were dealt with under the 1939 Code provisions referring to "partial liquidations" and received sale treatment unless "essentially equivalent to a dividend." The Senate Finance Committee Report on the 1954 Code explains that now the two types of situations are treated separately: distributions which may have capital gain characteristics because they are not made pro rata among the stockholders are tested at the stockholder level under § 302, while "distributions characterized by what happens solely at the corporate level by reason of the assets distributed" are treated as partial liquidations under § 346. The Finance Committee Report states that primarily § 346(a)(2) involves the previously developed concept of corporate contraction. The sole qualifying illustration given in the Committee Report and Regs. § 1.346–1(a) is a distribution of unneeded fire insurance proceeds where part of the business activities ceased after a fire; on the other hand, distribution of a reserve for expansion would not qualify.

Section 346(a)(2) does not expressly contain any reference to the necessary corporate contraction, but imports the concept merely by requiring that the distribution be "not essentially equivalent to a dividend," which according to the Committee Report must be interpreted here based on corporate level business contraction factors rather than reduction of proportionate stockholder interest as in § 302. Section 346(a)(2) also requires:

—redemption of stock

—pursuant to a plan

—within the taxable year in which the plan is adopted or the succeeding taxable year.

As with the vague stockholder level "not essentially equivalent to a dividend" test of § 302(b)(1), this section is of limited use for planning because of its uncertainty. Destruction by fire as in Imler (T.C.1948), on which the Committee Report and the example in the Regulations are based, is infrequent. Obviously merely accumulating earnings for several years, investing them in land, stocks, bonds, or short term paper, and then distributing such liquid assets, is a dividend and not a business contraction; Regs. § 1.346–1(a) indi-

[*135*]

cates that this is so even if the assets had been set aside under a business expansion plan now abandoned. Examples of genuine contractions which presumably would qualify under § 346(a)(2) even though the five year active business "safe harbor" test of § 346(b) could not be met include:

—assets unnecessary after cancellation of a major contract or franchise for distribution of certain products, Rev.Rul. 55–373 as modified by Rev.Rul. 60–232

—assets unnecessary after a change from a department store to a smaller discount apparel store in a smaller premises, Rev.Rul. 74–296

—possibly cases of termination of an active business which does not qualify under § 346 (b) because the five year requirements were not met or not all the assets were distributed.

(d) *Redemptions in Partial Liquidations*. Technically, the definition of "redemption" in § 317 applies only to part I of subchapter C (§§ 301–318), and the term as used elsewhere, as in § 346 (a)(2), is not defined, but may be assumed to have the same meaning. There is authority for waiving the redemption requirement of § 346(a) (2) where the distribution is pro rata among the stockholders, the theory being that in pro rata situations, e. g., a corporation with only one stockholder, the redemption of stock is meaningless.

Cf. Rev.Rul. 77–245 (stockholders presented certificates for notation thereon of amount distributed). I.R.S. may be the party seeking to waive the redemption requirement where the distributee is a corporation. See Fowler Hosiery, Inc. (T.C.1961 aff'd 7th Cir. 1962). Note that caution therefore must be exercised before distributing a hoped-for dividend in kind eligible for § 243 to corporate stockholders, if the Service might find a corporate contraction of the distributing corporation with more burdensome capital gain treatment under §§ 346/331 to the recipients. There is no express reference to redemption in § 346(b) but the Tax Court in Baan (1970) held that a distribution qualifying under § 346(b) must also meet the redemption requirements of § 346(a)(2). On appeal the Second Circuit did not find it necessary to decide this issue but indicated that a contrary reading of the statute was equally plausible. Baan aff'd sub nom. Gordon (1970).

Where the redemption is pro rata the Service has ruled that the number of shares treated as redeemed in a partial liquidation is "that number of shares the total fair market value of which equals the amount of the distribution." Rev.Rul. 77–245, clarifying Rev.Ruls. 56–513 and 59–240. If the stock is not publicly traded, its fair market value may be determined by the general principles stated in Rev.Rul. 59–60, e. g., in an appropriate case, based on fair market value of the corporate assets, less liabilities. Gain or loss is then measured by the difference between the amount distributed and the adjusted basis of the stock deemed surrendered. Sometimes cases have simply accepted the number of shares actually redeemed by the stockholders without questioning their value. If the stockholder owns blocks of stock with a high basis, and others with a low basis, he may select which of those to use in a § 302(a), § 303 redemption or a § 346(a)(2) partial liquidation.

§ 11. Consequences to the Distributing Corporation

(a) *Characteristics of Redeemed Stock.* Section 317(b) provides that (for purposes of §§ 301–318) stock is considered as redeemed whether or not it is cancelled, retired, or held as treasury stock. As a general rule under the Code, treasury stock has no significance, and is treated no differently from authorized but unissued shares. If after a redemption treasury stock is later sold by the corporation for a price different from the redemption cost, § 1032 provides that no gain or loss is recognized.

(b) *Distributions in Kind.* In nonliquidating redemptions, the provisions of §§ 311, 47, 1245 and 1250–1254, apply if the consideration used by the distributing corporation is not cash but other property. Section 311(d), which applies to redemptions regardless of their treatment at the stockholder level, provides for the recognition of gain (but not loss) if appreciated property is distributed in a nonliquidating redemption unless one of seven listed exceptions applies. The most important of the exceptions are:

　—a § 302(b)(3) complete redemption of a 10 percent or more stockholder who has held his stock one year, counting § 1223 tacking. § 311(d)(2)(A) and Regs. § 1.-311–2(b)(2)

and

　—a § 303 distribution. § 311(d)(2)(D).

If a redemption qualifies for one of the exceptions in § 311(d)(2), the distributing corporation generally recognizes no gain under § 311(a), but may still have to recognize gain under § 311(b) (distributions of LIFO inventory) or § 311(c) (distributions of property with liabilities in excess of basis). If § 311(d) does apply, all gain on the distributed property is recognized; accordingly § 311(d) provides that the more limited recognition rules of subsections (b) and (c) do not.

The character of the gain recognized under § 311(d) is determined by hypothesizing a sale of the property to the redeemed stockholder. Therefore, § 1239 may result in the corporation's recognizing ordinary income if depreciable (in the hands of the stockholder) property is used to redeem the shares of an 80 percent or more stockholder. (The 80 percent control test is applied prior to the redemption; special attribution rules are provided in § 1239(a).) Rev.Rul. 75–514.

Section 336 provides generally for the nonrecognition of gain or loss to the corporation if it distributes property (other than cash or its own obligations) in a partial (or complete) liquidation. The rule contains only one stated exception, for installment receivables governed by § 453(d). However, as with § 311, § 336 is overridden by the depreciation and investment credit recapture provisions; also the tax benefit rule (see Chapter 6) may cause the recognition of gain.

(c) *Earnings and Profits Effects.* If § 302(d) applies, the distribution simply reduces e & p like any other § 301 distribution as covered in Chapter 4 on Nonliquidating Distributions.

However, if the distribution is treated as a sale or exchange by the redeeming stockholder (because it is a partial liquidation or because § 302 (a) or § 303 applies), part of the distribution reduces e & p, and the part "which is properly chargeable to capital account" does not. § 312(e). The explanation in general is that part of the value of the redeemed shares represents the stockholder's share of corporate capital and should not reduce e & p, but part represents his claim on ac-

[*140*]

cumulated e & p, not actually distributed to him (even though he is not taxed in that manner) which must reduce the e & p account. It is not clear, however, exactly how the allocation between e & p and "capital account" is to be determined.

A logical but generally pro-government position was originally adopted by IRS in Rev.Rul. 70–531: on a "sale"-treated redemption, the redeemed shares' ratable share of e & p is charged to e & p; everything else is not, since it represents the ratable share of a "capital account" consisting of capital contributions and increases (or decreases) due to unrealized appreciation (or depreciation) in value of corporate assets (including positive and negative goodwill) which are not reflected in e & p.

Example: X Corp. has e & p of $700,000. Fred Fox, owns 60 percent of the stock of X Corp. and an unrelated individual, George Green, owns the remaining 40 percent. X Corp. redeems half of Fred's shares for cash equal to their fair market value, $300,000; the redemption reduces Fred's ownership to $^{3}\!/\!_{0}$ and qualifies for sale treatment under § 302(b)(2). The balance sheet "book value" of X Corp. was $800,000, i. e., e & p $700,000 plus $100,000 original capital. The total net fair market value of the assets of X Corp. was $1,000,000 before the redemption. X Corp. reduces the $700,000 e & p by 30 percent, $210,000; the remaining $90,000 is treated as representing "capital account," i. e., original capital plus unrealized appreciation in assets, including goodwill.

In Herbert Enoch (T.C.1972) the Tax Court refused to accept Rev.Rul. 70–531, electing instead to follow the Jarvis (4th Cir. 1941) approach, which would charge to e & p everything distributed except the redeemed stock's ratable share of the capital account as shown on the books, i. e., a charge of $270,000 ($300,000–[30 percent of $100,000]) in the above example. In 1979, the Service abandoned its earlier position (Rev.Rul. 70–531) and announced that it would henceforth follow the *Enoch-Jarvis* approach. Rev.Rul. 79–376.

If the corporation distributes property other than cash (or its own obligations) in a redemption the proper adjustment to e & p is even more difficult because of the problem of meshing the e & p rules for distributions in kind, §§ 312(a), (c) with the § 312(e) rules for redemptions generally.

Where both ordinary dividends and sale-treated redemptions occur in the same taxable year the Service has ruled that regardless of chronological order, dividends take priority over sale-treated redemptions in absorbing current e & p. When current e & p is exhausted sale-treated redemptions and dividends reduce accumulated e & p in chronological order. Rev.Ruls. 74–338, 339. Baker (8th Cir. 1972) is similar.

§ 12. Review Problem

For the past 20 years Z Corp. has been engaged in the retail sales business. Four years ago Z Corp. purchased a franchise and the necessary equipment to manufacture certain items which it then sells in its store. Due to the restrictive terms of the franchise agreement Z Corp. has made little profit from the manufacuring operation and prospects for increasing profits are minimal. At the beginning of the current taxable year, Z Corp. had accumulated e & p of at least $200,000. There are two classes of stock outstanding, voting common and nonvoting preferred. Both classes of stock have a fair market value of $1,000 a share and are held in the following manner:

Son (S)	80 common
Trust (T)	60 common
Mother (M)	40 common and 20 perferred
Daughter (D)	20 common and 20 preferred

Except for 40 shares of S's common stock which he received as a gift in 1965 all of the stock owned by T, D, and S was obtained by specific bequest from Father (F) who died last year. M obtained her stock as residuary legatee of F's estate. F's gross estate (for purposes of federal estate taxes), less administration expenses, debts and casu-

alty losses, amounted to $350,000. Federal and
state death taxes plus funeral and administration
expenses amounted to $50,000. The value of F's
Z Corp. stock at the date of death was $180,000.
($900 a share). Each distributee of the estate
took the stock with a $900 per share basis under
§ 1014. T has as its beneficiaries D with a life
estate and the remainder to charity. D's actuarial
interest in T is 75 percent. The preferred stock
is not "section 306 stock".

On April 1, Z Corp. redeemed all of M's stock
for $60,000.

Two months later in an unrelated transaction Z
Corp. sold all of its noncash assets in the manufacturing operation for a net return of $60,000,
and redeemed all of D's stock and 20 shares each
from T and S for a total of $80,000. As a result
of the two redemptions S and T are the sole remaining stockholders with S owning 60 shares of
common and T owning 40.

Question: What are the tax consequences of
the two redemptions to M, S, T, and D?

Answer: As a result of the first redemption M
qualifies for sale treatment on $50,000 under §
303. The remaining $10,000 will either receive
sale treatment under § 302(a)/(b)(3) or dividend treatment under § 302(d) depending on
whether or not M retains or reacquires a prohibited interest in Z Corp. In the second redemption

D qualifies for sale treatment on the entire $40,-
000 she received under § 302(a)/(b)(2). T probably qualifies for sale treatment under § 302
(a)/(b)(1) or §§ 331(a)(2)/346(a)(2) but the
uncertain requirements of these sections make a
definite answer impossible. S cannot qualify for
sale treatment under § 302(a) but may qualify under §§ 331(a)(2)/346(a)(2). Analysis: M)
First applying the tests of § 302(b)(2): before
the redemption M is deemed to own her actually
owned shares (40) (for purposes of computation
under § 302(b)(2) the nonvoting preferred shares
are ignored even though under Regs. § 1.302–3(a)
their redemption will qualify for sale treatment
if the redemption of the voting stock qualifies),
S's and D's actually owned shares (100), and the
shares D owns constructively through T (45 (75
percent of 60)), or 92.5 percent ($^{185}\!/\!_{200}$). Applying the same attribution rules after the redemption M is still deemed to own 90 percent ($^{145}\!/\!_{160}$)
although her actual stock interest has been terminated. M therefore fails under both § 302(b)
(2)(B) and (C). (M also fails under § 302(b)
(1) because the net effect of the redemption was
to reduce her interest by only 2.5 percent and such
a small reduction by a 92.5 percent stockholder
is without practical significance.)

M will qualify under § 302(b)(3)/(c) if she
files the required agreement and does not retain
a prohibited interest or reacquire such an inter-

est within 10 years. Since the redeemed stock was obtained by bequest from F, M may also qualify for sale treatment under § 303. The value of F's shares at date of death was $180,000 which is more than 50 percent of the gross estate (less deductions specified in § 303(b)(2)(A)(ii)) ($180,000/$350,000 = 51.4 percent); therefore the redemption of 50 of M's shares qualifies under § 303. (Section 303 being limited to tax and administrative expenses which reduced the redeeming stockholder's interest, here as residuary legatee the entire $50,000). This is so regardless of the fact that M qualifies (or may qualify) for sale treatment under § 302(a). Regs. § 1.303-2 (g). However, if M retains or reacquires a prohibited interest in Z Corp. only the $10,000 which did not qualify under § 303 will be given dividend treatment. If M does receive dividend treatment (either now or retroactively) on the $10,000, her $9,000 basis in the 10 shares not receiving sale treatment will be allocated to D and/or S (and possibly T). If M qualifies under both §§ 303 and 302(a) she will realize a $6,000 gain on the redemption because her shares have a basis of $54,000 ($900 x 60) and the amount realized is $60,000.

(D) Before the redemption D is deemed to own her actually owned shares (20) (again ignoring the nonvoting preferred) and 75 percent of the 60 shares owned by T (45), or 40.6 percent

($^{65}/_{160}$). After the redemption she is still deemed
to own 75 percent of T's 40 shares, or 30 percent
($^{30}/_{100}$), which is under 32.48 percent (80 percent
of 40.6 percent) and therefore qualifies under §
302(b)(2). Since D's redemption reduced her
voting-common interest sufficiently under § 302
(b)(2) the incidental redemption of her nonvoting preferred shares also qualifies. Regs. 1.-
302-3(a). D has a gain of $4,000 ($40,000
amount realized—$36,000 basis). (D cannot
qualify under § 302(b)(3) because attribution
from an entity (T) cannot be waived under § 302
(c).)

(T) Before the redemption T is deemed to own
its actually owned shares (60) and all the shares
owned by its more than 5 percent beneficiary, C
(20) (ignoring the nonvoting preferred), or 50
percent ($^{80}/_{160}$). After the redemption T no longer
owns any stock by attribution (since its beneficiaries own stock only by attribution from T),
but actually owns 40 shares, or 40 percent ($^{40}/_{100}$),
which is equal to 80 percent of 50 percent, so T
fails to qualify under § 302(b)(2). It is probable
that T will qualify under § 302(b)(1): the reduction in interest not only just missed qualifying
under § 302(b)(2) but it also reduced T's actual
and constructive ownership from 50 percent at
which T and D probably had veto power, to 40
percent which effectively gives S control of the
day-to-day operation of Z Corp.

T may also qualify for sale treatment under § 331(a)(2). Z Corp. sold all of its noncash assets in the manufacturing business for $60,000 and distributed $80,000 in the second redemption. The sale and redemption clearly does not qualify as a partial liquidation under § 346(b) because the business was purchased within the last 5 years. However, it may qualify as a corporate contraction under § 346(a)(2) since there was a good business reason for selling the assets (low profits) and the sale ended Z Corp.'s involvement in manufacturing operations.

If T qualifies for sale treatment it will have a gain of $2,000 ($20,000 amount realized—$18,000 basis). In the unlikely event that T receives dividend treatment, the $18,000 basis in the 20 redeemed shares will be allocated to T's remaining 40 shares.

(S) Before the redemption S is deemed to own only his actually owned shares (80), or 50 percent ($80/160). After the redemption he owns 60 percent ($60/100) and clearly does not qualify for sale treatment under § 302(a). Like T, S will qualify for sale treatment if the sale of the manufacturing operation qualifies as a partial liquidation. Unlike the other stockholders S has the option of using shares obtained from F's estate or other shares he owned before the bequest and can therefore alter the tax consequences of a sale-treated redemption by using shares with a basis different from the § 1014 basis for the inherited shares. If S receives dividend treatment the basis in the 20 redeemed shares will be allocated to his remaining 60 shares.

It is unimportant to S or T that $20,000 more than the proceeds of the asset sale were distributed in the second redemption. Regs. § 1.302–2(b) provides that if stock is redeemed in an amount in excess of that permitted under § 331 (a)(2) then any amount qualifying under § 302 (a) will be excluded in determining the amount available under § 331(a)(2). Since D qualified under § 302(a) the $40,000 she received will not be counted against the $60,000 which may be available under § 331(a)(2). (Also some part of the $20,000 is probably working capital attributable to the manufacturing operation which will be treated as any other asset of the discontinued business.)

CHAPTER 6

LIQUIDATIONS

Table of Sections

[*150*]

§ 1. Introduction

Complete liquidation of a corporation occurs when the stockholders turn in all of their stock and receive in exchange all of the assets of the corporation after arrangements have been made for paying liabilities to creditors. Except in the case of some liquidations of subsidiary corporations, the earnings and profits account with its potential for future dividend treatment of distributions disappears upon a complete liquidation. Under the general rule of § 331, the stockholder reports a taxable sale or exchange of all of his stock for his share of the liquidation proceeds, recognizing his gain or loss on his investment. Accordingly, under § 334(a) his basis in any property other than money received is its fair market value. If property is distributed in kind, under § 336, the liquidating corporation recognizes neither gain nor loss, except gain on certain installment obligations, under recapture provisions, under certain assignment of income principles or perhaps under tax benefit or accounting principles.

[151]

Stockholders are specially treated in two liquidation situations under § 332 and § 333. The liquidation of an at least 80 percent owned subsidiary by its parent corporation is tax free to the parent under § 332, upon compliance with certain conditions which make the application of § 332 practically elective. If the parent-subsidiary relationship in a § 332 liquidation is of sufficiently long standing, the parent succeeds to the subsidiary's basis in its assets under § 334(b)(1) and to its other tax attributes, such as earnings and profits, net operating loss carryforwards, and accounting methods, under § 381(a). If the stock of the subsidiary was recently purchased by the parent, the subsidiary's basis and attributes do not carry over to the parent but under § 334(b)(2) the parent takes a basis in the assets related to the price it paid for the stock of the subsidiary. An exception of less frequent significance is § 333, which permits electing stockholders to avoid recognition of gain if the liquidating distributions are concentrated in one calendar month, taking a basis in the assets under § 334(c) which reflects their basis in their stock. Exceptions which require dividend treatment of gain to the extent of earnings and profits, and further recognition of gain if stocks, bonds and cash are distributed, greatly limit the usefulness of § 333.

A corporation which is planning to liquidate commonly sells assets outside the ordinary course of business. Section 337 generally provides for nonrecognition of gain or loss on such sales except by collapsible corporations or in connection with a § 333 or § 332/334(b)(1) liquidation. Recognition occurs only at the stockholder level upon distribution, within 12 months of adoption of the plan of liquidation, of the sale proceeds and all other corporate assets. The requirements for qualification under § 337 make this provision practically elective.

Stockholders in "collapsible corporations", covered by § 341, suffer ordinary income treatment instead of capital gain on complete liquidations, as well as on sales, redemptions, and § 301 distributions in excess of basis. Sections 333 and 337 do not apply to "collapsible corporations".

§ 2. Treatment of Stockholders—General Rule: §§ 331(a), 346(a)(1), 334(a)

(a) *Recognition of Gain or Loss*. The liquidation of a corporation could be viewed for tax purposes in two different ways: (1) the distribution of any remaining balance in the earnings and profits account could be viewed as dividends, with any additional amounts being treated as return of capital applied against the basis of the shares and causing recognition of capital gain or loss; (2) the turning-in of stock for its appropriate share of the proceeds in liquidation could be considered simply as a sale upon which gain or loss is recognized. Congress has generally followed the latter view; thus under the general rule of § 331(a)(1) a stockholder treats his share of the corporation's assets distributed in complete liquidation as received in full payment in exchange for his stock. (Section 331(b) specifically makes § 301, with its possibility of dividend treatment, inapplicable to distributions in complete or partial liquidation.) Under the usual rules for sales and exchanges (§ 1001) a stockholder recognizes gain or loss on his shares; the stock normally is a capital asset under § 1221, giving him capital gain or loss. If a stockholder assumes (or takes property subject to) a corporate liability on liquidation, the liability reduces his gain or increases his loss.

If a stockholder has some stock with a high basis and some with a low basis, he may recognize gain on one block and a loss on another.

Example: On April 23, 1978, L Corp. distributes $1,000 in cash per share in complete liquidation; the stockholders turn in all of their stock for cancellation. Sam owns and surrenders 50 shares with an adjusted basis of $10,000 which he purchased 5 years ago, and 50 shares with an adjusted basis of $65,000 which he purchased 5 months ago. The stock is a capital asset in his hands. Sam recognizes long-term capital gain of $40,000 ($50,000 amount realized less $10,000 adjusted basis) on the older block of stock, and short-term capital loss of $15,000 ($65,000 adjusted basis less

$50,000 amount realized) on the newer block. If the facts are the same except that the stockholder is Sam Corp., a corporation which is a less-than-80 percent stockholder of L Corp., the recognition of gain or loss by the stockholder is the same. See Regs. § 1.331–1(e), *Example.*

If the corporation adopts a plan of complete liquidation but makes more than one liquidating distribution to stockholders, the stockholders have sale or exchange treatment under the partial liquidation provisions of §§ 331(a)(2) and 346(a) (1). Before recognizing gain on a block of shares, a stockholder must first recover its basis; before recognizing a loss, the amount of the loss must be determined with reasonable certainty. Rev. Rul. 68–348.

Example: The facts are the same as in the preceding example, except that L Corp. adopted a plan of complete liquidation in November 1977 and distributed $500 per share in cash as a liquidating distribution on December 13, 1977, and $500 per share in cash as a final liquidating distribution on April 13, 1978. Sam uses the calendar taxable year. As of December 31, 1977, the amount of the final liquidating distribution cannot be determined with reasonable certainty. For 1977 Sam reports a long term capital gain of $15,-000 ($25,000 amount realized less $10,000 adjusted basis) on the older block and nothing on the newer block (because he has not recovered basis but the amount of any loss cannot yet be determined). For 1978, Sam reports additional long term capital gain of $25,000 ($25,000 amount realized less zero unrecovered adjusted basis) on the older block and a short-term capital loss of $15,000 ($65,000 adjusted basis less $50,000 amount realized) on the newer block.

The liquidating corporation may distribute assets, such as disputed claims or contingent contract rights, the reasonably accurate valuation of which is impracticable. If this occurs, the tax effect of the liquidation to the stockholder receiving such assets will be held "open" until a value can be placed on the assets. (Regs. § 1.1001–1(a) takes the position that a transaction will be held "open" only in "rare and extraordinary" cases.) The effect of holding the transaction open is to delay the reporting of all or part of the stockholder's gain or loss on the liquidation; also it may result in the stockholder recognizing capital gain rather than ordinary income.

Example: M owns one-half the stock in C Corp. The stock is a capital asset in his hands and he has a basis in the stock of $10,000. In complete liquidation of C Corp. M receives $20,000 in cash and a contingent contract claim with a face value of $20,000 but whose true value cannot be determined. In the year he receives the distribution M will report a capital gain of $10,000 (cash received less basis in the stock surrendered). If M later

[*156*]

receives $10,000 in settlement of the claim he will treat it as a liquidating distribution from C Corp., made in the year of settlement (i. e., a capital gain). If at the time of distribution the claim had been valued at $5,000 (a closed liquidation) M would recognize $15,000 capital gain in the year of distribution, and $5,000 of ordinary income in the year of settlement (because the money received as a settlement was not received in a "sale or exchange"). See Logan (U.S.1931).

(b) *Basis to Stockholders.* If a stockholder receives property other than money in a liquidating distribution, under the usual sale or exchange rules of § 1001(b) he counts the property at its fair market value in determining his recognized gain or loss. Accordingly, § 334(a) provides a fair market value basis as the general rule for property (other than money) received in a partial or complete liquidation. The stockholder must generally recognize and pay tax on any gain even if he has not received any cash with which to pay the tax. If he promptly sells any property received in a liquidation, however, he normally recognizes little or no further gain or loss because of his fair market value basis in the property.

§ 3. Treatment of Stockholders—Liquidation of a Subsidiary: §§ 332, 334(b)(1) and (2)

(a) *Nonrecognition of Gain or Loss.* To encourage simplification of corporate structures, and

[*157*]

on the view that the transaction amounts to a change of form but not of substance, Congress in 1935 provided generally that a parent corporation recognizes no gain or loss on the complete liquidation of its subsidiary corporation. As contained in § 332, the provision now prevents recognition on a parent's stock investment in an 80 percent subsidiary if the complete liquidation complies with certain conditions. If the parent corporation does not own the required 80 percent of the stock or other conditions of § 332 are not met, however, the liquidation will result in recognition of gain or loss by the parent corporation under the general rule of § 331.

The 80 percent stock ownership test of § 332 (b) requires the parent to own 80 percent of the subsidiary's voting stock (measured in relationship to the total combined voting power of all classes of stock) and 80 percent of the total number of shares of "all classes" (interpreted as "each class") of nonvoting stock except for nonvoting preferred stock ("limited and preferred as to dividends"). The exception for nonvoting preferred distinguishes this test from the "control" test of § 368(c).

The required 80% ownership must exist continuously at all times beginning with the date of adoption of the plan of liquidation until the parent corporation receives the subsidiary's property. § 332(b)(1). The parent corporation might want

§ 332 to be applicable in order to avoid recognition of gain on its stock in the subsidiary or to be inapplicable in order to recognize a loss. The Tax Court has held, on facts involving the § 332 (b)(1) requirement, that § 332 "is elective in the sense that with advance planning and properly structured transactions, a corporation should be able to render § 332 applicable or inapplicable". Riggs, Inc. (1975) (Acq.) (parent corporation owning 72 percent of subsidiary and desiring a tax-free liquidation arranged for the redemption by the subsidiary of the 28 percent minority, disclosing that a liquidation of the subsidiary was "contemplated" after this redemption; held, over the IRS contention that an informal plan of liquidation had been adopted before the acquisition of the required 80 percent, that on these facts the date of the formal adoption of the plan controlled). The court relied in part on the analogous permission extended by the Regulations under § 337 (discussed later in this chapter) to make sales tax-free or taxable by controlling the date of formal adoption of the liquidation plan. The Commissioner's acquiescence in *Riggs* indicates that the Service will normally accept application of § 332 in cases where a parent first causes redemption of a minority interest to obtain 80 percent ownership and then formally adopts a plan to liquidate the subsidiary.

Prior to the 1954 Code, the predecessor of § 332 was avoided by the parent corporation if it owned *any* less shares in the subsidiary when it received the subsidiary's property than it owned at any time after the adoption of the plan, even if the parent at all times owned at least 80 percent. According to the Senate Finance Committee Report this feature was removed from the 1954 Code "with the view of limiting the elective features of this section". Apparently a more than 80 percent parent can still avoid the application of § 332 if it sells enough stock to end its 80 percent ownership either before adopting the plan of liquidation or after adoption but before completion of the liquidation. Similarly, issuance of new stock in the subsidiary to outsiders, or increasing an existing minority interest through a recapitalization may sometimes be used to reduce the parent's interest below the statutory 80 percent.

To qualify under § 332, the liquidation must come within either the one taxable year or four taxable years time limit of § 332(b)(2) and (3) (the "taxable year" referred to being that of the subsidiary. Rev.Rul. 76–317):

—a one-shot liquidation, or a series of distributions completely distributing all property of the subsidiary within one taxable year. § 332(b)(2). The one taxable year in which all distributions take place can be a later year

[160]

than the taxable year in which the plan of liquidation is adopted. Rev.Rul. 71–326.

—a liquidation completed within 3 years from the close of the taxable year in which the first liquidating distribution is made. The plan of liquidation must provide that distributions are to be completed in this period. § 332(b)(3). Under this procedure, the parent must file a waiver of the statute of limitations (to permit retroactive taxation of earlier distributions if the liquidation is not completed within the period) and may be required to post bond. § 332(b) (flush language); Regs. § 1.332–4(a)(2), (3).

The timing limits begin with relation to the first liquidating distribution of property; there is no specific limit on how long after the adoption of the plan this might occur. Section 332(b)(2) fixes the time of adoption as the adoption by the stockholders (i. e., the parent) of the resolution authorizing distribution of all the subsidiary's assets, in complete cancellation or redemption of the subsidiary's stock.

The Regulations, § 1.332–6(a), require, among other things, that the plan of liquidation be adopted by both the parent and the subsidiary. However, the Service may waive this requirement of the Regulations, so a parent cannot use its failure to comply to avoid the application of § 332. Service Co. (8th Cir. 1948). Similarly, it has been held that § 332 may apply if the liquidation is completed within 3 years even though the plan of liquidation did not provide for distribution within 3 years. Burnside Veneer Co. (6th Cir. 1948).

(b) *Basis of Assets to Parent: § 334(b)(1), (2).* In a liquidation under § 332, there are two alternative basis rules for the property received by the parent. The general rule under § 334(b) (1) is that the basis is the same as it was in the hands of the subsidiary. This follows the general theory of the transaction's being tax free because it is a mere rearrangement of the corporate form of ownership of property from the subsidiary to another corporation with essentially the same ownership. The alternative basis rule under § 334 (b)(2) applies if the parent adopts a plan of liquidation within two years after purchasing (within a 12 month period) the 80 percent interest in the subsidiary. The parent then takes as its basis in the assets its adjusted basis in its stock in the subsidiary (with adjustments, such as adding any liabilities assumed). This approach is referred to as the "statutory *Kimbell-Diamond* rule" and as providing for a "stepped-up" basis. Kimbell-Diamond Milling Co. (5th Cir. 1951) held that a corporation which purchased the stock of another corporation in order to obtain the corporation's assets by liquidation should determine its basis as if it had made a one-step purchase of the assets.

In the actual case, the Commissioner succeeded in winning a stepped-down basis for assets which were purchased for less than the subsidiary's basis in them. But more frequently, § 334(b)(2), the statutory embodiment of the *Kimbell-Diamond* principle, will result in a step-up in basis because its conditions can usually be avoided in situations where the result would be a step down.

Example (1): General Metals Corp. (GM)' liquidates its 100% owned subsidiary, Nit Corp. (N) (in whose stock GM has an adjusted basis of $50,-000), receiving the following assets: vacant land held for investment, with an adjusted basis to N of $100,000 and a fair market value of $175,000; cash of $25,000; and business equipment (§ 1231 property) with an adjusted basis to N of $50,000 and a fair market value of $40,000. The liquidation results in no recognition of gain or loss to GM under § 332. If GM owned its N stock for more than 2 years before adopting the plan of liquidation, under § 334(b)(1) its adjusted basis will be the same as N's in the land and equipment. The fact that GM's adjusted basis in its N stock was $50,000 becomes irrelevant as this basis disappears. (If N had $32,000 of liabilities which GM assumes, GM's basis in the assets will still be the same as N's.)

Example (2): The facts are the same, except that GM had just purchased all of the stock of N for $240,000. Upon liquidation of N under § 332, GM receives assets with a total fair market value of $240,000 ($175,000 plus $25,000 plus $40,000) and realizes no gain or loss, but if any had been realized it would not have been recognized because of § 332. Under § 334(b)(2), assuming no adjustments except for the cash received, the total basis of the property other than cash received is $215,000 ($240,000 adjusted basis of GM in its N stock, less $25,000 for the cash received), Regs. § 1.334–1(c)(4)(v)(b)(1) which is allocated to the assets received in proportion to fair market values, i. e., $175,000 to the land and $40,000 to the equipment. (If N had $32,000 of liabilities which GM assumed, GM would presumably have paid only $208,000 instead of $240,000 for the N stock; in that case, after an upward adjustment to $240,000 for the liabilities assumed, and reduction of $25,000 for the cash received, the total basis of the property other than cash would still be $215,000, allocated $175,000 to the land and $40,000 to the equipment.)

In the above examples, if the parent sold the land after example (1) it would recognize a gain of $75,000 ($175,000 amount realized, less carryover adjusted basis of $100,000); if the basis of the land had been stepped-up to reflect the price recently paid for the stock as in example (2), the parent would recognize a gain of zero on the sale of the land for $175,000.

The statutory requirements for § 334(b)(2) basis are:

—a "purchase" (as defined in § 334(b)(3)

—of at least 80 percent of the voting stock by voting power and at least 80 percent of all classes (each class) of nonvoting stock except nonvoting stock limited and preferred as to dividends (the same 80 percent test as in § 332, of the subsidiary by the parent, made

—in one purchase, or in several aggregating 80 percent within a 12 month period, and then

—a plan of complete liquidation adopted not more than two years after the last purchase (i. e., the last purchase which results in 80 percent control) within the 12 month period

—carried out in compliance with § 332 (i. e., the parent must maintain 80 percent ownership and must complete the liquidation within the prescribed one-year or four-year format).

"Purchase" is defined in § 334(b)(3) as any acquisition of stock except the following four:

—where the parent's basis in the stock is determined in whole or in part by reference to the previous owner's basis (i. e., by gift, § 1015, or other tax free acquisition such as in a B reorganization, § 358)

—where basis is determined under § 1014 (because the property was acquired from a decedent)

—in a § 351 exchange, or

—from a person related under § 318(a) (unless that related "person" is itself a corporation whose stock was acquired by the parent by purchase).

The purpose is to limit the stepped-up basis approach to cases generally like *Kimbell-Diamond*, where the parent's stock in the subsidiary is acquired from an unrelated party (although Kimbell-Diamond acquirers could be related or unrelated to the seller) and has a cost basis and the seller recognizes gain or loss. It is unclear whether the enactment of § 334(b)(2) was intended by Congress to limit the application of the *Kimbell-Diamond* rule to transactions which satisfy the mechanical tests of that section. The Court of Claims in American Potash and Chemical Corp. (1968) held that *Kimbell-Diamond* could provide a stepped-up basis if the taxpayer parent corporation promptly liquidated the new subsidiary upon purchase of all its stock but had been delayed in its intended purchase of all the stock beyond the "80 percent in 12 months" requirement of § 334 (b)(2) because of delays in negotiating the purchase price. The Court of Claims stated that its decision would permit the Service to use *Kimbell-*

Diamond against a parent which intentionally avoided the terms of § 334(b)(2) because it wanted a carryover basis under § 334(b)(1). Commentators have criticized the Court's decision as a reintroduction of uncertainty into an area of tax law that Congress tried to regulate by specific mechanical rules. Accord, Broadview Lumber Co., Inc. (7th Cir. 1977), (*Potash* is wrong; *Kimbell-Diamond* can't apply where § 334(b)(2) doesn't apply because of § 334(b)(3)(C); taxpayer gets desired § 334(b)(1) basis) and International State Bank (T.C.1978), (*Kimbell-Diamond* intent test is pre-empted by § 334(b)(2)'s objective rules.) It is clear that the judicial *Kimbell-Diamond* rule may still be applied if a noncorporate purchaser of stock promptly liquidates the corporation, but in most cases the difference between *Kimbell-Diamond* and § 334(a) fair market value basis would be small or nonexistent.

(c) *Carryover of a Subsidiary's Attributes:* § *381.* In keeping with the concept that a § 332 liquidation of a subsidiary into a parent is a tax-free combination of the corporations under § 332, with a carryover of the subsidiary's basis under § 334 (b)(1), § 381(a)(1) provides for carryover of the tax attributes of the subsidiary to the parent. The carryover does not apply if the parent's basis in the acquired assets is determined under § 334 (b)(2); this is in keeping with the *Kimbell-Diamond* treatment of the transaction as resembling a purchase of assets by the parent. Section 381 (a)(2) provides for carryover of corporate attributes in certain types of tax free corporate reorganizations; the details of § 381 are considered in Chapter 13 on Carryovers. The attributes of the subsidiary which carry over are listed in § 381(c); they include the subsidiary's net operating loss carryovers, earnings and profits account, capital loss carryovers and methods of accounting.

(d) *Effect of Subsidiary's Debt to Parent:* § *332(c)*. Typically an 80 percent parent may be a creditor as well as a stockholder of the subsidiary. The distribution of property to the parent in complete liquidation of the subsidiary is considered first as paying off the subsidiary's debt with the remainder of the property received by the parent for its stock interest. If the parent's adjusted basis in the debt equals the principal of the debt (for instance in cases of cash advanced by the parent) the parent has no tax consequences from collecting the debt. If the parent's adjusted basis is less than the principal amount (for instance because the debt is securities issued by the subsidiary in a § 351 transaction in exchange for low basis property of the parent or because the parent bought the subsidiary's bonds at a discount) collection of the debt will result in recognition of gain by the parent. Regs. § 1.332–7. This gain is not protected from recognition by § 332, which applies only to prevent recognition of the parent's gain or loss on the receipt of property in liquidation, i. e., in exchange for stock in the subsidiary. If there is not enough property in the subsidiary to pay off its debts, that is, if the subsidiary is insolvent, there is nothing available for the stockholder. In that case, § 332 does not apply at all; the parent has a worthless stock deduction under § 165. Regs. § 1.332–2(b).

The second sentence of § 334(b)(1) provides a carryover basis for property received by the parent in a § 332(c) transfer "if [§ 334(b)(2)] does not apply". However, § 334(b)(2), unlike (b)(1), makes no express reference to transfers in respect of the subsidiary's debt to the parent. The Service takes the position, in effect, that there is no "if" about it; § 334(b)(2) applies only to transfers in respect of the parent's stock investment and never applies to a § 332(c) transfer, Regs. § 1.334–1(c)(1). Thus the Service reasons that § 334(b)(1) must apply to all § 332(c) transfers. Rev.Rul. 69–426.

Example: Parent buys all of a corporation's stock for $1.5 million and all of its debt for $1.5 million. The subsidiary has a basis in its assets of $2.0 million (two pieces of land each with a basis of $1 million and a fair market value of $1.5 million). According to the Service the parent would have a basis of $1.5 million in the property received in exchange for the stock and a basis of

$1 million in the property used to pay off the debt.

(e) *Effect on Minority Stockholders.* Only the 80 percent parent, and not any minority stockholder, is covered by §§ 332 and 334(b). The tax treatment of whatever the minority stockholders receive in exchange for their stock in the subsidiary is governed by other provisions. Regs. § 1.-332–5. They may recognize gain or loss under the general rules of §§ 1001 and 331(a)(1). In appropriate cases, they may elect nonrecognition of gain under § 333. If the liquidation is accomplished by state-law merger, it may (or may not, depending on the facts relating to "continuity of interest") qualify as a tax-free reorganization under § 368(a)(1)(A), so that the minority stockholders of the subsidiary can exchange their stock for stock in the parent without recognizing gain or loss, under § 354. Such mergers to accomplish a § 332 liquidation are specifically contemplated by the last sentence of § 332(b), and Regs. § 1.332–2(d), (e). Under these provisions, the parent receives § 332 treatment for the property received in the liquidation by merger. Treatment of minority stockholders under § 337 (c) and (d) where the subsidiary makes sales of assets during liquidation is covered in § 6(c), infra.

§ 4. Elective Nonrecognition of Gain in One-Month Liquidations: §§ 333, 334(c)

A "one-month" liquidation under § 333 generally permits electing stockholders to receive property which has appreciated in value without recognizing gain on their investment. (§ 333 is not applicable to losses.) The liquidating distributions (which may include a reasonable amount set aside for contingencies, Regs. § 1.333–1(b)) must all occur in some one calendar month, which month need not be within any particular length of time after adoption of the plan of liquidation; reasons for this requirement would be resolution of the basis of the earliest distributed property (which depends in part on the value of later distributions) and preventing stockholders from splitting any dividend and capital gain between two taxable years. Under § 334(c), the basis in property received is the same as the stockholder's adjusted basis in his stock, (increased for any gain which is recognized). Noncorporate stockholders must recognize gain with dividend treatment to the extent of their ratable share of earnings and profits, and any further gain as capital gain to the extent that money and (post 1953) stock and securities received exceed their ratable share of earnings and profits. § 333(e). An electing stockholder which is a corporation recognizes its gain as capital gain to the extent of the greater of (1) money and post 1953 stock and securities received or (2) its ratable share of earnings and profits. § 333(f).

Because of the unpleasant aspects for noncorporate stockholders of dividend treatment of gain to the extent of earnings and profits, the principal use of § 333 is in liquidation situations with little or no earnings and profits but large unrealized gain in the stock because of large unrealized gain in the corporate assets.

Example: The sole asset of L Corp. is vacant land with an adjusted basis of $30,000 and a fair market value of $500,000. Individual A, the sole stockholder, has an adjusted basis of $50,000 in his stock. L Corp. has no e & p. A wants to dissolve L Corp. and obtain title in the land. Under the general liquidation provision, § 331, A would recognize $450,000 gain on the liquidation and take the land with a $500,000 basis under § 334 (a). Electing under § 333, he recognizes no gain and takes the land with a basis of $50,000 (the basis of his stock) under § 334(c).

Election under § 333 by a noncorporate stockholder is effective only if 80 percent of the voting stock owned by noncorporate stockholders so elects. A corporate stockholder's election is valid only if 80 percent of the voting stock owned by corporations other than excluded corporations so elects; a corporation which at any time since 1954 owned 50 percent or more of the stock entitled to vote on a plan of liquidation is an "excluded corporation" which cannot elect. § 333(b) and (c). Note, however, that no election under § 333 can be made if the corporation is a collapsible corporation to which § 341(a) would apply if a sale of its stock or a liquidation were to occur.

Example: O Corp.'s one class of stock is owned as follows:

A—30 shares, adjusted basis $3,000;

B—30 shares, adjusted basis $160,000;

AB Corp. (owned equally by A and B)—

40 shares, adjusted basis $4,000.

O Corp. has no liabilities. Its assets are cash $25,000; land, adjusted basis $30,000 and fair market value $500,000. It has accumulated e & p of $20,000 and no current e & p. O Corp. adopts a plan of liquidation on February 15, 1979, and its individual and corporate stockholders file § 333 elections on Form 964 within the 30 days allowed by § 333(d) (as well as Form 966 required for all liquidations). The cash and the land are distributed ratably on June 20, 1979 (within one calendar month, under § 333(a)(2)).

The amounts of gain or loss recognized are:

A:	30% interest in Land FMV	$150,000	Ratable Share of e & p (dividend income)	$ 6,000
	Cash	+7,500	Cash in Excess of Ratable Share of e & p (capital gain)	1,500
	Amount Realized	157,500		
	Basis of Stock	—3,000		
	Gain Realized	$154,500	Gain Recognized	$ 7,500
B:	30% interest in Land FMV	$150,000		
	Cash	+7,500		
	Amount Realized	157,500		
	Basis of Stock	—160,000		
	Loss Realized	$ 2,500	Loss Recognized	$ 2,500
AB Corp.:	40% interest in Land FMV	$200,000	Ratable Share of e & p (capital gain)	$ 8,000
	Cash	+10,000	Cash Received (capital gain)	10,000
	Amount Realized	210,000	Gain Recognized equals greater of Ratable Share of e & p or Cash Received	
	Basis of Stock	—4,000		
	Gain Realized	$206,000		$10,000

B does not mind electing under § 333 to permit A to obtain the necessary 80% of the noncorporate-owned voting stock, although his tax treatment, since he does not have a realized gain, is not governed by § 333. See Regs. § 1.333–4(a). (If either the corporate or noncorporate stockholders did not elect, § 333 nevertheless would apply to the other class which did elect.)

§ 5. Tax Consequences to Liquidating Corporation of Distributions in Kind: § 336

Generally under § 336 the liquidating corporation recognizes neither gain nor loss on disposing

[*174*]

of its property to its stockholders in partial or complete liquidation. However, the recapture provisions override § 336 and there are judicially created exceptions to the general nonrecognition rules; these will be discussed with the exceptions to § 337 in § 7 of this chapter.

Section 336 itself mentions only one exception: distributions of installment receivables on which the corporation has been reporting its profit on the installment method under § 453. Section 453B provides that generally gain or loss is recognized to the extent of the difference between the basis of the obligation (determined as face amount remaining unpaid, less profit remaining to be reported, under § 453B(b)) and the fair market value of the obligation. § 453B(a). However, in a §§ 332/334(b)(1) liquidation, § 453B(d)(1) provides that no gain or loss is recognized on distribution of an installment obligation, (because the parent corporation succeeds to the subsidiary's basis and its accounting method under § 381, and will report the remainder of the profit as collections are made). Nonrecognition also is provided on distribution in complete liquidation of an installment obligation which could have been sold on the date of distribution without gain or loss under § 337 (except for collapsible or recapture gain). § 453B(d)(2).

§ 6.   Sales by Liquidating Corporation: § 337

(a) *In General.* Prior to enactment of the 1954
Code, well-advised stockholders could liquidate
their corporation with recognition of capital gain
on their investment, receive the corporate property with a fair market value basis and sell the
property with no further gain. Stockholders who
were less fortunate might find that the sale of
the corporate property was considered to be made
by the liquidating corporation, with gain taxed
at the corporate level and a second gain to the
stockholders upon distribution of the after-tax
sale proceeds. This unhappy result was reached
by the Supreme Court in Court Holding Co.
(1945) where the corporation negotiated a sale
of its assets and distributed them to the stockholders who made the sale; the happy one-tax
result was the Supreme Court decision in Cumberland Public Serv. Co. (1950). To avoid a trap
for the unwary in this general situation and end
formal distinctions as to whether the sale of assets was made before or after the liquidation, §
337, the *"anti-Court Holding"* provision was
adopted as part of the 1954 Code. Section 337
provides generally that a corporation which
adopts a plan of complete liquidation, and distributes all assets (less assets retained to meet claims)
within a 12 month period beginning on the date
of the adoption of the plan, recognizes no gain or
loss on the sale or exchange of property within

[*176*]

the 12 month period. (Since the 12 month period begins "on the date" of the plan's adoption, property can be sold tax-free at lunch on that date and the plan adopted at dinner. Regs. § 1.337–1.) The provision is mandatory in form, but the Regulations permit the corporation effectively to elect to have its liquidating sales all taxable or all within § 337 by placing the date of formal adoption by stockholders of the plan of liquidation either before or after the sales of property. Regs. § 1.337–2(b). Section 337 is also avoided, whether intentionally or inadvertently, if the liquidating distributions extend beyond the permitted 12 months. The Service, in Rev.Rul. 77–150, citing cases and legislative history, held that a corporation may intentionally avoid the application of § 337, e. g., to a loss from a sale of assets made after adoption of the plan, by waiting beyond the 12 month period before distributing to stockholders all of its assets (other than those retained to meet claims). A "straddle", the best of both worlds, is achieved if loss assets are sold before adoption of the plan, and gain assets sold tax free after adoption of the plan. The Regulations, § 1.337–2(b), warn that if the dates of sale straddle the date of formal adoption, the Service may contend that the plan was actually adopted informally before the loss sales. (The Service has had little success in establishing such an informal adoption when the stockholders were careful to separate the sales by a formal stockholders' resolution. See e. g., City Bank of Washington (T.C. 1962).)

(b) *Limitations on the Applicability of § 337.* Nonrecognition of gain or loss under § 337 is available only on the "sale or exchange" of property. Normally it is clear whether property has been sold or exchanged but a problem exists for transactions which are not true sales but are treated as such under other Code sections. (E. g., losses on worthless securities, § 165(g), gain or loss on involuntary conversions, § 1231(a).) After several unsuccessful attempts to limit § 337 to actual sales, the Service agreed to include involuntary conversions. The practical effect of this change of position was temporarily limited by the Supreme Court in Central Tablet Manufacturing Co. (1974) where the Court held that the date of the casualty (or the passage of title in a condemnation case), not the date of cash recovery, controlled in determining whether the "sale" took place within the 12 month period. Under this rule, § 337 would provide nonrecognition of casualty gain from a major casualty only if the corporation adopted a plan of liquidation on the very date of the casualty or condemnation. (Presumably, a standby plan could be approved to be "adopted" without further action, effective on the occurrence of a major casualty, as defined in the plan.) Congress responded to this situation in 1978 by enacting new § 337(e), which allows a corporation with an involuntary conversion 60 days after the "disposition" within which to adopt a plan of liquidation under § 337 and thereby obtain nonrecognition of gain or loss on the involuntary conversion. As to other types of transactions treated as sales by the Code, the Service position seems to be that they will generally qualify as § 337(a) sales as long as the property with reference to which gain or loss was realized was actually owned by the corporation, (thereby excluding capital gain dividends received from a regulated investment company). Rev.Rul. 69–18.

Section 337(b) provides that "property" which is sold tax-free under § 337 does not include:

—inventory (unless substantially all inventory attributable to one trade or business is sold to one person in one transaction). (The term "inventory" used herein includes also property held for sale to customers in the ordinary course of the corporation's trade or business, such as land held by a dealer in real estate. See § 337(b)(1)(A).)

—installment obligations, representing sale of inventory at any time (unless to one person in one transaction) or a sale of noninventory property sold before adoption of the plan.

The rationale is that the profits or loss from nonbulk sale of inventory or from sales made before liquidation status begins though collected in installments, properly relate to ordinary business operations rather than to the liquidating process. The bulk sale exception is available for substantially all the inventory of a business "at the time of sale", Reg. § 1.337–3(b), so that sales with recognition (perhaps of loss) could be made of some inventory after adoption of the plan, with one bulk sale of the remaining inventory being made tax-free.

In the past, cases had also excluded *Corn Products* assets (assets that are not inventory but are sufficiently related to the corporation's normal operations so as to produce ordinary income or loss when sold) from the definition of § 337(a) "property", see e. g., Hollywood Baseball Ass'n (9th Cir. 1970). In John T. Stewart III Trust (1975), however, the Tax Court held that § 337 applied to gain on the sale of mortgage servicing contracts which would have been ordinary income if gain had been recognized. I.R.S. has acquiesced in this decision and in Rev.Rul. 77–190 accompanying the acquiescence stated that § 337 "property" includes all assets of the corporation except the specific statutory exceptions of § 337(b).

The term "installment obligation" as used in § 337 has been interpreted by the Tax Court as including noninstallment ordinary accounts receivable (accounted for under the cash or accrual method rather than under § 453) with the result that the sale of accounts receivable at a gain produces recognized ordinary income. A gain on the sale of accounts receivable can occur if the seller uses the cash method (such as accounts receivable for services rendered before adoption of the plan) or in the case of sale of an accrual method receivable (such as from sale of inventory) at more than face because it bears a higher than market rate of interest.

(c) *Limitations on Applicability of § 337 in Connection with Other Liquidating Sections.* Section 337(c) provides that § 337(a) does not apply to sales or exchanges made by the liquidating corporation if it is a collapsible corporation under § 341, or if the liquidation is governed by §§ 333 or 332/334(b)(1). The rationale for excluding collapsible corporations is their tax avoidance purpose of avoiding ordinary income dispositions; the effect is that the sale of assets not covered by § 337 may cause recognition of enough ordinary gain to remove the collapsible status, so that the subsequent liquidation will result in capital gain treatment at the stockholder level.

The rationale for excluding § 333 liquidations is that in general there is no gain recognized at the stockholder level, so that the need to avoid two-level recognition is inapplicable; the same rationale explains the exclusion of tax free liquidations of subsidiaries with carryover basis under § 334(b)(1), which are not simultaneous with the liquidation of the parent.

In a §§ 332/334(b)(2) liquidation which is not simultaneous with the liquidation of the parent, the application of § 337 to the liquidating subsidiary is limited under § 337(c)(2)(B) and Regs. § 1.337–4 to gains from sales at prices no higher than a price which reflects what was paid by the parent for the subsidiary's stock. Any further appreciation and any losses from sales below the subsidiary's asset basis are recognized because § 337 does not apply. The result as to gains is consistent with the statutory *Kimbell-Diamond* concept, because if the liquidation precedes a sale of the assets by the parent the stepped-up § 334(b) (2) basis of the parent normally insures that it will not realize or recognize any gain.

If the parent as well as the subsidiary is to be liquidated, § 337(c)(3), added to the Code by the Tax Reform Act of 1976, permits the subsidiary to sell its assets under § 337 regardless of whether the parent's basis in the subsidiary's assets is determined under § 334(b)(1) or (b)(2) and without the limitations of § 337(c)(2)(B). In order to qualify, the parent must liquidate within 12 months of the subsidiary's adoption of the plan of liquidation. If the subsidiary is not directly controlled by the parent, § 337(c)(3) requires that in addition to the parent and the selling subsidiary, all other subsidiaries in the direct line of stock ownership above the level of the selling subsidiary must also be liquidated within the same 12 month period.

A special mechanical rule in § 337 and Regs. § 1.337–5 benefits minority stockholders in a subsidiary which loses § 337 coverage solely because of § 337(c)(2)(A), relating to subsidiary liquidations. The minority stockholder credits against his taxes the amount of his pro rata share of the corporation's increased taxes caused by the inapplicability of § 337; his amount realized on the liquidation is increased ("grossed up") by the same amount. This generally puts him in the same position as if his corporation had avoided tax under § 337 and had thereby been able to make a larger liquidating distribution to him.

§ 7. Exceptions to the Nonrecognition Rules of §§ 336 and 337

Sections 336 and 337 are overridden by the recapture provisions of §§ 47(a), 1245, 1250, 1251, and 1252, except in a § 332 liquidation of a subsidiary in which the parent takes a carryover basis in the distributed assets under § 334(b)(1).

Under the "tax benefit rule", sales under § 337 are denied tax free treatment when the property, such as small tools, linens being rented out, or a farmer's seed and feed was previously expensed. The expensed assets are still "property" within the meaning of § 337(a) but the amount previously deducted is required to be restored as ordinary income to the extent recouped by a sale; any gain realized in excess of cost (the amount deducted) will go unrecognized. Spitalny (9th Cir. 1970).

The recognition of gain on the sale of expensed assets under § 337 has led the Service to contend that a corporation distributing these assets in kind under § 336 also should recognize gain. Rev.Rul. 74–396 (except for liquidations to which § 381(a) (1) applies, i. e., a §§ 332/334(b)(1) liquidation of a subsidiary). The IRS rationale is that § 336 and § 337 should, whenever possible, be interpreted to produce the same tax results whether the corporation distributes its assets in kind or sells them under § 337 and distributes the proceeds. The Service's position was rejected by the Ninth Circuit in South Lake Farms (1963) on the rationale that a corporation distributing assets in liquidation realizes no "recovery". On the other hand the Tax Court and the Sixth Circuit have upheld the IRS position in Tennessee-Carolina Transportation (1978), finding a "deemed" recovery equal to the lesser of fair market value of the expensed truck tires or the portion of their cost attributable to their remaining useful life. Even if the Courts ultimately should not accept the Service's position, items expensed in the year of liquidation might possibly be disallowed under § 446(b) (clear reflection of income). (But see *South Lake Farms* where the Service could not find another accepted method of accounting that would result in the elimination of the deduction.)

Application of the tax benefit rule is limited to recovery of amounts actually deducted by the corporation from gross income (or deducted from ending inventory under the farm price method of accounting, which has the same effect as deductions from gross income). Therefore the § 336 distribution or § 337 bulk-sale of LIFO inventory is fully protected even though the LIFO method of accounting permitted the corporation to artificially lower taxes in previous years. Rev. Rul. 74–431.

Another exception to the nonrecognition rules of § 336 and § 337 is the assignment of income doctrine (income is taxed to the person earning the income and not to the person who happens to collect it). The doctrine will apply to the liquidating corporation as an exception to § 336 when it distributes assets which represent income earned by the corporation but not yet recognized (e. g., accounts receivable by a corporation using the cash method of accounting). For the doctrine to apply the income must be fully earned by the corporation prior to completion of the liquidation. The doctrine may also apply to sales under § 337. For example, a corporation using the completed contract method of accounting may sell the partially completed contract during liquidation; while the courts have generally classified the contracts as § 337(a) "property" they have required the corporation to recognize gain so as not to give cash or completed contract basis corporations an advantage over accrual basis corporations in § 337 sales or cash basis corporations distributing the assets under § 336. In some cases the Service has argued that the corporation must recognize income under either the assignment of income doctrine, or under § 446(b) (requiring the corporation to change to a percentage of completion or accrual method of accounting). The courts, in ruling in the Service's favor, have not always made it clear which theory served as the basis of their decision. E. g., Kuckenburg (9th Cir. 1962).

§ 8.　Sale of a Corporate Business

The liquidation provisions play an important role in connection with the sale of a corporate business. From the seller's standpoint it is normally more advantageous to sell his stock and let the buyer worry about any contingencies which may affect the corporation. This advantage may be offset if the buyer is able to obtain various warranties as to the financial condition of the corporation, perhaps with an escrow or contingent payment of part of the purchase price. In a stock sale, the buyer can, if desired, then liquidate the corporation, obtaining a stepped-up basis in the assets under § 334(a) (for a noncorporate buyer) or § 334(b)(2) (for a corporate buyer). The corporation will incur tax liability for recapture income and similar items, thus reducing the amount available to the buyer if he liquidates. (In addition the stockholder, as transferee of the corporate assets, will be liable for claims against the liquidated corporation, including any tax liability arising out of the liquidation itself). The new owner can cause the corporation to sell any unwanted assets under § 337 (to the extent of paid-for gain in connection with § 334(b)(2)) before liquidating or can sell them with no further gain after receiving them in liquidation. Alternatively the corporation can be kept alive by the buyer, preserving its favorable tax attributes.

A second major alternative for the seller is to have the corporation sell the desired assets to the buyer under § 337 and then liquidate, distributing the sale proceeds and any remaining assets. This leaves the seller to worry about any contingencies which may affect the corporation. The buyer gets the desired assets with a cost basis.

A third alternative for the seller stockholders is to liquidate first, after finding a buyer through negotiations, under the *Cumberland* approach. With a fair market value basis under § 334(a), the seller incurs no further gain upon sale of the assets.

The liquidation of a corporation by a new corporate stockholder typically involves choices among:

§§ 331/334(a)   (if the 80 percent conditions of § 332 are not met)

§§ 332/334(b)(2)   (if the liquidation occurs relatively soon)

§§ 332/334(b)(1)   (if the plan of liquidation is not adopted until more than 2 years after the stock purchase)

§ 9.   Collapsible Corporations: § 341

Because § 331 provides that a complete liquidation of a corporation is to be treated by its stockholders as a sale of their stock, resulting usually in capital gain or loss, and § 334(a) provides the stockholders with a fair market value basis in the property acquired in the liquidation, taxpayers developed the device of the "collapsible corporation" to convert what would otherwise be ordinary income into capital gain. A typical example of this was the formation of a corporation by an individual to build an apartment house, the sale of which by the individual would have produced ordinary income to the extent of any gain because the individual was a dealer in real estate. After the construction was completed the individual liquidated the corporation, recognizing as long-term capital gain on his stock the appreciation in value of the property and then sold the apartment with no further gain (because of a stepped-up basis).

The Service had limited success in attacking these transactions as shams or under assignment of income and step transaction principles. As a result Congress responded with the enactment of § 341.

The detailed consideration of § 341 is generally beyond the scope of a basic corporate tax course. A glance at § 341(e)(1), the first sentence of which has been nominated as the world's longest sentence, will indicate the complexities of this section. However, the basic principle is simple: if the corporation is deemed to be collapsible a stockholder who sells or exchanges his stock, or receives a distribution from the corporation, in a transaction which otherwise would result in long-term capital gain, must instead treat the gain as ordinary income.

Collapsible corporations are defined in § 341(b) as corporations formed or availed of:

(1) Principally for the manufacture, construction, or production of property; or the purchase of "section 341 assets" (as defined in § 341(b)(3); basically inventory and § 1231 assets)

(2) With a view to (a) a sale, liquidation or distribution before the corporation has realized a substantial part of the taxable income to be derived from the property and (b) a realization by the stockholders of the gain attributable to the property.

Since many corporations are formed or availed of principally for the purchase or production of property usually the main issue is whether the stockholders (interpreted to mean those stockholders who determine corporate policy) have the requisite view. The Regulations, § 1.341–2(a)(2), state that the controlling stockholders merely have to recognize the possibility that there be a sale, liquidation or distribution before the corporation has realized a substantial gain from the property. The Regulations to some extent narrow the coverage of § 341 by specifying that the view must exist at some time during the construction, manufacture, production or purchase of the collapsible property. § 1.341–2(a)(3). (Some courts have stated that the Regulations are too restrictive and that the requisite view may exist at any time when the corporation is availed of for purposes stated in § 341(b), e. g., Glickman (2d Cir. 1958). But recent decisions by the Tax Court have accepted the validity of the Regulations, e. g., F.T.S. Associates, Inc., (1972).)

The often litigated issue of whether the sale occurs before the realization of a "substantial" part of the taxable income to be derived from the property has diminished in importance since the Service, in Rev.Rul. 72–48, (after a series of losses in the courts) reversed its position and held that the test is whether a substantial amount has been realized, not whether there is a substantial amount yet to be realized (in the ruling a realization of one-third of the potential taxable income was held to be substantial).

Section 341(c) creates a rebuttable presumption that a corporation is collapsible if the fair market value of its "section 341 assets" is (a) 50 percent or more of the fair market value of its total assets (cash, stock and certain securities and obligations are not counted in determining the corporation's total assets) and (b) 120 percent or more of its adjusted basis in such "section 341 assets".

Section 341(d) provides three exceptions to collapsible treatment if:

(1) the stockholder at no time after the commencement of the manufacture, construction, production or purchase of the collapsible property owned more than 5 percent of the outstanding stock nor owned stock attributed to a more than 5 percent stockholder (with modified § 544 attribution rules being applicable);

(2) 30 percent or more of the gain recognized is attributable to noncollapsible property; or

(3) the gain is realized more than 3 years after the completion of the manufacture, construction, production or purchase of the collapsible property.

Section 341(e) also provides exceptions to collapsible treatment. It applies to 4 situations: sales or exchanges of stock, eligibility for § 333, complete liquidations, and eligibility for § 337. Generally if the amount of unrealized appreciation of the assets of the corporation that if sold by the corporation or by a more than 20 percent stockholder (5 percent for the § 333 exception) would produce ordinary income is 15 percent or less of the corporation's net worth then the corporation will not be deemed collapsible for purposes of the 4 exceptions.

Section 341(f) provides additional exceptions generally allowing a stockholder to sell his stock without regard to § 341(a) if the corporation consents to recognize gain on its noncapital assets and real estate when it disposes of them in a transaction which otherwise would qualify for nonrecognition of gain (e. g., §§ 311, 336) unless the basis also carries over (e. g., §§ 351, 361). The buyer of stock in a corporation should protect himself by inquiry and by obtaining appropriate warranties against a possible § 341(f) election made by the seller or a prior stockholder.

This is at best an extremely general outline of § 341, the practical application of § 341 being outside the scope of this text. An important point which should be noted is that even if a corporation does not fit within the definition of a collapsible corporation in § 341(b) the Service may be able to achieve a similar result under assignment of income or step transaction principles.

§ 10. The Liquidation-Reincorporation Problem

There is a problem if some stockholders of the liquidated corporation are stockholders of another corporation which acquires the liquidated corporation's operating assets. The Regulations warn that IRS "may" claim that there has not been a complete liquidation, but rather a § 368 corporate reorganization, with gain to the continuing stockholders taxable as a § 301 distribution to the extent of any "boot" they receive. Alternatively, IRS may assert that the liquidation is a sham with the corporation itself continuing in existence, or that there has been a dividend functionally separate from a reorganization. Regs. §§ 1.331–1(c), 1.301–1(l). The problem is discussed further in Chapter 12. (Similarly, a purported *partial* liquidation by distribution to stockholders of the assets of one of the corporate businesses, followed by a prearranged transfer of the business to a new corporation was held in Rev.Rul. 77–191 to be a divisive reorganization under §§ 368(a)(1)(D) and 355 and not a partial liquidation under § 331(a)(2).)

The benefits of a liquidation-reincorporation, if taxed as a liquidation, are to step-up the basis of corporate assets, wipe out accumulated earnings and profits, and withdraw unwanted nonoperating assets without their being taxed as a dividend. The price, if the transaction is taxed as a liquidation, is limited to a capital gains tax on the stockholders' realized gain, if any, a price which is offset by a step-up in basis in their investment and the availability of withdrawn liquid assets to pay the taxes.

The two principal types of methods are:

(1) Transfer of operating assets by the old corporation to a corporation with (some of) the same stockholders using § 337, followed by liquidation under § 331 of the old corporation or;

(2) Liquidation under § 331, followed by a § 351 transfer to a corporation with common stockholders.

The Service has announced in Rev.Proc. 80–22 that it will not issue a ruling that there is a complete liquidation in these situations if 20 percent or more of the stock of both corporations is owned by the same persons.

[*194*]

Cases (except Davant (5th Cir. 1966) and Reef (5th Cir. 1966) which also found a reorganization) have generally not supported the IRS argument of a "sham" liquidation. The only exception to date has been Telephone Ans. Serv. Co. (T.C.1974) where a parent corporation which conducted its business directly and through two subsidiaries tried to sell one of the subsidiaries under § 337 by adopting a plan of liquidation, selling the subsidiary's stock, transferring its operating assets to a new subsidiary corporation, and distributing the cash sale proceeds and stock of its two subsidiaries pro rata to its stockholders. The Court held that whatever the transaction was (a complex question which it declined to answer), for purposes of § 337 a complete liquidation had not occurred because the operating assets of the old parent remained in corporate solution within the newly formed corporation.

§ 11. Special Problems

(a) *Installment Sales.* Until October 1980, installment sales of corporate assets posed a significant practical difficulty regardless of whether the sales were covered by § 337 or not. The problem arose because the possibility of reporting gain only as payments were collected, (e. g. under § 453), was not available (except in "rare and extraordinary" cases, Regs. § 1.1001–1(a)) to the stockholder, who was required to recognize gain

(e. g. under § 331) and pay tax based on the fair market value of the installment receivables distributed to him in liquidation. This was a hardship where no buyers were available for the property except on installment terms, as may be the case, for example, with vacant land held for potential appreciation. New § 453(h), added to the Code in October 1980, now permits the stockholder to report his § 331 gain on the installment method in cases where the liquidating corporation distributes installment obligations received by it during its 12-month liquidation period in a § 337 liquidation.

(b) *Stock Transfers and Liquidations.* The liquidation of a corporation may provide a stockholder with an opportunity to avoid or defer recognition of gain on the appreciated value of his stock. He may accomplish this by transferring all or part of his stock prior to completion of the liquidation process. For example, a gift of stock to a lower tax bracket family member may result in a substantial reduction in total tax on the gain at a cost (if any) of a small gift tax, or a gift of stock to charity may both shift the gain to the charity (which is tax exempt) and provide a deduction to the donor. As long as the gifts are made prior to formal adoption of a plan of liquidation they are generally effective in shifting the gain. However, if the transfer is made after adoption of a plan of liquidation the transferor may be taxed on gain under assignment of income principles.

The current trend in judicial thinking in this area is that the donor will be taxed on the gain on shares given after adoption of a plan of liquidation if the "realities and substance" of events at the time of the gift indicate that it is unlikely that the plan of liquidation will be abandoned. See Jones (6th Cir. 1976) following Hudspeth (8th Cir. 1972) and Kinsey (2d Cir. 1973) and overruling Jacobs (6th Cir. 1966). Factors which had been deemed important in determining the likelihood of abandonment of a § 337 plan include the fact that a reversal of the decision would result in recognition by the corporation of substantial gain, the margin of decision in the vote to liquidate, and whether the donee had the power to prevent liquidation.

While it is now clear that a gift of stock in a liquidating corporation by a major stockholder will usually be considered an assignment of income, an installment sale of the stock under § 453 may succeed in deferring the stockholder's gain. This result was achieved in Rushing (5th Cir. 1971) affirming (T.C.1969) where taxpayers adopted § 337 liquidation plans for their wholly-owned corporations, and after the corporations had sold their assets tax-free and shortly before the end of the 12 month period for completing the liquidation, the taxpayers sold their stock to

trusts for their children for cash and installment
notes. The courts stressed that the trustee (a
bank) was truly independent, that an affirmative
act on its part (the authorization of the final distribution of the assets) was required to complete
the liquidation and that taxpayers were not trying to avoid but merely to defer recognition of
gain. However, *Rushing* (which relied at least
partly on the now-overruled *Jacobs*) is undermined by *Jones* and by Rev.Rul. 73–157 and Rev.
Rul. 73–536 which generally hold that where a
taxpayer purports to sell appreciated property to
a related party for an amount payable in installments and the related party thereupon sells it to
a third party for cash, the transaction lacks reality and the taxpayer does not qualify for the installment method of reporting income under §
453(b). New § 453(e), added to the Code in
October 1980, legislates a compromise result in
such cases, permitting installment method reporting but treating payments received by the second
seller from the third party as if they had been received by the first seller if the second sale occurred within two years of the first.

(c) *The Corporation's Deduction of Liquidating Expenses.* It is well settled that the corporation's liquidating expenses are deductible under § 162 as ordinary and necessary business expenses. See e. g., Gravois Planing Mill Co. (8th
Cir. 1962). At one time this was expanded by two

courts to apply to the cost of selling property in a § 337 liquidation, the theory being that a § 337 sale of assets is as much a part of the liquidation as the distribution of assets in kind. Pridemark, Inc. (4th Cir. 1965), Mountain States Mixed Feed Co. (10th Cir. 1966). However, since 1966, every circuit considering or reconsidering the issue has held that selling expenses are not deductible. Of Course, Inc. (4th Cir. 1974) overruling Pridemark, Inc.; Benedict Oil Co. (10th Cir. 1978) overruling Mountain States Mixed Feed Co.; Connery (3d Cir. 1972); Lanrao Inc. (6th Cir. 1970); Morton (8th Cir. 1968); Alphaco, Inc. (7th Cir. 1967); Page (9th Cir. 1975).

CHAPTER 7

STOCK DIVIDENDS

Table of Sections

§ 1. Tax-Free Stock Dividends: § 305(a)

A corporation's distribution to its stockholders of its own stock is normally referred to as a stock dividend. The general rule is that stock dividends are tax-free to the recipient under § 305(a). There are significant exceptions in § 305(b), discussed below, but they do not apply to most cases.

Beginning tax courses normally cover Eisner v. Macomber (1920), in which the Supreme Court held that a recipient of a stock dividend of common shares on her common shares, the only class outstanding, could not constitutionally be taxed because she had not realized income. On these facts, she and all of the other stockholders simply had more shares, more pieces of paper, representing the same proportionate interest in the corporation.

The Eisner v. Macomber approach remains the basic rule today under § 305(a). Typical situations covered by the rule include the following:

—The outstanding stock of N Corp. is 200 shares of common stock. A and B each own 100 shares. N authorizes and issues pro rata a dividend on the common of 1000 shares of a new class of $100 par 7 percent preferred stock. A and B have no gross income from the receipt of the preferred stock.

—Each recent year, M Corp., listed on the New York Stock Exchange, has issued both a 5 percent stock dividend and cash dividends on its only class of stock. Judy and Alice each receive a 5 share stock dividend on their 100 shares of M Corp. stock. Alice sells her 5 shares. Judy and Alice each report no gross income on the receipt of the shares and Alice recognizes gain or loss on the sale of the stock. (See § 2 infra for determination of holding period and basis.)

§ 2. Basis of Tax-Free Stock Dividends: § 307 (a) and (b)

The stockholder who receives a tax-free stock dividend has no change in the total basis of his stock investment. This is in keeping with the concept that no taxable event has occurred because his investment interest is simply represented by more pieces of paper. Section 307(a) provides that his adjusted basis of his "old" shares, on which the "new" stock dividend shares are received, is allocated under Regulations among the old and new shares. The Regulations provide for allocation in accordance with fair market values immediately after the stock dividend distribution. Regs. § 1.307–1(a). In the ordinary case of a dividend of common on common this results simply in spreading the old shares' adjusted basis ratably over each share, old or new. (Normally the fair market value of the old shares will decline proportionately to reflect the stock dividend's transfer of part of the old shares' value into new shares.)

Example: Judy had a cost basis of $1680 in 100 shares of M Corp. stock, or $16.80 a share. Judy received 5 shares of M Corp. stock as a tax-free stock dividend. Since the relative fair market values of the old and new shares are 100:5 (each share being of equal value), she allocates ⁵⁄₁₀₅ of her $1,680 basis to the 5 dividend shares, and ¹⁰⁰⁄₁₀₅ to the 100 old shares, or ¹⁄₁₀₅ to each share. Her total basis is still $1,680, but allocated over 105 shares instead of 100, it is now $16 per share. The sale of 5 shares with a basis of $80 (5 x $16) at $17 per share for $85 accordingly would result in a gain of $5.

The holding period of new shares received as a tax-free stock dividend "tacks" on to the holding period of the "old" shares under § 1223(5). Thus gain in the example will either be long or short term capital gain depending on Judy's holding period for the 100 shares.

§ 3. Stock Rights Distributions: § 305(a), (d); § 307(b)

A corporation can receive new investment capital if instead of a stock dividend, it distributes to its stockholders rights to purchase stock. Such rights have two elements of value: (1) The extent (if any) that they entitle the stockholder to purchase stock at a price which is below the market price of the stock when the rights are issued; and (2) The chance that the holder will profit because the stock may go up in value before the deadline for buying it.

For purposes of § 305(a), § 305(d) provides that rights to buy stock are treated as stock. Thus a distribution of rights to buy common stock by a corporation with an all common stock capital structure, is tax-free under § 305(a).

The stockholder who receives a rights distribution is in an unstable position because the rights will expire soon, so he must exercise them himself, let them expire, or sell them for eventual exercise by someone else. The tax results depend in part on the basis of the rights.

Under the basis rules of § 307(a), stock rights are treated as "new" stock. Basis is allocated between the "old" stock and the "new" rights in proportion to fair market values on the date of distribution. Regs. § 1.307–1(a) (last sentence) provides that basis is allocated to tax-free stock rights only if they are exercised or sold. Thus if rights expire in the hands of the distributee no deductible loss occurs. There is a special de minimis rule if immediately after the distribution the fair market value of the rights is less than 15 percent of the fair market value of the stock on which the rights were distributed, as will normally be the case. Section 307(b) provides that the recipient stockholder shall have a zero basis in such low-value rights unless he elects in his tax return to allocate basis to his rights under § 307 (a). The zero basis "de minimis" rule simplifies the tax treatment of many rights distributions, while permitting the stockholder to have the benefit of the more complex treatment if he so elects.

Stock rights, like stock dividends, if received tax-free (so that their basis is determined under § 307) have a tacked holding period under § 1223 (5). This is so regardless of whether the rights' § 307 basis is zero or an allocated basis.

If the stockholder (or any later holder) exercises the rights, his basis, if any, in the rights is added to the exercise price in determining his cost basis in the stock. His holding period in the purchased stock, however, starts with the date of exercise under § 1223(6); he does not tack any previous periods because he basically makes a new investment when he buys the stock.

Example: In June, 1979, American Banana Corp. (ABC) issues 20 stock rights with a total fair market value of $100 to each holder of 100 shares. On the date of distribution (i. e., immediately after the distribution) 100 shares are worth $5,000. Each right entitles the holder to buy 1 share for $46. Sam, who owns 200 shares with an adjusted basis of $2,000 and a holding period of more than 1 year, receives 40 rights. Two weeks later he sells 20 rights for $115 and exercises 20 rights, paying $920 ($46 x 20 shares) to buy 20 ABC shares. Sam has no gross income from receipt of the rights. § 305(a). His 40 rights have a zero basis (unless he elects to allocate basis) because their fair market value ($200) is less than 15% ($1500) of the $10,000 fair market value of his stock at the time of distribution. § 307(b). Thus he reports long term capital gain of $115 ($115–zero) on the sale of his 20 rights and has a cost basis of $920 ($920 exercise price plus zero) and a new holding period in his new 20 shares of stock. § 1223(6). If he elects by a statement attached to his tax return to allocate basis to the 40 rights (which he must do as to all rights or none, Regs. § 1.307–2) then his basis in the 40 rights is

$$\frac{\text{FMV rights \$200}}{\text{FMV rights \& FMV stock \$10,200}} \times \text{\$2,000 total basis} = \text{\$39.22}$$

so his basis per right is \$.98 (\$39.22 ÷ 40). His sale of 20 rights for \$115 then produces a long term capital gain of \$95.40 (\$115–\$19.60), and his basis in the 20 purchased shares is \$939.60 (\$920 exercise price plus \$19.60 basis of exercised rights).

§ 4.   Taxable Stock Dividends: § 305(b), (c)

A stock dividend (or stock rights distribution) is taxable as a § 301 distribution to the extent of its fair market value, if and only if it falls within one of the exceptions listed in § 305(b).   Section 305(b), as expanded by the Tax Reform Act of 1969, will be discussed at some length, but because of the delayed effective dates of the amendments (in certain situations) and as an aid to understanding, a brief historical discussion of taxable stock dividends follows.

After the Supreme Court's decision in Eisner v. Macomber, Congress exempted all stock dividends from tax, even though Eisner v. Macomber dealt only with a dividend of common on common, the only class outstanding.   After the Supreme Court made it clear in *Koshland* (1936) (a case dealing with allocation of basis) that some

[*206*]

stock dividends were constitutionally taxable, Congress responded with a provision taxing all stock dividends which constitute income "within the meaning of the Sixteenth Amendment of the Constitution". This was interpreted by the Supreme Court as being limited to stock dividends which resulted in an increase in the stockholder's proportionate interest in the corporation.

Because of the uncertainty of the "proportionate interest" test Congress, in 1954, adopted a general tax-free rule with only two seemingly mechanical exceptions:

> If the recipient (or any other stockholder) could elect to take property instead of stock; or

> If the distribution was in discharge of preferred stock dividend arrearages for the last two years including the taxable year.

The Treasury attempted to expand these exceptions by regulations first proposed in 1956 and finally adopted in expanded form in 1969. (The 1969 regulations generally did not apply until 1991 to stock dividends on stock outstanding on September 2, 1968.) The 1969 regulations attempted to tax various devices such as the use of convertible stock with changing conversion ratios and the "Citizens Utilities" plan (discussed below) which had been used to make tax-free increases in the equity interests of certain stockholders while other stockholders received taxable cash dividends.

In the Tax Reform Act of 1969, Congress in its amendment of § 305 gave express statutory support to results reached only by strained interpretation in the 1969 Regulations, and specifically brought back a "proportionate interest" test.

As amended in 1969, § 305(b) contains five exceptions to the general rule of § 305(a):

(1) Optional distributions, i. e., distributions which at the election of any stockholder (whether exercised before or after declaration of the stock dividend) are payable either in stock or "property" (such as cash). This is the same as one of the two exceptions in the original 1954 Code version. Note that the precise amount recognized by a stockholder who receives the stock dividend is not the amount of cash which could have been received but rather the fair market value of the stock dividend, under the usual § 301 rules. Rev.Rul. 76–53.

(2) Disproportionate distributions, i. e., distributions which have the result of receipt of "property" by some stockholders and the increase by other stockholders of their proportionate interests in corporate assets or e & p. A detailed consideration of this key principle, beyond the scope of this work, ap-

pears in Regs. § 1.305-3, containing examples. A key example is the "Citizens Utilities Plan"; if a corporation has two classes of common stock outstanding and pays stock dividends on one class and cash dividends on the other, the stock dividends are taxable as § 301 distributions. There is no requirement of a "plan" to distribute cash to some stockholders and increase the proportionate interest of others; for example, quarterly stock dividends to one class of common will all be taxable if there are annual cash dividends on another class of common, even if all these events are "independent and unrelated". Regs. § 1.305-3(b)(2). However, a stock dividend to one class more than 36 months apart from the nearest cash payments to another class is presumed not to have a taxable "result", unless both are made pursuant to a plan, in which case the stock dividend is taxable. Regs. § 1.305-3(b)(4).

Many examples in the Regulations consider other situations such as the payment of cash in lieu of fractional dividend shares, or changes in conversion ratio, which may result in an increase in proportionate interest by some stockholders and a receipt of property by others. See Regs. § 1.305-3(c) and (d).

(3) Distributions of common and preferred, i. e., distributions of preferred stock to some common stockholders and of common stock to others. This includes, for example, a stock dividend of convertible preferred on common where it is reasonable to anticipate that some will convert their preferred to common and others will keep their preferred because of a 6 month time limit on the conversion privilege. Regs. § 1.305–4(b), *Example (2)*.

(4) Distributions on preferred, i. e. all stock dividends on preferred stock. (This greatly broadens the rule of the original 1954 Code provision, which taxed only stock dividends on preferred in discharge of the last two years' dividend arrearages.)

(5) Distributions of convertible preferred, i. e., distributions of convertible preferred stock unless the corporation establishes that they will not result in a disproportionate distribution. Regs. § 1.305–6 says that such a distribution is not taxable if the conversion right may be exercised over a period of many years and the dividend rate is consistent with market conditions at the time of distribution. In other situations, a disproportionate distribution will result if the conversion period is relatively short and it may be anticipated that some holders will convert and others will

not. This is very similar to the example given under (3) above.

Section 305(c), a new concept introduced in the Tax Reform Act of 1969, provides that, under regulations, transactions which increase the proportionate interest of a stockholder but are not actually stock dividends, are treated as property distributions to the stockholder. The transactions which may be treated as taxable stock dividends are:

> a "change" (in conversion ratio or redemption price);

> a "difference" (between redemption price and issue price);

> a "redemption" (treated as a § 301 distribution); or

> "any transaction" (including a recapitalization) having a similar effect on the interest of any stockholder.

If such a "change, difference, redemption or transaction" results in increasing any stockholder's proportionate interest in corporate e & p or assets and has the result described in § 305(b) (2)–(5), a "deemed" distribution of a taxable dividend may occur. Generally, the Regulations provide that if the transaction was not part of a plan to increase some stockholders' proportionate interest and not done regularly, it will not be deemed to be a taxable distribution. For example, an isolated redemption of a dissenting stockholder's shares will not result in a taxable deemed distribution to the nonredeeming stockholders even though their proportionate interest in the corporation has been increased, while the redeeming stockholder received cash. This is true whether or not the redemption was treated as a § 301 distribution. Regs. § 1.305–3(e), *Example (10)*. A stock dividend distributed at the same time would also be unaffected by the redemption. Regs. § 1.305–3(e), *Example (11)*. Similarly, an isolated "old to young" recapitalization enabling retiring employees to exchange common stock (the only class outstanding) for newly issued preferred while younger employees exchange their stock for additional shares of common will not have a taxable result. Regs. § 1.305–3(e), *Example (12)*.

Changes in conversion ratio will be treated as distributions unless made pursuant to a bona fide adjustment formula which compensates for tax-free increases in the proportionate interest of the underlying stock. Since a holder of a convertible security is considered a stockholder for purposes of § 305 (§ 305(d)(2)), changes in the conversion ratio of securities will be treated as if a change had been made on convertible stock.

The 1969 amendments to § 305 apply generally to distributions made after January 10, 1969, but there are transitional rules (contained in § 421 (b)(1) of the Tax Reform Act of 1969, usually printed as a footnote to § 305(b) in student editions of the Code) which delay the effective date in certain situations until January 1, 1991. Thus in blocking new adoptions of tax gimmick capital structures after 1969, Congress blessed existing ones for some 20 years.

§ 5. Effects of Stock Dividends on Distributing Corporation: §§ 311(a), 312(d)

If a corporation distributes its stock (or rights to acquire its stock), it recognizes no gain or loss on the transaction. § 311(a)(1). This § 311 rule for "distributions" to stockholders of stock or rights is paralleled by § 1032, which prevents recognition when the corporation "exchanges" its stock for money or other property. If the corporation had previously purchased its own stock and used the treasury shares for distribution or exchange, these Code provisions make clear (§ 1032 by specific reference to treasury stock) that the corporation does not recognize any gain or loss. Nonrecognition is the rule for the distributing corporation regardless of whether the stock dividend is taxable or tax-free to the recipient stockholder.

Distribution of a § 305(a) tax-free stock dividend (or stock rights) is not considered a distribution of earnings and profits. § 312(d). Distribution of a stock dividend (or stock rights) which is treated as a § 301 distribution under §

305(b), or a "change, difference, redemption or transaction" which similarly results in § 301 treatment under § 305(c), does reduce e & p (to the extent there are any) of the distributing corporation. The e & p are reduced by the fair market value of the taxable stock or rights distribution (regardless of whether the recipient is an individual or corporation), Regs. § 1.312–1(d). This is consistent with the rule that a corporate recipient of a § 305(b) taxable stock dividend (or rights distribution), like a corporate distributee of a corporate debt obligation, includes the fair market value of the distribution as the "amount" received under § 301. Regs. § 1.301–1(d).

CHAPTER 8

PREFERRED STOCK BAIL–OUTS AND "SECTION 306 STOCK"

Table of Sections

§ 1. The Basic Preferred Stock Bail-Out

A "bail-out" means withdrawal of corporate earnings and profits by the stockholders without their being taxed on a dividend or giving up proportionate ownership. A "preferred stock bail-out" if successful, means a bail-out through the issuance of preferred stock to a stockholder who then sells the newly issued stock at a capital gain to an unrelated investor, from whom the stock is soon redeemed by the corporation. The basic transaction, approved in *Chamberlin* (6th Cir. 1953), is generally prevented by § 306 as adopted in 1954. The student should know the basic preferred stock bail-out pattern, how § 306 operates if it applies, when it applies, and what similar transactions are still possible.

[*215*]

The steps in *Chamberlin* were:

—A tax-free stock dividend of a new class of preferred stock pro rata to the holders of the one class of common stock outstanding. The preferred stock terms were designed to be satisfactory to an investor (two insurance companies) waiting to buy it; it was required to be retired over an eight year period by annual redemptions of a fixed number of shares beginning in the second year.

—Virtually all the stockholders sold their preferred in one transaction to the investor for a total of $800,000. Each stockholder reported capital gain with his basis in the preferred stock being an allocated portion of his original common stock basis, under the approach now reflected in § 307.

—The stockholders thus received $800,000 cash from a sale of stock and not from the corporation; however in due course the preferred stock would be redeemed and disappear and the corporation would pay out $800,000. Thus the final result of the entire series of steps was the withdrawal of $800,-000 from the corporation, the receipt of that amount by the stockholders with sale and capital gain treatment, and the retention by the stockholders of their proportionate interests in the corporation.

In *Chamberlin* the Commissioner with the agreement of the Tax Court treated the transaction as a cash dividend to the stockholders, on the theory that cash was indirectly paid by the corporation. The Court of Appeals decision in *Chamberlin* held however that the preferred stock dividend was tax-free despite the plan for its sale and later redemption. Congress was then working on the 1954 Code, and responded with § 306.

§ 2. Section 306: Definition of "Section 306 Stock"

Section 306, new in the 1954 Code, blocks the preferred stock bail-out. It operates by "tainting" the preferred stock issued as a stock dividend, so that its sale or redemption will produce ordinary income. For example, on the *Chamberlin* facts, the stock dividend of preferred on common remains tax-free, but the sale of this "section 306 stock" to the investors for $800,000 results in $800,000 of ordinary income to the selling stockholders, provided that e & p of the corporation totalled at least that much in the year the preferred stock was distributed. (The § 307 allocated basis of the "section 306 stock" cannot be applied against the selling price, but is reallocated by the selling stockholder to his common stock. Regs. § 1.306–1(b)(2), *Examples (2) and (3)*. A preferred stock bail-out opportunity still possible under § 306 is sale or redemption of preferred stock which was included in the original capital structure of the corporation rather than having been issued in a tax-free stock dividend or similar transaction.

The basic definition of "section 306 stock", in § 306(c)(1), taints stock in three situations:

—Stock received by the selling stockholder as a stock dividend tax-free under § 305(a) (other than a stock dividend of common on common). This would cover the preferred stock received in *Chamberlin*. The 1969 changes in § 305 did not change the tax-free status of this preferred on common stock dividend. Of course, if the stock dividend is taxable (as with a stock dividend of preferred on preferred, § 305(b)(4)), the dividend stock is not "section 306 stock" and there is no bail-out possibility.

—When preferred (i. e., not common) stock is received at least partly tax-free by the selling stockholder in a reorganization (or under §§ 355/356 relating to corporate divisions) "to the extent that either the effect of the transaction was substantially the same as the receipt of a stock dividend," or the stock was received in exchange for "section 306 stock." This provision covers, for instance, a variation on the Chamberlin situation in which the same effect is achieved but the preferred stock is issued to the selling stockholder not as a stock dividend but in a recapitalization, in exchange for a surrender by each common stockholder of a pro rata part of his stock.

—When the selling stockholder's basis is determined by reference to his basis or someone else's in "section 306 stock". This goes beyond stock received in tax-free exchanges for "section 306 stock" to cover "section 306 stock" received by lifetime gift with § 1015 basis or common stock received in a § 351 transaction in exchange for "section 306 stock", Regs. § 1.306–3(e), or stock received under § 1036 in exchange for "section 306 stock" in the same corporation.

If the corporation has no e & p, so that no part of any money distributed instead of a stock dividend would have been a dividend, the stock is not "section 306 stock." § 306(c)(2); Regs. § 1.-306–3(a).

Note that in determining whether preferred stock (for example, received in "family" recapitalizations) is "section 306 stock", § 318 is not applied. Thus a father can receive preferred for all his common and not have it treated as "section 306 stock" even though his wife or children own all the common.

For purposes of § 306, rights to acquire stock are treated as stock, § 306(d)(1), so that if money distributed in lieu of the rights would have been a dividend the distributed rights (at least if they are rights to acquire preferred stock) will be "section 306 stock." If stock is acquired by exercise of the rights, the amount of ordinary income on nonredemption disposition of the stock as acquired tax-free is computed as if "section 306 stock" with a fair market value equal to that of the rights had been distributed in place of the rights. § 306(d)(2); Regs. § 1.306–3(b).

Section 306(e)(1) provides that if "section 306 stock" which was distributed with respect to common is downgraded by being exchanged for common stock in the same corporation, the common stock received is not "section 306 stock." Section 306(e)(2) provides that common stock convertible into preferred or into property is not "common stock" for purposes of § 306.

Section 306(g) provides that a change in the terms of previously issued stock may result in its classification as "section 306 stock."

§ 3. Operation of § 306

The general consequences of disposing of "section 306 stock" are provided by § 306(a), with exceptions in § 306(b).

If the "section 306 stock" is redeemed, the entire amount realized is treated as a § 301 distribution. § 306(a)(2). Assuming that the corporation has enough e & p, the redemption proceeds thus receive dividend treatment, as with any "nonsale" redemption. § 306(a)(2). If "section 306 stock" is disposed of other than by redemption the entire "amount realized" i. e., the selling price, is treated as ordinary income to the extent that the stock's fair market value on date of distribution was covered by e & p. (In Code language, "such stock's ratable share of the amount which would have been a dividend at the time of distribution if (in lieu of section 306 stock) the corporation had distributed money in an amount equal to the fair market value of the stock at the time of distribution." § 306(a)(1)(A)(ii).) This § 306(a)(1) limitation for later sales to third parties focuses on the potential bailout when the preferred stock was issued. Thus, if the corporation lacked e & p to cover the fair market value of the "section 306 stock" when originally distributed, or if the "section 306 stock" is later sold for more than its value when distributed, part of the sale price will not be ordinary income. In that case, under § 306(a)(1)(B), there is recovery of basis, and then capital gain, but there can never be a recognized loss. § 306(a)(1)(C). In contrast, if the § 306 stock is redeemed, the fair market value and e & p at the earlier date of distribution of the "section 306 stock" become irrelevant and the focus under § 306(a)(2) is on the e & p of the corporation at the time of the redemption.

The amount treated as ordinary income on sale of "section 306 stock" to a third party is not a corporate distribution; it does not affect corporate e & p and is not a dividend eligible for the § 116 exclusion or the § 243 intercorporate deduction. Corporate e & p remain intact until the third party redeems the preferred stock, which has lost its § 306 taint in his hands because of his § 1012 cost basis. If "section 306 stock" is redeemed, however, there is a § 301 distribution, i. e., a dividend to the extent of e & p, and a reduction of e & p under § 312.

Example (1): "Section 306 stock" with a fair market value of $100,000 is distributed as a stock dividend to 10% stockholder Irving; 10% of e & p is $60,000. His § 307 allocated basis in the "section 306 stock" is $90,000. Irving later sells the stock for $98,000 to an investor. Irving has $60,000 of ordinary income, § 306(a)(1)(A), the $98,000 amount realized but only to the extent that the earlier $100,000 distribution was covered by his $60,000 ratable share of e & p. Applying his $90,000 basis against the remaining $38,000 amount realized leaves him with no capital gain, and $52,000 of unused basis which he adds to his basis in the stock with respect to which the "section 306 stock" was distributed. Regs. § 1.306–

1(b)(2), *Example (2)*. If instead of selling his "section 306 stock" to an investor for $98,000, Irving sells it to the corporation, the entire $98,-000 is a § 301 distribution; if there are at least $98,000 of e & p at that point, Irving has a $98,-000 dividend. § 306(a)(2).

Example (2): "Section 306 stock", FMV $100,-000, is received as a stock dividend by a stockholder whose pro rata share of e & p exceeds $100,000. Later sale of the stock for up to $100,000 produces ordinary income equal to the selling price. Later sale for more than $100,000, e. g., $105,000, produces $100,000 ordinary income and a $5,000 reduction of basis of the stock (or gain to the extent that $5,000 exceeds basis). The unused basis is transferred to the seller's other stock. See Regs. § 1.306–1(b)(2).

§ 4. Exceptions

Four exceptions, one vague and three safe-harbor, are provided by § 306(b). In general, they limit the bite of § 306 to bail-out situations. The three safe-harbor rules are:

—A sale or redemption of "section 306 stock" which terminates the stockholder's entire stock interest is excepted. § 306(b)(1). There is no bail-out because the stockholder is not at all retaining his interest in the corporation. For this exception to apply, a non-redemption sale of "section 306 stock" must be to a buyer unrelated under § 318(a), and § 318(a) applies in testing whether the seller owns any stock after the sale.   § 306(b)(1) (A). If the "section 306 stock" is redeemed, this exception requires that the redemption qualify under § 302(b)(3) as a complete termination of interest.   § 306(b)(1)(A). Thus, in case of a redemption of "section 306 stock" a waiver of family attribution under § 302(c)(2) can provide safe-harbor treatment.   In case of a nonredemption sale of "section 306 stock" which terminates the stockholder's actual, but not his constructive stock interest, there is no safe-harbor but he might perhaps obtain IRS approval under the vague subjective exception, § 306(b)(4).

—A redemption of "section 306 stock" which qualifies as a partial or complete liquidation is excepted.   § 306(b)(2). There is no bail-out of e & p in theory, because of the corporate-level contraction or termination which qualifies the transaction for sale treatment, even if the stockholder retains his proportionate interest.

—A tax-free disposition (under nonrecognition provisions) of "section 306 stock," is excepted.   § 306(b)(3). There is no bail-out because the nonrecognition provisions preserve the e & p in the corporation or its successor, and the § 306 "taint" under § 306(c)

(1)(C); for example, stock can be acquired tax free under § 354 in a merger, or other § 368 reorganization, in exchange for "section 306 stock", but the acquired stock is "tainted". The exception is "to the extent that" gain or loss is not recognized; if the boot provision, § 356, applies, the transaction is treated under the § 306(a)(2) redemption approach, with the boot treated as a § 301 distribution. § 356(e), Regs. §§ 1.306–3(d), 1.356–4.

The fourth exception is a vague subjective provision for a transaction established to the satisfaction of IRS to be "not in pursuance of a plan having as one of its principal purposes the avoidance of Federal income tax." § 306(b)(4). Under this exception, a non-tax avoidance purpose must be established for the disposition of the "section 306 stock"; purity must be shown also for the original distribution of the "section 306 stock" unless the stockholder simultaneously or previously disposes of the underlying stock with respect to which the "section 306 stock" was issued. The Regulations give 2 examples: (1) minority stockholders who receive stock dividends of "section 306 stock" and make "isolated redemptions"; (2) "ordinarily" a stockholder who receives a stock dividend of 100 preferred "section 306 stock" shares on his 100 voting common shares and sells the common before disposing of his "section 306 stock." Regs. § 1.306–2(b).

CHAPTER 9

REORGANIZATIONS: IN GENERAL

Table of Sections

§ 1. General Effects of Qualification as a "Reorganization"

If a corporate transaction qualifies as a "reorganization," as that term is defined in § 368, partly or wholly tax-free treatment follows under other Code provisions.

At the stockholder level, under §§ 354 or 355, 356 and 358: No gain or loss will be recognized by stockholders or security holders on certain exchanges by, or distributions to, them "in pursuance of the plan of reorganization" in which they receive nonrecognition property, §§ 354, 355, except that additional receipt of boot will cause limited recognition of gain, § 356. (On the question of what constitutes a "security" see § 2(d) of Chapter 3.) The participating stockholder or security holder will take a substituted basis in nonrecognition property received, and a fair market value basis in boot property. § 358 (which was discussed in Chapter 3 on Incorporations).

At the corporate level, under §§ 357, 361, 362, and 381: If a corporation, as a "party" to the reorganization exchanges property for stock or securities in another corporate "party" generally no gain or loss is recognized, § 361; the assumption of liabilities, with certain exceptions, also is tax-free, § 357; the corporate transferee of the property takes it with a carryover basis, § 362, and also succeeds to other tax attributes of the transferor corporation under § 381. The reorganization provisions provide nonrecognition of realized gain or loss for investors and corporations, deferring the nonrecognized gain or loss through basis provisions. The reason, as with similar nonrecognition provisions like § 1031, is a Congressional determination not to impose current tax effects upon these transactions involving continuity of investment under modified corporate forms.

To qualify as a "reorganization", a transaction must be one of six types described in § 368(a)(1), paragraphs (A) through (F), and known as A reorgs, B reorgs, etc., from their Code paragraphs. These are of four general categories:

—Acquisitive reorgs: In general, one corporation acquires all or substantially all the assets of the other (or a controlling stock interest in the other) by issuing stock in exchange; the stockholders of the acquired corporation maintain a continuing proprietary interest by exchanging their stock for stock in the acquiring corporation tax free under § 354 (or with limited recognition of gain under § 356 if boot is received). Typical patterns are acquisition by one corporation of all of another corporation's assets, at least partly for stock of the acquiring corporation in a state-law merger (A reorg), a similar "practical merger" acquisition of assets for voting stock by contractual arrangement (C reorg), or voting stock for stock acquisition of a new subsidiary (B reorg). The details of these patterns, including triangular reorgs in which the acquisition is made by a subsidiary using its parent's stock rather than its own as the consideration, are discussed in Chapter 12, on Acquisitive Reorganizations.

Divisive D reorgs: A corporation divides by transferring part of its operating assets to a subsidiary and retaining other operating assets; the stock of the subsidiary is then distributed or exchanged tax free under § 355 (§ 356 if boot is also distributed) to some or all of the parent's stockholders. These separations are discussed in Chapter 11 on Corporate Divisions.

—Recapitalizations (E reorgs): A reshuffling of the capital structure of one corporation. Pursuant to a corporate plan, some or all stockholders exchange part or all of their stock for stock in the same corporation tax free under § 354 (or with limited recognition of gain under § 356 if they also receive securities or other boot). Also covered are exchanges by owners of securities for new securities and/or stock under §§ 354/356. Recapitalizations are the subject of Chapter 10.

—F reorgs: "a mere change in identity, form, or place of organization, however effected." F reorgs are discussed in Chapter 12, as is the non-divisive D–§ 354 reorg.

The underlying assumption of these reorganization provisions is that there is a continuity of investment, with investors maintaining an economic interest in their reorganized enterprise ("in modified corporate form") through continuing ownership of stock. The Regulations in § 1.368–1 state that to qualify under the reorg provisions a transaction (or series of transactions) must comply not only with one of the expressly specified patterns in § 368 but also with the underlying assumptions and purpose of the provisions. Thus, qualification requirements include:

—continuity of proprietary interest (except E reorgs Rev.Rul. 77–415; with modifications in divisive D reorgs), a requirement discussed further in Chapter 12 on Acquisitive Reorganizations

—business purpose

—continuity of business enterprise (which for some years has had the limited meaning of continuity of *a* business enterprise, not necessarily the one in which the corporation was engaged before the reorg, Rev. Rul. 63–29. The Treasury Department in December 1979, however, proposed regulations that, if finalized, would require that the transferor's historic business activity be continued or at least that a significant portion of the transferor's historic business assets be used by the transferee.)

In addition, attention must also be paid to such judicial doctrines as the "step transaction" doctrine (tax effect will be governed by the overall result of a prearranged series of transactions (steps) rather than by the results of each of the steps viewed in isolation).

Since the tax-free benefits of the reorganization provisions accrue only to a corporation which is a "party to a reorganization," see e. g. §§ 354 (a)(1), 361(a), it is sometimes important (especially in more complex transactions) to pay close attention to the question of which corporation is a "party". The term is defined in § 368(b) to include (1) a corporation resulting from a reorg (such as the resulting corporation when two corporations are consolidated into a new corporation) and (2) both corporations in a reorg in which one corporation acquires stock or assets of another. Obviously included also is the corporation in a one-corporation reorg (i. e., a recapitalization). Detailed provisions also define a corporate "party" so as to cover the use of a parent's stock in a subsidiary acquisition in a triangular A, B or C reorg, discussed in Chapter 12. See Regs. § 1.368–2(f) for examples.

§ 2. Nonrecognition Treatment of Stockholders and Security Holders: §§ 354, 355

Under § 354, no gain or loss is recognized if, pursuant to a reorg plan:

—a stockholder exchanges his stock for stock in a corporation which is a party to a reorganization. By continuing as a stockholder he maintains a continuity of invest-

[231]

ment, i. e., equity interest or ownership, in the corporate enterprise in its reorganized form.

—a security holder exchanges his securities (bonds) for stock, thereby increasing his commitment from that of a long-term creditor to that of an equity owner, Regs. § 1.354–1.

—a security holder exchanges his securities for securities of the same or lesser principal amount as those exchanged, or for that amount of securities plus stock, § 354(a)(1), (2). This long-term creditor at least remains a long-term creditor, without increasing the amount of money he will eventually withdraw as principal from the reorganized enterprise when his debt instrument is paid.

In these examples, the permissible consideration to be received, "stock or securities," § 354 (a)(1), is interpreted as "stock and/or securities" so that "stock and securities" may be received. Regs. § 1.368–2(h). But securities received are nonrecognition property only to the extent securities are surrendered in at least equal principal amount. § 354(a)(2). Otherwise, securities (or the fair market value of their excess principal amount) are "other property," i. e., boot, under § 356(d).

Nonrecognition under § 354 applies to these exchanges if they are "in pursuance of a plan of reorganization." The reorganization may be any of the six letter types, A through F, except a corporate separation, that is, a divisive D reorg. Exchanges in a divisive D reorg are specifically excluded from § 354 by § 354(b) and thereby channelled into § 355, which contains the special requirements as to 5-year active business for corporate separations.

§ 3. Limited Recognition of Gain for Stockholders and Security Holders Receiving Boot: § 356

If an exchange by a particular taxpayer is pursuant to a plan of reorganization, and is partly for consideration which would receive nonrecognition treatment under § 354 (or § 355 in corporate separations) if it were the only consideration he received (sometimes referred to as "nonrecognition property"), and partly for "other property," ("boot"), § 356 applies. As with other boot provisions, the Code first provides for nonrecognition if solely nonrecognition property is received, and then provides separately for limited recognition of gain if partly nonrecognition property is received. Compare §§ 354/355 and 356 with § 351(a) and (b) and with § 1031(a) and (b). The rule of § 356(a)(1), like the other boot provisions just cited for comparison, provides that the taxpayer receiving the boot recognizes any realized gain to the extent (money plus fair market value of other property) of the boot received; likewise, § 356(c) resembles §§ 351(b)(2) and § 1031(c) in barring recognition of losses realized on exchanges partly for nonrecognition property and partly for boot.

Example: In a reorg, A, B, and C each exchange 100 shares of stock for stock, FMV $1,500, and bonds, FMV $800 of the corporation which acquires their former corporation. The adjusted basis of each in his 100 shares is: A, $2,000; B, $1,000; C, $3,000. A's realized gain of $300 (amount realized $1,500 plus $800 = $2,300, less adjusted basis $2,000), is recognized but not in excess of the $800 boot received; since his $300 gain is not in excess of $800, the entire $300 gain is recognized. B's realized gain of $1,300 ($2,300 amount realized less $1,000 adjusted basis) is recognized to the extent of the $800 boot, that is, $800 gain is recognized, § 356(a). C's realized loss of $700 ($3,000 adjusted basis less $2,300 amount realized) is not recognized. § 356(c).

The boot provision, § 356, applies on a taxpayer-by-taxpayer basis. It applies only to a taxpayer who receives some nonrecognition property and some boot. If none of the property received is nonrecognition property the term "boot," which implies something "additional," is not appropriate to describe the property received.

Example: In a reorg, D exchanges all of his stock solely for securities, which are not nonrecognition property to him since he surrendered no securities. D has a taxable exchange not governed by § 356. If the reorg is a recapitalization, his taxable exchange of stock for bonds of his own corporation results in capital gain or loss under § 302(a), or in a § 301 distribution to him if by § 318 attribution he owns too much stock after the redemption to qualify for sale treatment.

§ 4. Dividend Within Gain: § 356(a)(2)

Section 356(a)(2) provides that if gain is recognized under § 356(a)(1) as just discussed, and the exchange "has the effect of the distribution of a dividend", then each distributee shall treat as a dividend so much of his recognized gain as is not in excess of his ratable share of the corporation's accumulated e & p. Any remaining gain is treated as gain from the exchange of property, i. e., normally capital gain. Whether the exchange "has the effect of the distribution of a dividend" is in general determined by applying the tests of § 302 for determining dividend equivalence in redemptions, Rev.Ruls. 74–515, 516. The proper way to apply these tests, however, is currently in dispute. The Eighth Circuit views the boot as being received from the transferee corporation and therefore the tests of § 302 are to be applied by looking at the difference between the ownership interest in the acquiring corporation which the taxpayer would have obtained if the transaction had been arranged without his receiving boot and the interest he actually obtained. Wright (1973). The Service has expressly declined to follow this decision and contends that the distribution should be treated as though it were made by the acquired corporation. Rev.Rul. 75–83. The Fifth Circuit, in Shimberg (1978), approved the Service's view. Clearly, further litigation will be required to resolve the issue.

Example: In a merger which qualifies as an A reorg, M Corp. acquires N Corp.; A, B, C, and D, are the equal stockholders of N. A, B, and C each exchange their stock for a $12,000 package consisting of M stock, FMV $10,000 and M debentures, FMV $2,000; D exchanges his N stock for a different $12,000 package, consisting of M stock FMV $1,000 and M debentures, FMV $11,000. Assume that upon proper application of § 302 tests, the bonds received by A, B, and C have the effect of a dividend but the bonds received by D do not have a dividend effect. At the time of the merger A, B, and C's ratable shares of accumulated e & p are each $1,500. The adjusted basis of each N Corp. stockholder is: A, $9,000; B, $11,000; C, $13,000; D, $10,000. A, whose realized gain is $3,000 (AR $12,000 – AB $9,000), recognizes $2,000 of the gain under § 356(a)(1) because of the $2,000 boot received; under § 356(a)

(2) $1,500 is treated as a dividend and the remaining $500 is capital gain. B, whose realized gain is $1,000, (AR $12,000 – AB $11,000) recognizes his entire $1,000 gain under § 356(a)(1) because of the $2,000 boot received; his dividend under § 356(a) is limited to the $1,000 of recognized gain. C has a realized loss of $1,000 (AB $13,000 – AR $12,000) which he does not recognize because of § 356(c). He has no dividend; § 356(a) (2) is inapplicable because there is no recognized gain under § 356(a)(1). D, whose realized gain is $2,000 (AR $12,000 – AB $10,000), recognizes the $2,000 gain under § 356(a)(1) because he received at least $2,000, i. e., $11,000 of boot. Because the boot does not have the effect of a dividend as to D, § 356(a)(2) does not apply and the $2,000 is capital gain.

A corporate recipient of a boot dividend in kind treats its fair market value as its § 301 "amount" and its basis in the property, Regs. § 1.356–1(d). It then takes a § 243 deduction for 85 percent or 100 percent of this amount. Rev. Rul. 72–327.

Boot in what would otherwise be a tax-free *distribution* under § 355 (as distinguished from an *exchange*) is always treated as a § 301 distribution of property. § 356(b). This rule applies to boot in § 355/§ 356 spinoffs, in which stock of a subsidiary normally is distributed pro rata to stockholders of the parent corporation. Any boot received in such a transaction obviously resembles a dividend to the parent's stockholders; § 356(b) thus automatically treats this boot under § 301, without regard to the § 356(a)(2) requirements of (1) the existence of gain, (2) a finding of dividend equivalence, (3) existence of accumulated e & p and (4) limitation to the stockholder's ratable share of e & p. N.B. Under § 356(e), surrender of § 306 stock makes the boot-gain rule of § 356(a)(2) inapplicable; the boot is taxed as a § 301 distribution.

§ 5. Treatment of Stockholder/Security Holder: Basis, § 358

The basis of property permitted to be received by a stockholder or security holder without recognition of gain or loss under §§ 354/355 or 356 is generally the same as that of the property surrendered (with adjustments if applicable). § 358(a)(1). The basis of other property (boot) except money received is the fair market value of the property. § 358(a)(2). This treatment (already encountered in connection with § 351 exchanges) follows the general pattern of nonrecognition provisions (as with § 1031(d)): realized gain or loss which is not recognized is deferred through substituted basis in the new nonrecognition property; boot property which causes recognition of any realized gain is taxable at its fair market value and thus receives a fair market value basis (even if the boot is received on a nongain exchange, it is not the type of property in which the realized loss should be deferred); money received cannot be given a "basis" but is treated in the computation as if it had a basis equal to its amount.

If a taxpayer receives or retains more than one block of nonrecognition property, his total basis for his nonrecognition property computed under § 358(a)(1) is allocated under the Regulations among those properties, § 358(b)(1); Regs. § 1.-358–2 provides generally for allocation among his retained and received stock and securities by classes, in accordance with relative fair market values. If more than one block of boot property is received, each takes a fair market value basis under § 358(a)(2), so no allocation among boot properties is necessary.

In determining basis under § 358, simply refer to § 358(a)(1) and go through the increase and decrease steps provided there, even though they frequently cancel each other out.

Example: Pursuant to a reorg in which N is acquired by M, stockholder A exchanges his stock in N with an adjusted basis of $10,000, for a $15,000 package consisting of M stock FMV $11,000, M bonds (securities) FMV $3,000 and $1,000 cash. His realized gain of $5,000 (AR $15,000 − AB $10,000) is recognized to the extent

of $4,000 (FMV of "other property" $3,000, plus
$1,000 money received) under § 356(a)(1). Part
or all of this $4,000 may be treated as a dividend
under § 356(a)(2), depending on facts not stated.

A's adjusted basis in the stock he receives is
computed as follows:

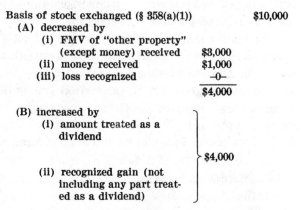

Basis of stock exchanged (§ 358(a)(1))		$10,000
(A) decreased by		
(i) FMV of "other property" (except money) received	$3,000	
(ii) money received	$1,000	
(iii) loss recognized	–0–	
	$4,000	
(B) increased by		
(i) amount treated as a dividend		
(ii) recognized gain (not including any part treated as a dividend)	$4,000	

Thus the basis of A's new M stock is $10,000, i.
e., ($10,000 – $4,000 + $4,000), the same as his
basis in his N stock. Under § 358(a)(2), A's basis in the boot bonds is their fair market value,
$3,000. To check this result, note that (a) un-
realized gain in nonrecognition property received,
$1,000 ($11,000 FMV – $10,000 AB) equals (b)
the nonrecognized gain of $1,000 ($5,000 realized
gain – $4,000 recognized gain).

Example: The facts are the same as in the preceding example, except that A's basis in the N

stock is $16,000 so that he has a realized loss of
$1,000 on receipt of the $15,000 package. His basis in the boot property (bonds) is always FMV,
$3,000, under § 358(a)(2). His basis in the stock
is $12,000, i. e., $16,000 − $3,000 boot − $1,000
money − $0 loss recognized ($1,000 loss is realized but not recognized) + $0 treated as a divi-
dend and $0 other gain recognized. The unreal-
ized loss in the nonrecognition property (M stock)
received is $1,000 (AB $12,000 − FMV $11,000),
which is equal to the realized but nonrecognized
loss of $1,000 on the N stock exchange (AB
$16,000 − package AR $15,000).

§ 6. Transferor Corporation: Nonrecognition of Gain Under §§ 361, 357

In some reorgs, particularly asset acquisitions,
the transferor corporation (the assets of which
are being transferred to and acquired by the
transferee or acquiring corporation in exchange
for stock or securities) is prevented from recognizing gain or loss realized on the exchange by §
361; if the transferor also is relieved of liabilities
assumed or taken subject to, § 357 (already studied in connection with § 351 transfers) provides
generally for preservation of the nonrecognition
treatment.

The general rule § 361(a) provides that no gain
or loss is recognized by a corporation which as a
party to a reorg and in pursuance of the reorg

plan exchanges property for stock or securities in another corporation which is a party to the reorg.

Example: In a "practical merger" C reorg, B acquires all of the assets of T, except for a small amount of cash retained by T to pay off its few creditors. B issues voting stock, FMV $2,000,-000, to T in exchange for the transferred assets in which T has an aggregate adjusted basis of $1.6 million. T realizes, but under § 361 does not recognize, gain or loss on various assets transferred to B.

The acquiring corporation may use other consideration in addition to stock or securities, within the limits permitted for the type of reorg being carried out. The transferor of assets which receives this boot in exchange nevertheless recognizes no loss realized on any assets, § 361(b)(2), and recognizes no gain realized on any other assets so long as it distributes the boot in pursuance of the reorg. § 361(b)(1)(A). In the relatively rare case in which the transferor corporation remains alive after the reorg retaining undistributed boot, § 361(b)(1)(B) requires it to recognize its realized gain, but in an amount not in excess of the boot (money and fair market value of "other property") received but not distributed under the reorg plan.

Example: (a) In the practical merger C reorg considered in the previous example, the next step pursuant to the reorg plan is that T liquidates, distributing the B voting stock to its stockholders in exchange for their T stock. This liquidation (at least for the T stockholders) is not governed by the liquidation provisions covered in Chapter 6; their exchange of T stock for B stock is tax free under § 354 because it is pursuant to the plan of reorganization. It is generally assumed that T recognizes no gain or loss on the distribution to its stockholders although the specific statutory authority is unclear.

(b) The facts are the same except that instead of $2 million FMV of B voting stock, B uses a package consisting of $1.7 million B voting stock, $100,000 FMV of B nonvoting stock, $100,000 FMV of B securities (bonds) and $100,000 FMV gold bars; assume that this is still a C reorg by reason of § 368(a)(2)(B). T nevertheless recognizes no gain or loss on its exchange of assets for the package: under § 361(a) the $200,000 of nonvoting stock and securities of B, a party to the reorg, are nonrecognition property, Regs. § 1.-361–1. The gold bars are boot but do not cause T to recognize gain because they are distributed by T to the T stockholders. § 361(b)(1)(A). A T stockholder's exchange with T of his T stock for his share of the B stock-bonds-gold package is governed by § 356; under § 356, the B voting and nonvoting stock are nonrecognition property but both the B securities (since he surrendered no securities) and the gold bars are boot, causing recognition pro tanto of the T stockholder's realized gain.

The acquiring corporation, B in the examples, may be transferring only its own stock in exchange for the acquired assets; even if its stock is treasury stock, B recognizes no gain or loss on exchanging its stock for property. § 1032 (discussed in connection with § 351 transactions in Chapter 3 on Incorporations). If the acquiring corporation issues its own securities, it is promising to pay cash and cannot realize gain or loss. If in part it transfers boot which is neither stock nor securities, such as gold bars, it recognizes any gain or loss on that property, § 1001(c), but it gets no increase in basis of assets acquired. § 362. In triangular A, B, or C reorgs, the acquiring subsidiary may transfer stock or securities of its parent corporation which is a party to the reorg; see the discussion of triangular reorgs in Chapter 12 on Acquisitive Reorganizations.

In asset acquisitions, the acquiring corporation may assume or take subject to some or all of the acquired corporation's liabilities. In a merger, for example, all of the acquired corporation's liabilities at the date of the merger are assumed by the acquiring corporation by operation of the state merger law. Liabilities relieved are part of the amount realized by the acquired corporation; in general, under § 357(a), the acquired corporation recognizes no gain from this because liabilities relieved are not considered as boot and do not prevent the exchange from being covered by § 361. (In the odd case of liabilities relieved for a tax avoidance or nonbusiness purpose, the total liabilities relieved from the acquired corporation are considered boot; this would cause the acquired corporation to recognize all of its gain (to the extent of this boot) under § 361(b)(1)(B) because there is no way for it to distribute this boot.) In D reorgs only, which resemble § 351 transactions, liabilities relieved from the transferor corporation which exceed the total basis of all the transferred assets cause the transferor to recognize the excess as gain under § 357(c), already discussed in regard to § 351 transactions in Chapter 3 on Incorporations.

§ 7. Transferee Corporation: Basis of Transferred Assets: § 362

In general, property acquired by a corporation in a reorg has a carryover basis under § 362(b) (first sentence). In the unusual case in which a transferor corporation recognizes gain under §§ 357(c), 357(b), or 361(b)(1)(B), the assets transferred have their basis increased by the amount of the recognized gain; otherwise the transferee corporation simply succeeds to the transferor corporation's basis in its assets. The basis carries over in each asset on an asset-by-asset basis. The rule of § 362(b) (first sentence) is the same as that of § 362(a), considered in connection with § 351 transactions, which provides carryover basis with a step-up for the transferor's recognized gain in the case of § 351 transfers and transfers "as paid in surplus or as a contribution to capital."

If the acquiring corporation issues securities, transfers § 361(b) boot which is distributed by the transferor corporation, or assumes or takes subject to liabilities of the transferor (and if, as will normally be the case, no gain is recognized to the transferor corporation) there is no step-up in the basis of the transferred assets. Note that there is no step-up in the asset basis even though the stockholders of the transferor corporation recognize gain on the exchange of their stock for stock plus securities or plus distributed gold, as in the example in the discussion of § 361. This follows under § 362 because the transferee corporation in a reorg is a continuation in modified form of the transferor corporation.

Example: In a qualifying reorg L Corp. transfers land with a basis of $30,000 and subject to a mortgage of $50,000 to B Corp. for B stock FMV $40,000 and securities of a fair market value and principal amount of $10,000. L thereupon distributes the B Corp. stock and securities to its sole stockholder in redemption of all of the stock of L. L recognizes no gain or loss on the exchange, § 361(b)(1)(A), and the stockholder who has a basis of $30,000 in his L Corp. stock realizes $20,000 but recognizes only $10,000 of gain (the excess principal amount of the securities), § 356(a), (d). Despite the recognition of gain by the L stockholder and B's assumption of the mortgage, B takes the land with L's carryover basis with no step-up, since no gain was recognized by the *transferor* (L Corp.). If, however, L were to recognize gain of $70,000 by reason of §§ 358(d) and 361(b)(1)(B), then B would step up its basis in the land to $100,000, § 362(b).

The second sentence of § 362(b) excludes stock or securities in a corporation a party to a reorg from the carryover basis rule, unless acquired by exchange of stock or securities of the transferee (or its parent). In general, together with § 358(e) this simply assures that § 362 will apply to the transferee corporation in an asset acquisition, but not to the transferor, e. g., for the voting stock of the transferee which it receives in a C reorg which is not a practical merger because the transferor does not liquidate; the transferor's basis in the transferee's stock is governed by § 358 (under the reference in § 358(a) to exchanges under § 361, and without exclusion by § 358 (e)).

§ 8. Transferee Corporation: Carryover of Corporate Attributes: § 381

In general, the acquiring corporation in an A, C, nondivisive D, or F reorg succeeds to the corporate attributes of the acquired corporation, § 381(a)(2), such as net operating loss carryovers, earnings and profits, capital loss carryovers, accounting methods and other attributes listed in § 381(c). Fuller discussion, including discussion of §§ 269 and 382 which may limit such carryovers, is in Chapter 13 on Carryover of Corporate Attributes.

CHAPTER 10

RECAPITALIZATIONS: E REORGANIZATIONS

Table of Sections

§ 1. In General

Among the specific types of reorganizations, recapitalizations are discussed here first for two reasons: 1) unlike acquisitive and divisive reorgs, they involve only one corporation, which is the same corporation both before and after and 2) they may resemble stock dividends and may involve issuance of § 306 stock, so that they can be considered conveniently following Chapters 7 and 8 on those topics.

The Code does not define the E reorg other than as simply "a recapitalization." § 368(a)(1) (E). The term has been defined by the Supreme Court as "a reshuffling of a capital structure within the framework of an existing corporation." Southwest Consolidated Corp. (U.S.1942). The

Regulations, § 1.368–2(e), which should be examined, do not attempt a definition as such but give 5 brief examples of transactions which are "a recapitalization" and hence an E reorg. The examples illustrate two of the three types of tax-free recapitalization permitted:

—securities are exchanged for stock. (*Example (1)*, old bonds for preferred.) Under § 354(a), this exchange is tax-free.

—securities are exchanged for other securities. (Not covered by the Reg. examples). Under § 354(a), this exchange is tax-free to the exchanging bondholder unless the new securities have a greater principal amount than the old; in that case the fair market value of the excess amount is boot under §§ 354(a)(2) and 356(d)(2)(B).

—stock is exchanged for stock. (*Examples (2)* and *(4)*, in which 25 percent or all of the preferred stock is exchanged for common and *Example (3)*, common is exchanged for new preferred.) This exchange is tax-free under § 354(a). The new preferred received may, however, be "section 306 stock", see § 306(c)(1)(B) and Chapter 8, § 2 supra. A fourth type of exchange, old stock for new securities, is never tax-free, under §§ 354(a)(2) and 356(d)(2)(B) (particularly, last sentence). See Regs. § 1.354–1(d), *Example (3)*.

In all recapitalizations the exchanges are directly between the stockholder or bondholder and the corporation. In Hartzel (B.T.A.1939), Acq., a distribution of new preferred and common in place of existing common was followed by an exchange between stockholders, the older stockholders giving the new common for the preferred of the young. The court treated the "detour", with the final result contractually predetermined, as being part of the reorg and therefore tax-free. Frequently, in form, an offer which may be accepted or rejected by each is made by the corporation to individual holders of an entire class of stock or bonds. Rev.Rul. 56–654 treated as a "recapitalization" a charter amendment increasing the liquidation value of preferred, finding a constructive exchange of the old preferred and some common for the new preferred. Similarly, exchanges of stock pursuant to a conversion privilege were held to be E reorg recapitalizations in Rev.Rul. 77–238; provisions in the certificate of incorporation which require a retiring employee to convert his common stock into preferred or have it redeemed for cash, or which permit preferred stockholders to convert into common, were "a continuing plan of reorganization."

In addition to the three pure types of possible recapitalizations, mixtures of these types are possible, such as old bonds for new bonds and stock.

If, pursuant to a recapitalization plan, any stockholder does exchange all his stock solely for securities (bonds), his exchange is a redemption, tested for dividend equivalence directly under § 302, rather than a boot distribution under § 356. See Regs. § 1.354–1(d), *Example (3)*, last sentence. His surrender of stock to the corporation in exchange for property, the bond, is a redemption as defined in § 317. If he received any stock at all, he would have not a redemption but, generally a § 356 exchange with the bond as boot, §§ 354(a)(2)(B) and 356(d); he would recognize any realized gain to the extent of the boot; § 356(a), but loss would not be recognized, § 356 (c). (Can a stockholder avoid dividend treatment of the full amount distributed and limit his dividend to his gain under § 356 merely by receiving one share of stock along with the bond? I.R.S. could use Regs. § 1.301–1(l) to prevent this.)

Example: A, B, and C are the three equal unrelated holders of X's one class of stock. Pursuant to a plan, each stockholder exchanges some of his stock with X as follows: A exchanges 50 percent of his stock for X bonds; B exchanges 25 percent of his stock for new X preferred stock and 25 percent for X bonds, and C exchanges 50 percent of his stock for new X preferred stock. A's exchange is governed by § 302, B's by § 356 and C's by § 354.

[252]

Rev.Rul. 74–269 reminds that if the values differ when common is exchanged for new preferred in a capitalization, there is a side transaction to be identified for tax purposes and treated accordingly as for instance, a gift or compensation.

§ 2. Old-to-Young Recapitalization

One classic pattern of tax-free recapitalization is the old-to-young or Hartzel (B.T.A.1939), Acq. —Dean (T.C.1948), Acq. recapitalization. In a closely held corporation with only one class of stock, the younger stockholders exchange part or all of their common for more common or make no exchanges while older stockholders each exchange part or all of their common for preferred (which may be § 306 stock). This serves the business purpose of transferring control and greater share in risk and possible growth of value to the younger stockholders, and giving the older stockholders safer although limited current income and capital value. In a family corporation, if the current values of common and preferred exchanged are reasonably equivalent, there is no gift (for gift tax purposes) from older to younger relatives, and the value of the stock for eventual estate tax purposes is readily ascertainable and limited. Creating preferred also "thins" the value of the common so that younger employee-stockholders can afford to buy newly issued common; upon the death of the retiring stockholders, voting control will not pass to persons unfamiliar with the business. Regs. § 1.305–3(e), *Example (12)* poses a recapitalization in which common may be exchanged for a package of a small amount of new common and a large amount of new preferred or entirely for new common. The 5 major stockholders nearing retirement exchange their common for the mostly preferred package, while the young take the all common package. The example concludes that none of the exchanges in this "single and isolated" transaction is within the purview of § 305. The example carries out the intent evidenced in a Senate floor colloquy on the 1969 amendments to § 305, to protect the old-to-young recapitalization from current taxation; §§ 305(c) and 305(b)(3) otherwise might tax these transactions as having the effect of dividends of preferred to some common stockholders and common to other common stockholders. A fortiori a recapitalization of new preferred for some common seems equivalent to a preferred-on-common stock dividend and tax-free under § 305 (a). However, the value of this kind of recapitalization may be impaired by the fact that the new preferred will be § 306 stock, § 306(c)(1)(A). This result is not altogether unfavorable in the old-to-young recapitalization area, of course, because the old persons typically keep their preferred stock until death at which time it is cleansed of its taint because, under § 1014, the subsequent holder's basis is no longer determined by reference to the decedent's basis therein. See Regs. § 1.306–3(e).

§ 3. Dividend Treatment under § 356(a)(2) or Regs. § 1.301–1(*l*)

As discussed in Chapter 9 on Reorganizations: In General, the reorg boot provisions tax an exchange which "has the effect of the distribution of a dividend" by treating as a dividend the portion of the stockholder's recognized gain covered by his ratable share of accumulated e & p. § 356 (a)(2). This "boot dividend" rule will generally thwart attempts to bail out e & p by issuing bonds pro rata tax-free. An avoidance possibility may still exist, however, if some or all of the stockholders have a high basis in their stock, (for instance because they recently inherited it, § 1014) so that their small realized gain, or loss, will result in little or no dividend under § 356(a)(2). The Service threatens to combat some such cases by Regs. § 1.301–1(*l*), which provides that a § 301 distribution may occur at the same time as another transaction. Thus, if the stockholders of a corporation with only common stock outstanding exchange their stock with the corporation for new common plus bonds, the stock-for-stock exchange may be pursuant to an E reorg and tax-free under § 354 but the bonds are a § 301 distribution to the extent of fair market value. Because the gain limitation of § 356(a)(2) appears to be more of an accidental development than a considered Congressional policy judgment, the IRS appears to have a valid point. On the other hand, a reasonable argument can be made that the Regulation provision is contrary to § 356(a)(2).

Example: More than half of the fair market value of X Corp. (which has only common stock outstanding) is represented by accumulated and current earnings and profits. Sole stockholder S has an adjusted basis of 8 in his shares which have a fair market value of 10. In an E reorg S exchanges all of his common for new common FMV 5 and bonds FMV 5. Under the § 356(a) approach S would recognize gain of 2 on the transaction and this gain would all be treated as a dividend. Under Regs. § 1.301–1(*l*), however, S would have a dividend of 5.

§ 4. Application of § 305(c)

Under § 305(c), a recapitalization in which preferred stock with dividend arrearages is surrendered in exchange for other stock generally is treated as a taxable stock dividend on preferred under § 305(b)(4). For example, if in an E reorg recapitalization, outstanding preferred issued for $100, with $20 of dividends in arrears, is exchanged for new preferred with a FMV of at least $120 (or $100 FMV of new preferred and $20 FMV of common), the preferred stockholder is deemed to receive a $20 § 301 distribution. Regs. § 1.305–5(d), *Example (1)*; see also Regs. § 1.368–2(e), *Example (5)*. These preferred with arrearages for other stock recapitalizations are taxable if they result in increasing the stockholder's proportionate interest in corporate assets or e & p, i. e., if the FMV (or liquidation preference if greater) of the new stock received exceeds the "issue price of the preferred stock surrendered." Regs. § 1.305–7(c). For this purpose "issue price" means the greater of the issue price or the liquidation preference, not including dividends in arrears.

Also treated as a taxable stock dividend is a recapitalization that is "pursuant to a plan to periodically increase" a stockholder's proportionate interest in the assets or e & p. Examples (3) and (6) of Regs. § 1.305–5(d) illustrate that if preferred stock was not originally issued pursuant to a "periodic increase" plan (e. g., there was no plan to exchange it for common) and if there are no dividend arrearages, there will be no taxable stock dividend under § 305(c) if it is surrendered in an E reorg for other stock; the other stock may be, the examples show, common (even with FMV greater than the issue price of the preferred), or a new convertible or nonconvertible preferred.

§ 5. Section 1036

Section 1036 is an odd and little used provision which provides for nonrecognition of gain or loss on the exchange of common stock solely for common stock or preferred solely for preferred, in the same corporation. Such an exchange may involve, for example, an exchange of nonvoting common for voting common, or of one class of preferred for another with different terms. If the exchange occurs pursuant to a corporate plan of recapitalization, an E reorg, it is thus tax-free under § 354; § 1036 also covers cases of exchanges directly between 2 common or preferred stockholders not pursuant to a corporate plan, Regs. § 1.1036–1(a).

A practical effect of § 1036 is that for common-for-common or preferred-for-preferred recapitalizations it is unnecessary to show a business purpose to qualify for tax-free treatment.

If the exchange is for nonrecognition property plus boot, (and it is not in connection with a reorg), the boot provisions of § 1031(b) (limited recognition of gain) and (c) (nonrecognition of loss) apply and the basis of property received in the exchange is determined under § 1031(d). Almost any exchange by a stockholder with the corporation, however, would be pursuant to a recapitalization reorg; in that case, the boot is governed by §§ 356 or 301, not by § 1031(b). See Rev.Rul. 72–57.

CHAPTER 11

CORPORATE DIVISIONS: § 355, DIVISIVE D REORGANIZATIONS

Table of Sections

§ 1. In General

The division of a corporate enterprise into two corporations each owned by stockholders of the original corporate enterprise can be accomplished tax free if and only if it comes within the conditions of § 355 (or § 356, if it comes within § 355 except that boot is received).

There are three prototype patterns for a tax free division, known in tax parlance (but not in the Code) as spin-off, split-off and split-up. The

[*259*]

term "spin-off" is also used to refer generally to all three patterns.

—Spin-off. A corporation distributes to its stockholders the controlling stock of a subsidiary corporation. The transaction does not require the distributee stockholders to surrender anything in exchange; thus normally the distribution will be pro rata to all stockholders. This form resembles that of a § 301 distribution, and would normally constitute a dividend by the parent under corporate law.

—Split-up. A corporation liquidates completely, distributing to its stockholders in exchange for their stock its controlling stock interest in two or more subsidiary corporations. It can be strictly pro rata, or it can be used to give the stock of one sub to one group of stockholders and the stock of the other sub to another group.

—Split-off. A corporation distributes to its stockholders the controlling stock of a subsidiary corporation in exchange for part of the stock of the distributing corporation. This resembles the spin-off except that, like the split-up, it requires the stockholders of the distributing parent corporation to surrender some of their stock in the parent in exchange for controlling stock of the subsidiary. This form resembles that of a redemption or partial liquidation. It can be strictly pro rata, or some stockholders can surrender more shares and thus receive more stock of a sub.

Section 355 of the 1954 Code does not mention the three patterns and applies equally to qualifying transactions in any of the three forms. The three patterns were treated differently for tax purposes before the 1954 Code, and still have tax significance under § 356 as to the dividend or non-dividend treatment of boot received and as to the treatment of the entire transaction if it fails to qualify under § 355. They are also pertinent in analyzing whether a transaction meets some of the tests of § 355. Important features of the tax-free division, shared by all three patterns, are:

—There must be at least one subsidiary ("controlled corporation") of the dividing (or "distributing") corporation. See § 355(a)(1)(A). Control is defined in § 368(c). If the distributing corporation lacks a subsidiary it must create one (or two, for a split-up) as the first step in the transaction.

—Tax-free treatment is permitted only for the receipt of stock (or securities if securities of the parent are surrendered) in the subsidiary. §§ 355(a)(1)(A), 355(a)(3), 356 (a)(1), 356(d). Thus the corporate businesses must remain in corporate solution.

—After the transaction, there will be two corporations both controlled by stockholders of the parent. § 355(a)(1)(A), (D). In a pro rata transaction, such as the usual spin-off and some split-ups and split-offs, the corporations will be "brother and sister corporations," i. e., corporations with the same (or substantially the same) individual stockholders. A corporate division may also be non-pro rata in the sense that it gives different corporate interests of equivalent values to different groups of stockholders, typically to resolve a dispute among the stockholders. § 355(a)(2)(A), (B).

Example: F Corp. has been conducting business actively for 10 years and has accumulated substantial e & p when its two stockholders, A and B decide to separate their business interests. They do not want the tax consequences of a complete or partial liquidation, or a redemption terminating one of their interests, which would give one or both of them assets out of corporate solution and a capital gain on the surrender of all of his stock. A taxable dividend is of course unthinkable. Assuming that the transaction can meet the requirements of § 355, they can accomplish a tax-free division as follows: (1) Non pro

rata split-off: F transfers half of its assets to
Sub-A, a newly-formed subsidiary, in exchange
for all of the stock of Sub-A; A surrenders all of
his F stock to F in exchange for all of the stock
of Sub-A. This leaves B as sole stockholder of
F, which now contains half of the business assets.
(2) Split-up: F transfers half of its assets to
new Sub-A and half to new Sub-B, becoming momentarily a holding company; F then completely
liquidates, distributing all of the stock of Sub-A
to A and all of the stock of Sub-B to B in exchange
for their F stock.

§ 2.   Relationship of § 355 to D Reorgs

Under the 1954 Code, it is intended that corporate divisions be tax-free only if they pass the
anti-bail-out tests of § 355; if they do meet these
tests, the distribution will qualify for tax-free
treatment under § 355 (or for limited recognition
of gain under § 356 if there is boot) either independently or in pursuance of a D reorg. Section
355 is unique in providing tax-free treatment either without a reorg, like § 351, or as part of a
reorg, like § 354. The Code provisions (§§ 354
(b), 368(a)(2)(A)) are designed to insure that
all divisive distributions of a subsidiary's stock
by a parent must clear § 355 to qualify for tax-
free treatment, while nondivisive D reorg distributions are routed through § 354 (and discussed in Chapter 12). A § 355 transaction is

pursuant to a D reorg if, as a first step, the parent corporation transfers assets to the subsidiary (or subsidiaries) before distributing its stock. See § 368(a)(1)(D). All tax free divisions of corporations which do not have a subsidiary (until it is created in the transaction) are D reorgs since an asset transfer will be made in creating the subsidiary. If assets are not transferred, e. g., the stock of an existing subsidiary is distributed without a predistribution transfer of assets to it, the transaction is not a D reorg but it is nevertheless tax free under § 355 independently. See § 355(a)(2)(C).

The transfer of assets to a subsidiary for stock or securities of the subsidiary as the first step in a D reorg is tax-free to the parent by reason of § 361 and the asset basis carries over to the subsidiary under § 362. If the subsidiary assumes liabilities of the parent, § 357 normally preserves nonrecognition of gain, except as provided in §§ 357(b) (tax avoidance purpose) and (c) (liabilities in excess of basis).

There is a large area of overlap between § 361 and § 351 as to the transfer of assets by the parent to its controlled corporation (subsidiary) in exchange for stock or securities of the subsidiary. See § 351(c) (a corporate transferor can distribute to its stockholders stock of the transferee without dislodging control "immediately after".) Normally the distinction as to under which of these sections the transaction qualifies for non-recognition will not be important. However, a distinction may be important if boot is received by the parent in exchange for the assets it transfers. Section 361(b) (which only applies to reorgs) provides nonrecognition of gain if boot received by the parent is distributed in the reorg. Such nonrecognition is not available if the transfer qualifies only under § 351. If the parent recognizes gain (within 5 years of the distribution) because of boot received, the business of the subsidiary could be disqualified for § 355 distribution under § 355(b)(2)(B) since it was acquired "in a transaction in which gain or loss was recognized in whole or part." The Second Circuit in Gordon (1967), rev'd on other grounds (U.S.1968), took the position that gain or loss recognized within a group of controlled corporations would not cause disqualification under § 355. The 1977 Proposed Regulations under § 355 follow *Gordon*, stating that an acquisition by one member of an affiliated group (as defined in § 1504, with some modifications as to ownership of nonvoting preferred stock) from another would be disregarded even if gain or loss was recognized. Prop.Regs. § 1.355–3(b)(4). This is consistent with the position taken by the Service in several post-*Gordon* published rulings. Rev.Rul. 69–461; Rev.Rul. 78–442.

§ 3.   The Division Bail-out Problem

The corporate division pattern has bail-out potential. "Bail-out" of earnings usually means a stockholder's withdrawal of earnings, in effect, with tax at capital gain rates, while he maintains his proportionate interest in the corporation, as against the other stockholders. If liquid assets can be placed in a subsidiary and the stock of the subsidiary spun-off tax free pro rata to the stockholders, the stage is set for a bail-out similar in result to the preferred stock bail-out discussed in Chapter 8 and blocked by § 306. The liquid corporation can then be liquidated and its assets (or their proceeds after tax free sale under § 337) received with capital gain treatment by the stockholders; any non-cash assets will have a fair market value basis and can be sold by the stockholders without further gain. Or the stockholder can sell his stock in the former subsidiary with capital gain treatment to an outside investor, who can liquidate with no gain because of his cost basis in the stock.

In Gregory (U.S.1935) the Supreme Court held a scheme of this nature taxable as a dividend in one of the most famous of tax opinions. In order to obtain saleable assets (1000 shares of stock which she wanted to sell) from her wholly owned corporation without a dividend, Mrs. Gregory had the corporation form a subsidiary, transfer the 1000 shares of stock to the sub in a § 351 transaction, and then spin off the stock of the sub to her. This was in literal compliance with the then requirements for a tax free reorganization. She liquidated the corporation a few days later, reporting a capital gain on receipt of the desired assets, and sold them immediately as she intended. The Supreme Court taxed her as having received a dividend of the desired assets. Agreeing that her motive of tax avoidance was irrelevant if she did what the reorganization statute intended, the Court found that she did not. The transaction had "no business or corporate purpose" and was a "mere device" to disguise as a corporate reorganization the transfer of the desired assets to Mrs. Gregory (out of corporate solution) by preconceived plan. Meanwhile Congress in 1934 ended the tax-free spin-off to prevent such possible avoidance transactions; when spin-offs were reinstated in 1951, they came with anti-avoidance safeguards, refined in 1954 in § 355.

§ 4. The Requirements of § 355

Section 355 permits tax free receipt only of stock or securities of an 80 percent controlled subsidiary, within the definition of § 368(c). Receipt of boot places the transaction under § 356.

Besides the usual stock or securities requirement § 355 poses three other explicit requirements, referred to herein somtimes as tests, anti-avoidance or anti-bailout safeguards, or limitations:

> (1) *The "Device" Test.* The transaction must not be used principally as a device to distribute corporate e & p. § 355(a)(1)(B).

> (2) *Active Business Test.* Each corporation must be engaged in an active business with a 5-year history. §§ 355(a)(1)(C), 355(b).

> (3) *Amount of Stock.* The parent must distribute all of the stock and securities it owns in the sub, or at least an amount of stock constituting "control." § 355(a)(1)(D).

A fourth requirement, not stated in the Code, is that the distribution of the sub's stock have a business purpose. Regs. § 1.355–2(c), 1977 Prop. Regs. § 1.355–2(b).

Because these requirements are technical, and because they are designed to tax transactions which have bail-out potential even if no bail-out has yet occurred, they may tax transactions which are not intended as bail-outs and in which no bail-out will occur. Because the stakes are frequently high, taxpayers often seek an advance ruling from the Service.

§ 5. Active Business

The principal requirement of § 355 designed to block bail-outs is the "active business" test. §§ 355(a)(1)(C), 355(b). It requires that each of the corporations involved be engaged in the active conduct of a trade or business immediately after the distribution. To assure that the business does not represent a relatively temporary investment of liquid assets, the "active business" definition requires further that the business "has been actively conducted throughout the 5-year period ending on the date of distribution," § 355(b)(2)(B), and that it not have been directly or indirectly acquired by the corporation within that period except through a nonrecognition transaction. § 355(b)(2)(C), (D). See the discussion of the similar "active business" rules of § 346, *supra* Chapter 5, § 10(b).

The active business requirement alone specifically prevents a bail-out of cash or investment assets in the pattern followed in *Gregory*. The spin-off of a sub containing only shares of stock held as an investment, cash or other liquid assets, would fail under § 355 because immediately after the transaction only the parent corporation and not the spun-off sub would be "engaged in the active conduct of a trade or business." Thus the individual stockholder would have a dividend under § 301 in the amount of the fair market value of the distributed property, the stock of the sub.

(This dividend treatment would result even assuming that there was a real spinoff of stock of the sub, and not a mere cloak for the distribution of the liquid assets as in *Gregory*; in *Gregory*, the dividend was found in the liquid assets rather than the stock of the sub.)

Under § 355(b)(1) both distributing and controlled corporations must each be engaged in the active conduct of a trade or business immediately after the transaction (or if the distributing corporation was a mere holding company with no other assets, or a de minimis amount, Prop.Regs. § 1.355–3(a), each of the controlled corporations must be engaged in an active business immediately after the transaction).

A corporation is engaged in a trade or business if it carries on a group of activities for income-producing purposes, ordinarily including the collection of income and the payment of expenses, and including every step in the income-earning process from that group of activities, or if substantially all of its assets consist of stock and securities of a controlled subsidiary which is so engaged. Whether the business is "active" is a fact question. "In general, the corporation must perform active and substantial management and operational functions." Prop.Regs. § 1.355–3(b)(2)(iii). Thus holding property for investment, or owning and leasing property without performing significant services with respect to the operation

and management of the property are not "active."
In Prop.Regs. § 1.355–3(c), *Example (4)*, a bank
has owned an eleven story office building for sev-
en years, occupying the ground floor and renting
out the other ten with its own employees providing management and maintenance services. If
the bank puts the building into a sub and spins
off the sub, and the new corporation's employees
continue to manage the building, both bank and
building corporations will be engaged in active
business after the transaction. But if the bank
had occupied nearly the entire building, renting
out only a small part as storage space, and if the
spun-off corporation will rent the bank's space to
the bank under a net lease in which the bank does
the maintenance and repair and pays property insurance and taxes, the new corporation is not engaged in an active business. Compare *Example
(5)*.

The Service had once contended that there
must be two separate active businesses, each with
a separate five-year history; the present Regulations reflect that theory. But the Service indicated in Rev.Rul. 64–147 after losing Coady (6th
Cir. 1961) and Marett (5th Cir. 1963) on this issue, that it would no longer follow the Regulations
on this point and would eventually amend them;
thirteen years later the 1977 Proposed Regulations resulted. Thus if A and B are two equal
stockholders of a construction business corpora-

tion, a "vertical division" will qualify, e. g., if to resolve a dispute, some construction contracts and part of the equipment are placed in a sub and split-off to A, while B keeps the original company with other contracts and equipment. Both corporations are engaged in active business; there are now two businesses and each of them has a five-year active business history from the time when both were part of one business.

A functional division, in which one group of activities is separated, may also qualify. Thus if a nine year old department store business is conducted by the parent corporation and includes a suburban branch store opened three years ago (with its operations so integrated as to be part of the one business), and the branch is transferred to a sub and spun off, and thereafter the sub's employees operate the suburban store as a separate business, both corporations will satisfy the active business requirement. Prop.Regs. § 1.-355–3(c), *Example (12)*. However, if there is still a close business relationship between the operations of the two corporations, there may be business purpose and bail-out device problems, as discussed in §§ 6 and 7 of this chapter.

§ 6. Device

The active business requirement alone is, however, insufficient to prevent all forms of tax avoidance. It requires merely that each corporation conduct an active business, but it in no way limits the amount of liquid assets or other assets, related or unrelated to the active business, that the corporation may contain. Thus a corporation can meet the active business tests by spinning off a sub containing both (1) an active peanut stand business operated by the corporation for more than 5 years, FMV $30,000, and (2) $300,000 in cash or other unneeded non-active assets from profits of another continuing business unrelated to the peanut stand.

Buttressing the specific active business requirements therefore is the vague requirement that "the transaction was not used principally as a device for the distribution of the earnings and profits" of the parent or the sub. § 355(a)(1)(B). The term "device", derived from the *Gregory* opinion, suggests the general purpose to block spin-offs in which the stockholders plan promptly to withdraw liquid or saleable assets from either the parent or the spun-off sub at capital gain rates by a liquidation or sale of the stock. If this were the only effect of the clause it could amount to a mere exhortation to the courts to continue to declare such transactions outside the intended meaning of the tax free provision. It could, and in the view of the Service does, go further however, by disqualifying transactions in which the stockholder could readily at any time through liquidation or sale complete a bail-out of liquid assets of either the parent or the sub but has not yet done so.

The 1977 Proposed Regulations considerably clarify the IRS position as to when a distribution is "used principally as a device for the distribution of the earnings and profits" of either or both corporations. This position may be best understood by looking at three situations: stock sales, use of assets in a manner suggestive of a device, and non pro rata transactions.

Stock Sales

A prearranged sale (or exchange, such as by liquidating) of stock of either corporation results automatically in treatment of the transaction as principally used as a device and thus in disqualification under § 355 if the amount of stock sold is 20 percent or more of the corporation's stock; if a smaller amount of stock, or securities, is sold, this fact is "substantial evidence" that the transaction was principally used as a device. A sale is prearranged if it is actually negotiated, and is ordinarily considered prearranged if it was discussed by buyer and seller and was "reasonably to be anticipated by both parties." An actual sale, not prearranged, is "evidence" to be taken into account on the device question. In all cases, (except the over-20 percent of stock prearranged sale), other evidence is also to be taken into account. Prop.Regs. § 1.355–2(c)(2). Although the IRS probably lacks authority to fix a definite 20 percent standard, a court could well interpret the rule as an expert agency's determination that such a sale is "almost invariably convincing evidence" of use principally as a device. That would at least allow a taxpayer argument in such cases as Rev.Rul. 59–197, in which a prearranged sale of stock by the controlling stockholder of a more than 20 percent interest to a key corporate employee was part of the business purpose for the distribution, rather than evidence of use principally for a bail-out. The Proposed Regulations make no direct reference to the cryptic outer and inner parentheticals of § 355(a)(1)(B) that the mere fact of a sale other than by prearrangement does not mean principal use as a device; they infer the worst from a prearranged sale but still use a nonprearranged sale as evidence of a bail-out.

An exchange pursuant to a tax-free reorg in which no gain (or "an insubstantial amount of gain") is recognized is not a sale under the Proposed Regulations. Thus there may be a prearrangement to have either corporation acquired in a merger after the spin-off, as was approved by Morris Trust (4th Cir. 1966). The stockholder in such cases is simply maintaining his proprietary interest through stock in the merged corporation.

Use of Assets in a Manner Suggestive of a Device

A transaction may be used principally as a bail-out device even if the bail-out has not been consummated by a withdrawal of earnings at capital gain rates through sale or liquidation. The Proposed Regulations would base such a finding on the "nature and use of assets" by the corporations. Bad assets, evidencing principal use of the transaction as a device, include:

—New business. A business acquired in a taxable transaction in the preceding five year period. If either corporation contained only such a purchased business, the transaction would fail the active business test under § 355(b)(2)(C) or possibly (D). The device test thus backstops the active business test if an insufficiently aged business is spun off with an active business.

—Liquid assets. Cash or liquid assets such as "securities" (here presumably including stock) and receivables, not related to the reasonable needs of the business, if present in either corporation. As in *Gregory*, an asset which can readily be converted to cash will facilitate a bail-out.

—Related function. One corporation functioning principally to perform services for the other both before and after the transaction. Similarly, the Proposed Regulations

state that the examples of a captive coal
mine spun off by a steel mill, or an exclusive
sales agent spun off by a manufacturer, both
given as satisfying the active business test,
are relationships which evidence a bail-out
device as the principal use of the transaction.
Obviously something is questionable if the
recently divorced couple still acts as if mar-
ried. The question seems to be as to the
business purpose of the separation, however.
Rather than indicating bail-out potential, the
close relationship of the two corporations
may evidence that one could not readily be
sold without the other. However, there is
bail-out potential if one is liquidated and continues to operate as a partnership with a
stepped-up basis obtained at capital gain
rates, even though this would normally be
possible more directly by partial liquidation
under § 346. The justification for the IRS
position may lie in the potential for selling
such a coal mine operation and contracting
for supply of coal with the new owner, or
elsewhere, without really affecting the nature of the stockholders' underlying business
investment; however, that observation would
seem to go more to the question of whether
there are two active businesses after the
separation.

Non Pro Rata Transactions

The Proposed Regulations provide an important ordinarily safe harbor for non pro rata transactions. A transaction that would qualify with respect to each distributee for sale treatment under § 302(a) if it were taxable, will ordinarily not be considered to be a device. A less significant safe-harbor treats similarly a distribution when none of the corporations involved has e & p. Prop.Regs. § 1.355–2(c)(1).

§ 7. Business Purpose

Gregory is also authority for the requirement of a business purpose for any reorg or § 355 transaction. The Regulations, § 1.355–2(c), impose this requirement by barring distributions for purposes not "germane to the business of the corporations" and state that the reason for this limitation is to restrict tax-free treatment to "such readjustment of corporate structures as is required by business exigencies" and which have a continuity of interest in ownership. Regs. § 1.-355–2(c). The 1977 Proposed Regulations elaborate on this in § 1.355–2(b) as follows:

—The distribution must be carried out for real and substantial nontax reasons;

—the reasons must be germane to the business of the corporations, but a stockholder purpose is sufficient if "so nearly coextensive with a corporate business purpose as to preclude any distinction between them"; the transaction will not qualify if the sole purpose of the transaction is "fulfilling the personal planning purposes of a stockholder." This appears to be an endorsement of the concept of a "business-related" stockholder purpose. A disagreement on major operating decisions between two managing stockholders is a sufficient business reason for a non pro rata split-off, Prop.Regs. § 1.355–2(b)(2), *Example (2)*, and possibly an illustration of a business-related stockholder purpose.

—a purpose for transferring a business to a subsidiary is not as such sufficient to justify distributing the stock of the subsidiary. Parshelsky's Est. (2d Cir. 1962) (under 1951 statutory restrictions); Wilson (9th Cir. 1965). Thus the desire to protect one business from the risks of another will supply a business purpose for putting the risky business into a subsidiary, but not for distributing the stock of the sub. If a lender to the safer business however requires, based on customary business practice, that the stock also be distributed "to prevent the potential diversion of funds to" the risky business, there is a sufficient business purpose. Prop. Regs. § 1.355–2(b)(2), *Examples (3)* and *(4)*.

§ 8.   Continuity of Interest

Regs. § 1.355–2(c) state that qualification under § 355 requires continuity of interest in all or part of the enterprise by the persons who, directly or indirectly, were the owners prior to the transaction. See also Prop.Regs. § 1.355–2(b) (1). This concept overlaps with that of the "device" clause, as interpreted by IRS, as a prohibition upon an immediate or prearranged sale of the distributed stock. If the transaction begins with a transfer of assets to a sub, both § 351 and § 361 (which requires a D reorg, i. e., that the distribution qualify under § 355) can protect the transfer from nonrecognition only if the stockholders of the distributing corporation are in control of it "immediately after" the distribution, §§ 351(a) and (c), 368(a)(1)(D); a prearranged sale may violate this statutory continuity requirement (except in situations like that in Rev.Rul. 59–197, supra). The general reorg continuity of interest requirement, stated in Regs. § 1.368–1 (b) says it applies "except as provided in § 368 (a)(1)(D)"; this seems to be a reference to the permissibility of stockholders giving up their interest in one part of the enterprise in exchange for a larger interest in another part.

§ 9.   Treatment of Boot

As does § 354, § 355 treats as boot, rendering § 355 itself inapplicable, the receipt of excess principal amount of securities received over those surrendered, and all securities received if none is surrendered, i. e., bonds received for stock. § 355(a)(3). As under the provisions of § 356 relating to § 354, § 356 treats the fair market value of the excess principal amount (or of the entire bond if none was surrendered) as boot, i. e., "other property". § 356(d). In split-ups and split-offs, the exchanging holders of stock or securities recognize gain to the extent of boot received under § 356(a)(1); exchanging stockholders treat gain as a dividend to the extent of their ratable share of e & p if the transaction is sufficiently pro rata to have the effect of a dividend, under § 356(a) (2). Under § 356(c), loss is not recognized. Spin-offs, however, being distributions to stockholders without anything surrendered in exchange on which gain or loss could be realized result in the treatment of all boot as a § 301 distribution to the recipient stockholders. § 356(b). This automatic dividend treatment, to the extent of e & p accords with the normally pro rata nature of a spin-off. A special § 355 provision, § 355(a)(3) (last sentence) treats as boot any stock of the controlled corporation which was acquired in the past 5 years by the distributing corporation in a taxable transaction.

Example: A Corp. has owned 85 percent of the stock of Sub for more than 5 years, and purchased the remaining 15 percent within the last year.

If it distributes all the Sub stock to the A stock-holders, § 356 rather than § 355 applies (if all the § 355 tests except as to boot are met) because the recently purchased stock is boot under § 355(a)(3) (last sentence). If the transaction is a spin-off (a distribution but not an exchange), A stockholders have a dividend to the extent there are e & p of A to cover the fair market value of the boot. § 356(b). If the transaction is a non pro rata split-off (an exchange), stockholders who participate by exchanging stock of A for stock of Sub will recognize any gain to the extent of the boot stock received. § 356(a)(1). Stockholders with a loss will not recognize the loss. § 356(c). (Perhaps A could distribute an "all boot shares" package to the loss or non-gain stockholders, cutting down the proportion of boot shares received by the gain stockholders below 15 percent.) Section 302 tests, perhaps including attribution rules, apply in testing each gain-recognizing stockholder's exchange for dividend equivalence, and if it has the effect of a dividend, his ratable share of A's e & p is a dividend under § 356(a)(2); any remaining gain (or all the gain if he has significantly reduced his actual and constructive ownership in A) is capital gain. Under Rev.Rul. 74–516 boot in a split-off is tested for dividend equivalence by determining the percentage decrease that would have occurred if the stockholder had remained a stockholder of the parent and had received only the boot in redemption of some of his shares in the parent.

An example of the application of § 302 tests to boot in a non pro rata split-off under Rev.Rul. 74–516 is as follows. A and B each own 50 shares of the 100 outstanding shares of the only class of X Corp.'s stock. In a transaction which qualifies under §§ 355 and 356, X Corp. redeems all of B's 50 shares in exchange for all of the stock of a sub of X, plus $10,000 boot. The FMV of X stock is $1,000 per share. B's receipt of boot is tested under § 302 as if he surrenders 10 shares of X stock for $10,000, while keeping 40 shares. The hypothetical reduction (from $^{50}\!/\!_{100}$ to $^{4}\!/\!_{90}$) misses the § 302(b)(2) safe harbor but may qualify under § 302(b)(1).

§ 10. Basis to Distributees

Under § 358, boot received has a fair market value basis, § 358(a)(2). The basis of the non-recognition property in a § 355 (or §§ 355/356) transaction is determined by allocating basis among the nonrecognition property (stock and securities of the controlled corporation) received and any stock and securities of the distributing corporation which are retained. § 358(a)(1), (B)(1) and (2), and (C). The process is similar to allocating basis under § 307 in case of a tax-free stock dividend under § 305. The basis to be allocated is the recipient stockholder's adjusted basis of his stock and securities in the distributing corporation, decreased for boot received and increased for dividend and gain recognized, under § 358(a)(1).

Example: In a pro rata spin-off of its sub Y which meets the § 355 tests and thus qualifies under § 356, A receives Y stock, FMV $10,000 and $1,000 FMV of Y bonds. Under § 356(b), A treats the $1,000 as a dividend. A's basis in the Y bond is its $1,000 FMV. § 358(a)(2). A's adjusted basis in his X stock held before the transaction is $4,200 and its FMV was $22,000; immediately after the transaction the FMV of A's X stock was $11,000. This $4,200 basis (the original basis, with offsetting $1,000 decrease and increase under §§ 358(a)(1)(A)(i) and (B)(i)) is allocated in proportion to FMV among the $11,000 FMV retained X stock and the $10,000 nonrecognition Y stock received: $11/21$ to the stock of X retained and $10/21$ to the stock of Y. The basis of the X stock is $2,200 and the basis of the Y stock is $2,000. See § 358(c) and Reg. § 1.358–2(c), *Example (4)*.

If A had owned more than one class of stock, or also owned securities, the allocation would have had to be made separately as to each class. Regs. § 1.358–2(a)(4).

The holding period of nonrecognition property received generally includes the holding period of the exchanged or retained stock in the parent. § 1223(1).

§ 11. Effects to Distributing Corporation

Transfers to Sub. The distributing corporation recognizes no gain or loss on the transfer of property to the controlled corporation for stock or securities of the controlled corporation, § 361 (also, § 351), for example, when a new sub is created to be spun off. Section 361 applies because the transfer is pursuant to a D reorg. If the parent also takes boot (e. g., cash or notes) from the sub, § 361(b) will prevent the parent from recognizing gain if it distributes the boot to its stockholders. (§ 351(b) would cause recognition of gain to the extent of the boot).

The sub takes the parent's basis, § 362, and holding period for the transferred assets.

Distribution. Section 311 (or § 336 if there is a partial or complete liquidation of the parent) prevents the parent from recognizing gain or loss on its distribution of its stock or securities of the sub. See Regs. § 1.311–2(a)(2) (in general, § 311(d) does not apply).

Effects on E & P. Section 312(h) requires "proper allocation" of e & p between parent and sub. This allocation is generally made by relative FMV of assets if the sub is newly created; e & p deficits are not allocated. Regs. § 1.312–10.

§ 12. Flunked Divisions

A spin-off that fails to qualify under § 355 will be a § 301 distribution, and thus a taxable dividend if there are sufficient e & p of the distributing corporation. A corporate distributee would have a dividend in the amount of the lesser of the fair market value of the distributed stock or its basis in the hands of the distributing corporation, § 301(b)(1)(B), and would deduct 85 percent or 100 percent of that amount under § 243. A split-up that flunks might be taxed as a complete liquidation under § 331, but is more likely to be treated as a liquidation-reincorporation if the IRS can find a way to do so. The IRS problem is that it cannot be a D reorg for the very reason that it flunks § 355 (and is divisive and thus outside § 354). Telephone Ans. Service (T.C.1974, affirmed 4th Cir. 1977) supports a "no liquidation" theory with perhaps one corporation continuing and the stock of the other treated as a dividend distribution by the continuing corporation. A split-up distribution of stock of pre-existing subs (not formed in the overall plan) would seem to be immune from attack under Telephone Ans. Service, however. If there is no complete liquidation, note Rev.Rul. 75–223 holding that a distribution of a business in corporate form cannot qualify for partial liquidation treatment under § 346. Further discussion of liquidation-reincorporation is in Chapter 12. A split-off that flunks § 355 will be a redemption, seeking § 302(a) or § 346/331 capital gain treatment but if pro rata risking § 302(d) reference to § 301 and treatment as a taxable dividend. A corporate stockholder would obtain an 85 percent or 100 percent deduction if there is a dividend, however.

Because of the high stakes involved if a transaction thought to be tax-free is taxed as a dividend, a spin-off or any pro rata division should be undertaken only after at least carefully considering the advisability of seeking an advance ruling from the Service.

CHAPTER 12

ACQUISITIVE REORGANIZATIONS: A, B AND C; MISCELLANEOUS REORGANIZATION TOPICS

Table of Sections

§ 1. A, B and C Reorgs in General

The A, B and C reorgs are three tax-free acquisition patterns. § 368(a)(1)(A), (B), (C). The basic requirements are:

—A: a merger (or consolidation) under state law (or Federal law, as in the case of federally chartered banks). In the merger, the acquiring corporation acquires the assets of the acquired corporation in exchange for assumption of liabilities (by operation of the

[*288*]

state merger law) plus stock of the acquiring corporation and (perhaps) other consideration. The acquired corporation disappears and its stockholders exchange their stock for stock of the acquiring corporation.

—C: usually, a practical or de facto merger, in which the acquiring corporation by agreement issues its voting stock (or a strictly limited amount of other consideration) and may assume the acquired corporation's liabilities for substantially all the assets of the acquired corporation; as a usual but not essential further step under the plan, the acquired corporation then liquidates distributing the voting stock of the acquiring and any other consideration and any of its non-acquired assets to its stockholders in a § 354 or § 356 exchange for their stock in the acquired corporation.

—B: the basic acquisition consideration is, as in the C, solely the voting stock of the acquiring corporation; unlike the C with its limited exception for other consideration, the B permits none. Unlike the A and C, the acquisition is not of the acquired corporation's assets; instead its stock is acquired, so that the acquiring corporation becomes its controlling stockholder, with 80 percent control as defined in § 368(c).

§ 2. A Reorgs

There is no specific statutory limitation on the permissible acquisition consideration in an A reorg, so long as the transaction is a merger (or consolidation) under state law. The principal tax issue is whether the stockholders of the acquired (or merged or disappearing) corporation have sufficient continuity of proprietary interest. For example, if the articles of merger provide that N shall be merged into M and the former stockholders of N shall surrender their shares in exchange for M debentures, the transaction is clearly not an A reorg because there is no continuity of proprietary interest. If in the merger some N stockholders receive only stock, some receive partly stock and partly bonds and some receive only bonds of M, there is an issue as to continuity of proprietary interest.

The current IRS guidelines for issuing advance rulings that a merger is an A reorg require a 50 percent level (by value) of continuity. It is not necessary that each stockholder of the acquired corporation receive stock of the acquiring corporation worth at least 50 percent of the value of his acquired corporation stock so long as in the aggregate the stockholders of the acquired corporation receive stock of the acquiring corporation equal in value to 50 percent of the acquired corporation's stock. Sales or redemptions made pursuant to the plan of reorganization are considered in determining whether there is 50 percent continuity. Rev.Proc. 77–37. Thus sales of stock made after the exchange can violate continuity of interest and disqualify the entire transaction. The continuity of interest should last long enough to show a definite and substantial ownership intent. Rev.Rul. 66–123.

The Service will not rule favorably on a proposed A, B or C reorg if there has been a change of ownership of over 50 percent of stock of the acquired corporation (even in a nontaxable transaction) within a two-year period prior to the ruling request, unless the parties establish by independent evidence that the change is unrelated to the later acquisition. See 8 Tax Adviser 234 (1977) (based on unpublished IRS position). This represents a two year "look back" rule for determining whether a cash purchase of stock (or an acquisition by tax-free spin-off or contribution of capital) is "old and cold" or prevents continuity of interest. The approach follows Yoc Heating Corp. (T.C.1973) in which a purchase by P of 85 percent of the stock of S, followed by a (reverse triangular) merger nine months later did not qualify as a reorg for lack of continuity of interest on the part of the sellers.

Failure to meet the guideline gives no assurance as to the IRS position in advance; IRS might on audit treat the transaction as an A reorg, or it

might not. Where certainty is desired, as will
normally be the case, a corporation desiring tax-
free treatment will normally comply with the
guidelines and may decide to obtain an advance
ruling from the Service.

The continuity of proprietary interest does not
have to be in the form of voting stock; an A
reorg only requires continuity of equity ownership, not participation in the management of the
acquiring corporation. John A. Nelson Co. (U.S.
1935). Thus, unlike the B and C reorgs, nonvoting stock may be used in an A reorg to provide
the needed continuity.

§ 3. C Reorgs

In the C reorganization the definitional requirement that the acquisition of the acquired
corporation's assets be solely for voting stock of
the acquiring corporation normally assures that
the stockholders of the acquired corporation will
have continuity of proprietary interest (except if
too much of this stock is sold). In the typical
case, the acquired corporation stockholders will
exchange their stock for the voting stock of the
acquiring corporation (and any limited other
consideration permitted) upon the liquidation of
the acquired corporation; in the rare case in
which the acquired corporation remains alive
holding the voting stock of the acquiring corporation, the stockholders of the acquired corpora-

tion have a proprietary interest in the acquiring through their holding company.

The C definition requires an acquisition of "substantially all of the properties" of the acquired corporation. The term "properties" means assets. The "substantially all" (rather than all) requirement allows a little leeway. The advance ruling guideline, Rev.Proc. 77–37, requires the transfer of at least 90 percent of the fair market value of the net assets and at least 70 percent of the fair market value of the gross assets held by the corporation immediately prior to transfer. All payments to dissenters, redemptions, and irregular dividends, made pursuant to the plan of reorganization are considered as assets held immediately prior to transfer.

Liabilities of the acquired corporation can be assumed without disturbing the qualification as a C reorganization as long as the only other consideration is the acquiring corporation's voting stock. § 368(a)(1)(C) ("but" clause).

The permissible use of other consideration under § 368(a)(2)(B) is so strictly limited as to be unavailable if the acquired corporation has substantial liabilities. It permits the use of money or other property in addition to voting stock to a limited extent, but for the purpose of this computation only, liabilities assumed (or taken subject to) by the acquiring corporation are counted as

money paid by the acquiring corporation. § 368
(a)(2)(B) (last sentence). Under the exception,
boot can be used so long as enough voting stock
is given to pay for 80 percent of the fair market
value of all of the assets of the acquired corporation. Note that the voting stock must buy 80 percent of all the assets, which is more than 80 percent of the acquired assets unless all the assets are
acquired.

Example: N has $100,000 FMV of assets and
no liabilities. Under the exception of § 368(a)
(2)(B), M can acquire N in a C reorg by issuing
to N in exchange for all its assets M voting stock,
FMV $80,000 or more, and cash or other prop-
erty, $20,000 or less.

Example: N has $100,000 FMV of assets and
$25,000 of liabilities. M can acquire N in a C re-
org by issuing to N M voting stock, FMV $75,000,
and assuming the $25,000 of liabilities, in ex-
change for all the N assets. This qualifies under
§ 368(a)(1)(C) because the "but" clause of that
sentence provides that the assumption of liabilities is disregarded and the acquisition is thus considered to be "solely for voting stock". If M issues $74,000 of its voting stock, pays $1,000 cash
and assumes $25,000 of liabilities the transaction
will not qualify. The $1,000 cash takes the trans-
action outside § 368(a)(1)(C) itself; the § 368
(a)(2)(B) exception does not apply because only

$74,000 or 74 percent, less than $80,000 or 80 percent of all of the N assets, are acquired for voting stock; the other $26,000 or 26 percent are acquired for money, counting liabilities as money paid under the last sentence of § 368(a)(2)(B).

A liability created by the reorganization, e. g., liability to pay dissenters, if assumed by the acquiring corporation, is treated as boot (and thus may disqualify a C reorg). Rev.Rul. 73–102. However, the acquiring corporation's payment of the acquired corporation's share of reorganization expenses, e. g., legal fees, transfer taxes, is not considered boot. Rev.Rul. 73–54. (But payment of stockholder expenses will constitute boot).

§ 4. B Reorgs

In a B reorg, the acquiring corporation acquires stock of the acquired corporation solely for voting stock, and immediately after, the acquiring corporation is the controlling parent and the acquired corporation its subsidiary. (Voting stock of the acquiring corporation's parent may be used as the sole consideration; the following discussion ignores this possibility, and it is discussed below under the heading "Triangular Reorgs".) The acquiring corporation typically offers to exchange its voting stock directly with any of the acquired corporation's stockholders. The acquiring corporation must be in control, within the 80 percent tests of § 368(c), immediately after the transaction (or series of transactions) but it need not obtain control by the reorg. For example, a parent corporation could exchange its voting stock for stock held by minority stockholders of the sub in a B reorg. See the second parenthetical clause in § 368(a)(1)(B). If the acquiring corporation is in control immediately after the exchange, there is no minimum amount of stock that must be acquired in the transaction. For example, an exchange by M corporation of its voting stock for stock of N corporation can be a B reorg if, in the transaction:

M acquires all of the N stock;

M acquires 80 percent of the N voting stock and 80 percent of each class of N non-voting stock (§ 368(c) control as interpreted by Rev.Rul. 59–259);

M acquires 20 percent of the N stock, having previously owned 79 percent;

M acquires 1 percent of the N stock, having previously owned 81 percent.

M acquires 3 percent of the N stock, but its percentage ownership of N drops from 100 to 82 because N simultaneously issues new stock to others.

The reorg must be a transaction in which all of the stock acquired is acquired solely for voting stock of the acquiring corporation. No securities, cash or other property may be given. There is no limited exception, like that provided by § 368(a) (2)(B) for C reorgs. This point was made clear in Turnbow (U.S.1961) in which a taxpayer argued that § 356 permitted him to receive some boot in a purported B, merely recognizing his gain to the extent of the boot, because § 354 would have applied if all stock had been given and no boot. The Supreme Court held that the taxpayer could not use the boot provision because the transaction was not a B reorg, since no boot is permitted in a B reorg, which must literally be solely for voting stock.

Example: M Corp. bought 75 percent of the stock of N for cash in 1975. (Note that if this separate 1975 transaction had been for M voting stock instead of cash, it would still have been a taxable transaction.) In 1977, in a separate transaction it acquired another 10 percent solely for M voting stock. The 1977 transaction is a B reorg. However, if in 1977, M acquires 85 percent of the stock of O for a package of 98 percent M voting stock and 2 percent cash, the transaction is not a B. Similarly, the transaction will not be a reorg if M in 1977 acquires 75 or 82 percent of the stock of Q for M voting stock from some Q stockholders, and also in the same transaction acquires 10 percent of the Q stock from other stockholders for cash or bonds.

This "solely" for voting stock requirement puts great stress on the concept of a transaction (or series of transactions). A series of related steps are treated as one transaction. The Regulations state that a series of acquisitions taking place over a relatively short period of time, such as 12 months, may qualify as a B reorg. Regs. § 1.368–2(c). This rule protects an acquisition of less than 80 percent for voting stock if it is part of a later acquisition resulting in more than 80 percent ownership.

For example in the much-publicized ITT acquisition of Hartford Casualty, ITT had purchased 10 percent of the Hartford stock for cash when it decided to acquire control by offering Hartford stockholders a tax-free swap for ITT voting stock. If the cash acquisition of 10 percent had been "old and cold" there would have been no problem, but it was sufficiently related in time and thinking as to be considered part of the whole transaction, thereby making the stock swap taxable.

The solely for voting stock requirement prevents any continuity of proprietary interest problems such as may arise in a merger based upon the mix of acquisition consideration. However the IRS ruling guideline applies its 50 percent continuity test to a B reorg after taking into account prearranged redemptions or other dispositions of stock.

The solely for voting stock requirement in a B or a C is not violated if, as an incidental part of the exchange that is not bargained for, the acquiring corporation pays cash in lieu of issuing fractional shares of stock. Rev.Rul. 66–365, following Mills (5th Cir. 1964).

The acquiring corporation's basis in the acquired corporation stock in a B is determined under § 362(b). See §§ 362(b) ("unless" clause of second sentence); 358(e). The basis in different blocks of shares will differ, because it was acquired from different stockholders and carries over its basis in their hands. The acquiring corporation will have to ascertain this basis by asking the exchanging acquired corporation stockholders. Obviously, basis in the acquired corporation stock will be relevant if the stock is later sold or exchanged in a taxable liquidation.

After the B reorg, the acquired corporation is intact but has the acquiring corporation as its controlling stockholder. If there is a plan to liquidate the subsidiary after the purported B, IRS has taken the position generally that the transaction is really a two-step acquisition of the acquired corporation's assets, which must qualify for tax-free treatment (if at all) as a C. (It could fail as a C if it fails the "substantially all of the properties" test.) Rev.Rul. 67–274, Regs. § 1.382(b)–1(a)(6).

§ 5. Triangular Reorgs

The pre-1954 predecessors of the A, B and C reorgs (also known as A, B and C for their paragraph designations in the 1939 Code) were interpreted to require that the stock used as acquisition consideration be stock of the acquiring corporation itself. For business reasons, it might be useful to have the acquisition made by a subsidiary using the stock of its parent so that exchanging stockholders of the acquired corporation would become stockholders of the parent (or grandparent, in a B pattern) of the corporation which carried on the acquired's business. In Groman (U.S.1937) and Bashford (U.S.1938), it was held that this remote or indirect interest of the acquired corporation stockholders in their former stock (or assets of their former corporation) through stock in the acquiring corporation's parent did not supply the continuity of interest needed for a reorg. See Rev.Rul. 63–234. The C and B definitions were amended in 1954 and 1964 respectively by insertion of the parenthetical "(or in exchange solely for all or a part of the voting stock of a corporation which is in control of the acquiring corporation)" in order to specifically permit triangular C and B reorgs. Also, § 368 (a)(2)(C) specifically permits a planned "drop down" by the acquiring corporation to a sub of acquired assets in a regular A or C, or stock in a regular B, thus reaching a triangular end point to the transaction. However, the straight acquisition plus drop-down runs the acquired assets or stock through the acquiring parent momentarily, and thus may contaminate the parent with liabilities which may follow the assets.

In 1968 and 1971, Code amendments authorizing two triangular A reorgs were added as §§ 368(a)(2)(D) and (E); parallel amendments were made to the § 368(b) definition of a "party" to a reorg. The "(a)(2)(D)" triangular A reorg is a state law merger of the acquired corporation into the acquiring corporation for stock of the acquiring corporation's parent. The transaction is more flexible than a triangular C because the acquisition consideration can include nonvoting stock of the parent, bonds and cash or any other property (except stock of the acquiring corporation itself, specifically excluded by § 368(a)(2)(D)(ii)). As in a straight A reorg, the only limit on the acquisition consideration is the general continuity of proprietary interest principle, (applied under § 368(a)(2)(D)(i) as if the merger were into the parent of the acquiring corporation, so there is no problem of indirect continuity). § 368(a)(2)(D). This triangular A borrows from the C however the requirement that "substantially all of the properties" of the merged corporation must be acquired. § 368(a)(2)(D).

The "(a)(2)(E)" triangular A reorg is a "reverse statutory merger" in which the state law merger is of the acquiring (parent) corporation's subsidiary into an unrelated corporation which survives, and the voting stock of the parent is exchanged for controlling stock of the surviving corporation. Typically, in order to acquire 100 percent control of an outside corporation without terminating its corporate existence, P puts P stock into its wholly owned Sub S (which may but need not have other assets), and then S is merged into the outside company X with the former X stockholders receiving the P stock and P receiving the X stock in exchange for its S stock. The result is that X is a sub of P. The IRS had ruled that this type of transaction amounted to a B reorg if the P stock was voting stock, Rev.Rul. 67–448, but the 1971 amendment makes the transaction an A reorg so that some nonvoting P stock and other consideration can be used, so long as an amount of X stock constituting control (80 percent under § 368(c)) is exchanged by its former owners for P voting stock. § 368(a)(2) (E)(ii). Also the surviving subsidiary, X, must retain "substantially all of its properties" and of the properties of S other than the P stock and other consideration furnished to S and distributed in the transaction.

§ 6. Flunked A, B and C Reorgs

If a non-triangular statutory merger fails to qualify as an A or a non-triangular practical merger fails to qualify as a C, e. g., because stock-holders of the acquired corporation do not receive or keep sufficient stock or voting stock of the ac-quiring corporation:

—The exchange of acquired corporation stock for stock and other consideration is taxable: each former acquired corporation stockholder recognizes his gain or loss under § 1001.

—The acquired corporation recognizes gain or loss unless § 351 applies (including gain under the recapture provisions on re-capture property) on assets transferred to the acquiring, except to the extent that the merger plan in an A, or the plan for sale of assets and liquidation in a C, is a plan of liq-uidation and the asset transfers are (except for the recapture aspects) protected from recognition by § 337. The acquired corpora-tion is protected by § 336 from recognition on its liquidating distribution to its stock-holders.

—The acquiring corporation takes the transferred assets with a § 1012 cost basis equal to the FMV of its stock and other con-sideration paid to the acquired, except that liabilities assumed and new debt instruments issued are counted at their principal amount rather than FMV. (If inadequate interest is

provided on deferred payment obligations, §
483 may reduce the "principal amount" and
replace part of it with "unstated interest"
which will be deductible when paid.)   The
transfer of its own stock for property is protected from recognition by § 1032.

If a purported B reorg fails, e. g., for inclusion
of consideration other than voting stock of the
acquiring corporation or because too much of the
new stock is promptly sold by the former acquired
stockholders:

—The exchange or sale of acquired corporation stock is taxable, with recognition of
gain or loss under § 1001, unless § 351 applies.

—The acquired corporation is not affected,
in general, because there is merely a change
in the identity of its stockholders.   The
change of stock ownership (whether a B or
not) may lead to a loss of carryovers under §
382, discussed in Chapter 13 on Carryover of
Corporate Attributes.

—The acquiring corporation will have a
cost basis in the stock of the acquired corporation obtained in the transaction.   If it later
liquidates the acquired subsidiary within §
332, the § 334(b)(2) (statutory *Kimbell-
Diamond*) basis rules may apply, e. g., if

[*304*]

enough of the acquired stock was purchased within a 12 month period.

§ 7. Contingent Consideration

For business reasons such as uncertainty about the value of stock or of business assets, an acquisition transaction may provide for some form of contingent consideration. Payment of additional voting stock if certain conditions are met in the future does not generally spoil a B or C reorg; the transaction is still solely for voting stock. A portion of each stock payment, however, will normally be taxable (and deductible by the payer) as interest imputed under § 483. See, e. g., Jeffers (Ct.Cl.1977); Cocker (T.C.1977). IRS advance ruling guidelines require among other things a 5 year deadline, that the rights to the contingent stock not be negotiable or readily marketable, and that they not constitute more than 50 percent of the total consideration. Rev.Proc. 77–37. An alternative approach is to issue the consideration in escrow subject to being repaid if the hoped-for contingencies do not occur. Details are in Bittker & Eustice, Federal Income Taxation of Corporations and Shareholders (4th Ed. 1979) ¶ 14.56.

§ 8. F Reorgs

An F reorg is defined in § 368(a)(1)(F) as "a mere change in identity, form, or place of organization, however effected." The Regulations give no further explanation of the nature of this type of reorg, and for a long time it had not been the focus of much attention as it was thought to apply only to changes in the structure of a single corporation similar to that in Rev.Rul. 57–276 (reincorporation of a corporation in another state achieved by the creation of a new corporate shell followed by merger was an F reorg). Also, as the pattern of an F reorg is frequently the same as that of an A, C or D reorg and the tax results of qualification under any one are frequently the same, it was often unnecessary to distinguish between the different reorg types. Many of the recent F reorg cases, however, have involved situations in which F reorg qualification was the only path to the desired tax results.

The significance of qualifying a transaction as an F reorg is in § 381(b) which generally disallows the carryback by an acquiring corporation of net operating losses against the pre-acquisition income of an acquired corporation except in the case of an F reorg acquisition. Thus § 381(b) has been the source of an awakened taxpayer interest in the F reorg. Taxpayers' success in asserting application of the F reorg to the fusion of two or more corporations where there was identity of proprietary interest and uninterrupted business continuity in Stauffer's Estate (9th Cir. 1968) and Associated Machine (9th Cir. 1968) was met with the Service's refusal to follow those

decisions and its assertion that the F reorg was
limited in its application to changes in the structure of a single corporation, a position in which
it was supported by the Tax Court. Rev.Rul. 69–
185. After a series of losses on this issue in the
Courts of Appeals, however, the Service revoked
Rev.Rul. 69–185 and conceded that a combination
of two or more corporations might qualify as an
F reorg if: 1) there was a complete identity of
stockholders and their proprietary interests in
the transferor corporation(s), 2) the corporations were engaged in the same business activities
or integrated activities before the combination,
and 3) the business enterprise of the combined
corporations continued unchanged after the combination. Rev.Rul. 75–561.

Whether this more receht Service position may
be subject to relaxation by the courts is as yet
unclear. The complete identity of stockholders
element may have been undermined by the decision in Aetna Casualty and Surety Co. (2d Cir.
1976). In that case a parent corporation merged
its 62 percent subsidiary ("Old Aetna") into a
newly created 100 percent subsidiary ("New Aetna"), exchanged the 38 percent minority's stock
for stock in the parent and spun off New Aetna.
The minority's interest in New Aetna was, of
course, reduced by this transaction. The court
held that the transaction was an F reorg for purposes of § 381(b)(3) and stated that total identi-

ty of stockholders in both the acquired and the acquiring corporations was not indispensable to qualification as an F reorg, but indicated that less than 50 percent identity would not suffice. In denying the Government's petition for a rehearing the court emphasized, however, that its decision was limited to classification of the transaction as an F reorg for purposes of § 381(b)(3) only and was limited to a reorg in which a corporation is merged into a corporate shell with no prior tax history. This proved to be the ground on which the Tax Court (which continues to take a restrictive view akin to that outlined in Rev. Rul. 69–185, supra) distinguished *Aetna Casualty* in Berger Machine Products (1977), a case in which four operating corporations owned by related persons in differing amounts were merged into one. The court applied Rev.Rul. 75–561 and noted that there had been a change in the percentage of ownership by the stockholders of the merged corporations which in its view amounted to more than "a mere change in identity, form, or place of organization". The dissent felt, however, that the shifts in minority ownership were relatively insignificant when compared with those that occurred in *Aetna Casualty* and that the *Berger Machine* decision was only contributing to uncertainty in the law.

The Service has subsequently relaxed its requirement of a complete identity of shareholders and now will allow a de minimis change. Rev. Rul. 78–441. Just how far the Service will go in defining de minimis is uncertain. Consequently, a clear statement of what constitutes an F reorg must await further administrative and judicial development.

§ 9.   D–§ 354 Reorgs: the Non-divisive D Reorg

The D reorg definition requires two things: 1) an asset transfer by one corporation to another "controlled" corporation (i. e., controlled by the transferor or by some or all of its stockholders including stockholders immediately before the transfer, "or any combination thereof") and 2) distribution of stock or securities of the controlled corporation under §§ 354 or 355 (or the related provisions of § 356). The application of the D reorg to divisive transactions under § 355 was discussed in Chapter 11 on Corporate Divisions. The divisive D reorg is one of two different basic patterns covered by the D reorg definition: a parent transfers assets to a new or existing subsidiary, the stock of which is distributed in a spin-off, split-off or split-up under § 355. The other basic pattern is a D reorg in which the distribution is an exchange which qualifies under § 354. Under § 354(b), this can occur only if the transferee corporation acquires "substantially all" the assets of the transferor, § 354(b)(1)(A), and the transferor distributes "the" (i. e., all of the,

Regs. § 1.354–1(a)(2)) stock, securities and any other properties received, and any retained properties, under § 354, i. e., it is completely liquidated, § 354(b)(1)(B). An example of this non-divisive D–§ 354 reorg is:

T Corp. transfers all of its assets, FMV $1,-000,000, to a newly formed subsidiary S in exchange for all of the S stock, FMV $700,000 and S bonds, FMV $300,000; T then distributes S stock to some T stockholders in exchange for their T stock, and distributes a package of a small amount of S stock and a large amount of S bonds to the other T stockholders. The result is that T is succeeded by a new corporation S which carries on the same business enterprise as T with continuity, but not identity, of stock ownership. T could transfer its assets subject to existing liabilities or instead it could retain assets to pay some or all of its liabilities without violating the requirement that it transfer "substantially all" of its assets. See Regs. § 1.354–1(a)(2) (second sentence). Retention of 30 percent of its gross assets would violate the "substantially all" requirement under the advance ruling guidelines of Rev.Proc. 77–37, discussed in § 3 of this chapter, supra. T also could retain an insubstantial amount of its assets, which it would then have to distribute in its complete liquidation along with the S stock and securities. T stockholders who receive all S stock recognize no gain or loss under

§ 354; T stockholders who receive S stock and debentures recognize gain to the extent of the boot received under § 356.

A transaction "described" in both §§ 368(a)(1)(C) and (D) is treated as described only in the D reorg definition paragraph, under § 368(a)(2)(A). To make sense of this provision, it must be read to mean that a transaction is "described" in § 368(a)(1)(D) even though the distribution of the controlled corporation's stock does not qualify under either § 354 or § 355. Thus a transaction which fits the D reorg pattern except that there is a nonqualifying distribution cannot be saved as a reorg by qualifying under the C reorg definition.

Example: In Rev.Rul. 74–545, a corporation transferred substantially all its assets to a new subsidiary for its stock and distributed the sub's stock to its stockholder, but the transferor remained in existence as a passive investment corporation with an insubstantial amount of assets. This distribution is not a D reorg because it fails the active business requirements of § 355(b)(1)(A) and the complete liquidation of the transferor requirement of § 354(b); although this transaction is within the language of the C reorg, it is sufficiently "described" in D (i. e., (1) controlled transferee (2) distribution of some stock) that it is prevented by § 368(a)(2)(A) from being a

C reorg. Thus the distribution of the subsidiary stock is a dividend to the stockholder. Such a transaction would not be undertaken with knowledge of its tax consequences unless the stockholder is a corporation which can deduct 100 percent of the dividend under § 243.

§ 10.   D–§ 354 or F Reorg Treatment of Liquidation-Reincorporations

The D–§ 354 reorg is an IRS weapon in the liquidation-reincorporation area. If corporation X transfers substantially all its assets to sister corporation Y, which has identical stockholders, for Y stock and cash, and liquidates distributing the remaining assets, the Y stock and cash to the X stockholders, the transaction is a D–§ 354 reorg, with the remaining assets taxed as a boot dividend under § 356. If an attempt is made to avoid reorg treatment by instead having X sell its operating assets to Y for cash and then liquidate, the transaction may still be treated by IRS and the courts as a D–§ 354 reorg because

(1) it is not necessary that at least one share of Y stock be issued by Y to X and distributed by X to its stockholders, as literally required by § 368(a)(1)(D);

(2) "substantially all" can mean all operating assets, even though they do not represent a high percentage of the value of all the assets. Moreover, Y need not have identical

stock ownership with X so long as it is 80 percent controlled by some (one or more) of the former X stockholders. And in Grubbs (T.C.1962) the requirement that the transferor corporation distribute all of its assets was met by finding "constructive distribution" of retained assets to a stockholder whose stock was not redeemed. Taxpayers almost invariably have been successful in avoiding a finding of a D–§ 354 reorg if former stockholders of the transferor corporation own less than 80 percent of the new corporation. See, e. g., Gallagher (T.C.1962) (former stockholders (who owned 62 percent of the stock) received 73 percent of the stock of new corporation). IRS, however, despite its lack of success in the courts, will not give a favorable advance ruling if former stockholders own more than 20 percent of the new corporation. Reform proposals in this area might amend the Code to reduce the 80 percent ownership requirement to 50 percent, eliminate the "substantially all" the assets requirement in § 354(b)(1)(A), and/or apply § 318 constructive ownership rules.

Other limited IRS success in the liquidation-reincorporation area has been based on finding an F reorg accompanied by a separable redemption of those former stockholders who do not participate in the new corporation. See Reef Corp. (5th

Cir. 1966). This is especially difficult, however, if the new corporation contains additional new assets contributed by new stockholders.

See also the discussion of the liquidation-reincorporation problem in Chapter 8, § 10.

CHAPTER 13

CARRYOVER OF CORPORATE ATTRIBUTES

Table of Sections

§ 1. In General

In certain liquidations of subsidiary corporations and tax-free reorganizations listed in § 381 (a), the corporation acquiring assets acquires with them the tax attributes of the acquired corporation, listed in § 381(c). Most significant of these attributes are the net operating loss carryovers of the acquired corporation, § 381(c)(1), the earnings and profits account, § 381(c)(2), and methods of accounting, § 381(c)(4).

Example: Acme Corp., a calendar year taxpayer, has unexpired net operating loss carryovers to 1978 totalling $200,000. Acme is acquired by Baker Corp. for voting stock of Baker,

[*315*]

a calendar year taxpayer with no loss carryforward, in a statutory merger which constitutes an A reorganization, on December 31, 1977. Under §§ 381(a)(2),(c)(1), Baker succeeds to the right to use Acme's $200,000 of unexpired carryovers and can claim a deduction for them under § 172 in computing its taxable income for calendar 1978. If any carryover still remains unused, and did not expire in 1978 it can be carried forward by Baker for any remaining years of carryforward period in the usual manner.

The term "carryover" is used in at least three different senses to which one should be alert.

1. Carryover (including carry forward and carry back) of net operating losses by one taxpayer from his or its loss year to earlier, or if necessary later, taxable years of that taxpayer, under § 172.

2. Carryover of attributes (including § 172 net operating loss carryovers) from one taxpayer to another, under § 381, in certain tax-free corporate transactions.

3. Carryover of basis in a particular piece of property as it changes hands from one taxpayer to another, in a tax-free exchange under such basis provisions as § 362.

The carryover of attributes under § 381 is subject to complete or partial elimination under § 382 (as applicable beginning in 1980) in transactions in which the former stockholders of the loss corporation fail to continue as at least 40 percent stockholders of the combined corporation. Section 382 also terminates completely or partially the available carryovers of a single corporate taxpayer in circumstances where its stock ownership undergoes similar change. Similar limitation of certain corporate attributes other than net operating loss carryovers is provided by § 383.

Section 382 contains two subsections which cover substantially different areas of transactions. Section 382(a) applies when the stock ownership of a single corporation undergoes substantial change by purchases of stock or similar transactions. Section 382(b) applies in A, B, C, D–354 and F reorgs in which one corporation acquires the stock or assets of another and the stockholders of the loss corporation do not maintain at least 40 percent ownership of the combined enterprise.

The rules of § 382 were substantially revised in 1976 with a delayed effective date to allow for technical amendments. Originally, § 382(a), as amended, was to apply to taxable years beginning after June 30, 1978, and amended § 382(b) was to be effective for reorganizations pursuant to plans adopted after 1977. Late in 1977, it became clear that the technical amendments would not be imminently forthcoming, so Congress extended the effective dates for two years in both cases. In general, discussion of § 382 in this chapter focuses upon the amended version, although it seems likely that further modifications of uncertain import will be made.

Until the § 382 rules are clarified, the student may consider the material herein as indicative of some among a range of potential solutions. Basic issues in the area thus may be particularly worthy of broad consideration, for example:

> (1) Should the Code, through § 382, impede sale of loss carryforwards? See discussion in § 3 infra.

> (2) Should carryforwards be eliminated if and when (but only if and when) the loss corporation (or its successor) ceases to conduct the same business activities that produced the losses? Compare Libson Shops, Inc. (U.S.1957). This policy is subject to the criticism that it encourages artificially prolonging uneconomic loss activities which would not be continued except for the tax advantage.

If there is a device to exploit any gap in § 382, carryovers may also be disallowed under the more general provisions of § 269 relating to certain acquisitions for the principal purpose of tax avoidance.

§ 2. Mechanics of § 381

Section 381(a) states the transactions eligible for carryover. Liquidations of a subsidiary which are tax free under § 332 qualify unless the basis of the subsidiary's assets becomes the parent's stock cost under § 334(b)(2) (the statutory *Kimbell-Diamond* rule). § 381(a)(1). A transfer of assets tax-free at the corporate level under § 361 is also a carryover transaction if connected with an A, C, D–354 or F reorg. The absence of the B reorg in the definition is not discriminatory; the effect of a carryover is automatic in a B reorg in that the stock of the acquired corporation is acquired tax-free and the corporation, with all of its attributes, remains alive as a subsidiary.

Section 381(b) provides mechanical operating rules which apply to all of the covered transactions except an F reorg. The exception for an F reorg, which is a mere change in identity, form, or place of organization, permits the corporation surviving the transaction not only to take account in the future of the tax attributes of its predecessor or predecessors, but to carry back its own future losses against past income of the predecessor or predecessors. In a combination of two unrelated corporations, the acquired corporation's previous losses carry forward under § 381 but, under § 381(b)(3), the acquiring corporation can not carry back a net operating loss or net capital loss for a post-acquisition taxable year to a taxable year of the acquired (referred to as the distributor or transferor) corporation. Similarly an earnings and profits deficit of one corporation cannot reduce *prior* e & p of another corporation. § 381(c)(2)(B). Another significant mechanical rule is § 381(b)(1), which closes the taxable year of the distributor or transferor. Thus, unless the transaction is arranged to occur at the normal end of the acquired corporation's taxable year, the acquired corporation will have a short taxable year. In that event the short final taxable year of the acquired corporation and the continuing taxable year of the acquiring corporation each count as a year for purposes of determining whether the five or seven years of loss carryforward permitted under § 172 have elapsed. See § 381(c) (1). Prior to its amendment by the Tax Reform Act of 1976, § 172 allowed a carryback of three years and a carryforward of five years for a net operating loss (except for longer periods for certain special categories of taxpayers, such as railroads). Now, a net operating loss for any taxable year ending after 1975, i. e., for 1976, carries over for 7 taxable years. § 172(b)(1)(B). A taxpayer may elect to forego the entire three year carryback period for any post-1975 operating loss, under § 172(b)(3)(C), added by the Tax Reform Act of 1976. This could be advantageous, for example, if income of a corporate taxpayer in the carryback years was below $100,000 and therefore taxed at a low rate, but the carryforward years appear likely to be taxable at 46 percent.

In addition to the big three carryover items discussed previously (net operating loss carryovers, earnings and profits, and method of accounting, § 381(c)(1), (2), and (4), there are many other listed items which carry over, § 381 (c)(3), (5)–(26).

An example of the mechanical operating rules of §§ 172 and 381 is as follows: Loss Corp., which uses a calendar taxable year, is merged into Gain Corp., which also uses a calendar taxable year, on July 2, 1977 in an A reorganization. At the time of the merger, Gain Corp. has no net operating loss ("NOL") carryforwards and Loss Corp. has $200,000 of unused NOL carryforwards from the following taxable years: 1974 ($100,-000); 1975 ($50,000); 1976 ($40,000); short year ending 7/2/1977 ($10,000). For 1977 (including results of the former Loss Corp. business for the period after July 2, 1977), Gain Corp. has taxable income (before deducting under § 172 any NOL carryforwards acquired from Loss Corp.) of $180,000. The $200,000 of Loss Corp. carryforwards are first carried to Gain Corp.'s taxable year 1977, under § 381(c)(1)(A), (B), but under these rules Gain's § 172 deduction is limited to the fraction of the year's (pre- this deduction) taxable income corresponding to the fraction of the year the two corporations were combined. On the prescribed daily basis, this is $^{183}/_{365}$, here treated as ½ for simplicity. Thus Gain Corp. wipes out only ½ of its $180,000 (pre- this deduction) 1977 taxable income by deducting $90,000 under § 172, reports taxable income of $90,-000, thereby using the oldest $90,000 of the $200,000 inherited carryforwards and carries forward to 1978 the newest $110,000. If for 1978 Gain Corp. has taxable income (before deducting the NOL carryforwards) of at least $10,000, it will use up the remaining $10,000 of its loss carryforward from loss year 1974 by a § 172 deduction; otherwise part or all of the remaining 1974 loss would expire. The five taxable years to which the 1974 losses carry forward are three years of Loss Corp., 1975, 1976, short 1977; and Gain Corp. taxable years 1977 and 1978.

§ 3.   Limitations on Net Operating Loss Carryovers in Certain Stock Acquisitions: § 382 (a)

The net operating loss carryover, if any, from a taxable year of a corporation, and any of its prior taxable years, can be reduced or eliminated under § 382(a) if during that taxable year or a lookback period of two preceding taxable years there has been an increase of more than 60 percentage points in the percentage of stock owned by a defined group, which increase is attributable to stock purchases or certain other acquisitions listed in § 382(a)(1)(C). If, as in most cases, the situation for application of § 382(a) involves a purchase of all of the stock of a loss corporation, the carryforwards are totally eliminated. § 382 (a)(2). If the new ownership group increased its percentage by more than 60 but less than 100 percent, the net operating loss carryover is reduced by 3½ percent for every percentage point from 60–80, and 1½ percent for every percentage point from 80–100. Thus an acquisition of 60 or less percent new ownership does not impair the net operating loss carryovers, an acquisition of 80 percent by new owners eliminates 70 (3½ × 20) percent of the carryovers and an acquisition of 90 percent eliminates 85 percent of the carryovers.

A series of important exceptions is provided in § 382(a)(5). They protect acquisitions of ownership from related parties, by long-term full-time employees, by gift or inheritance, and generally by creditors who take stock in relinquishment of their claims, among other worthy cases.

Prior to its amendment by the Tax Reform Act of 1976, § 382(a) differed in a number of important respects. Probably the most significant was that it required as a condition of the termination of carryforwards, not only change in ownership of the corporation (of 50 percent) but that the corporation failed to continue to carry on (at least until the end of the next taxable year) a trade or business substantially the same as it conducted before the stock acquisition. The elimination of this provision makes § 382(a), like § 382 (b), terminate carryovers of a corporation merely because the former owners of a corporation have sold out their interest.

Section 382 originated in the 1954 Code supposedly as a response by Congress to "trafficking" in net operating loss carryovers, i. e., the purchase of a corporation largely because of the tax value of its loss carryovers to the acquiring corporation. It was designed to apply mechanical rules which would make for more certainty than existed under § 269 with its "principal purpose" test. (See § 5 infra.) As a policy matter, however, it is arguable that so long as corporations and stockholders are treated as separate for tax purposes, with the stockholders unable to obtain the benefit of corporate losses and (in effect) double-taxed on distributed corporate earnings, there is no justification for denying the economic benefit of net operating losses to stockholders who actually suffered the economic detriment of the losses. Under this line of reasoning, simplification and greater tax equity could be achieved by eliminating § 382 and permitting the former owners to derive the economic benefit of their carryovers through the higher price that would be obtained for their stock if the new owners knew that they could freely use the carryovers. This reasoning puts to one side cases where the business has degenerated to the point that nothing but the carryovers remain; survival of such carryovers would normally be blocked by the principal purpose rules and the mechanical patterns of § 269 or in some cases by the doctrine that the corporation ceases to exist for tax purposes if its business inactivity continues for a certain period. It may be argued, however, that selling of the favorable tax attributes should be permitted even in these situations.

On the other hand, if "trafficking" were allowed, a substantial windfall would accrue to the buyer because he probably would not have to pay dollar for dollar for his tax savings. Allowing the buyer to obtain windfall tax-free profits in his purchased corporation, when others in similar businesses are paying taxes appears inequitable. Further, under present law, individuals who sustain a loss on their investment do obtain some tax relief because they may have at least a capital loss on their stock which can be deducted to some extent against ordinary income and can be carried over indefinitely.

§ 4. Limitation on Net Operating Loss Carryovers in Reorganizations: § 382(b)

If a corporation acquires the stock or assets of another corporation in an A, B, C, D–354 or F reorg and either corporation ("loss corporation") has a net operating loss carryover for the taxable year of the acquisition or to such year from a prior year, these net operating loss carryovers of the loss corporation to the acquisition year and later years may be substantially reduced almost to the point of elimination. § 382(b). They can be fully preserved only if the stockholders of the loss corporation receive for their stock at least 40 percent of the total fair market value of the participating stock or all of the stock of the acquiring corporation. Since an acquisition for stock between unrelated corporations normally presupposes that the acquiring corporation is publicly owned, only rarely would the loss corporation be worth enough to permit its stockholders to obtain 40 percent ownership in the acquiring corporation. If the loss corporation stockholders obtain 1 percent ownership in the acquiring corporation, 98½ percent of the carryovers will be eliminated; for each additional percentage obtained up to 20 another 1½ percent of the carryovers is saved and for percentages between 20 and 40, each additional percent of ownership obtained saves another 3½ percent of the carryforwards. This is essentially the same formula as under § 382(a). See § 382(b)(2). The Tax Reform Act of 1976, which inserted the two-tier "shaving" system just stated, also tightened § 382(b) by applying it to B reorgs and in a more stringent manner to triangular reorgs. The definitions of "stock" and "participating stock" are in § 382(c).

§ 5. Acquisitions for the Principal Purpose of Tax Avoidance: § 269

Under § 269 certain tax benefits of acquisitions may be lost because their attainment was the principal purpose of the acquisition. Section 269 applies to acquisitions of control of a corporation, or by one corporation of carryover basis property from another non-controlled corporation. The control level in this provision is set at 50 percent. If the principal purpose of the acquisition is avoidance of federal income tax by securing the benefit of a tax deduction or other allowance which would not otherwise be enjoyed, IRS may disallow the deduction or allowance. Unlike § 382 which is strictly mechanical in its operation, § 269 applies only to transactions which both follow a prescribed mechanical pattern and also are motivated by the "principal purpose" to obtain a tax saving. The Regulations provide that "If the purpose to evade or avoid Federal income tax exceeds in importance any other purpose, it is the principal purpose." § 1.269–3(a)(2).

The Committee Reports on the 1976 amendments to § 382 state that § 269 is retained in the Code to deal with transactions not expressly within amended § 382, such as "built-in loss" transactions, i. e., acquisition of carryover basis property with adjusted basis in excess of fair market value, and other "apparent devices to exploit continuing gaps in the technical rules." The reports say, however, that § 269, "should not be applied to disallow net operating loss carryovers in situations where part or all of a loss carryover is permitted under the specific rules in § 382, unless a device or scheme to circumvent the purpose of the carryover restrictions appears to be present." This appears to limit the function of § 269 in the area of net operating loss carryovers to preventing some plans based on exploiting some possible technical loophole in § 382; a principal purpose to save taxes by acquiring loss carryovers with a nearly worthless active business will not trigger § 269. But in such cases the loss corporation (mainly its losses) will normally not be worth enough to give its former stockholders a large share (such as 20 to 40 percent) of the continuing or combined enterprise, and the carryovers will be largely or entirely lost under § 382.

CHAPTER 14

SUBCHAPTER S

Table of Sections

§ 1. Introduction

In 1958 Congress enacted Subchapter S (§§ 1371–1378) with the objective of minimizing federal income tax considerations in the choice of business form for small businesses. This objective is accomplished by allowing certain electing "small business corporations" ("Subchapter S corporations" or "electing corporations") to be, for the most part, exempt from federal income tax. Although a Subchapter S corporation maintains a normal corporate character for purposes other than federal income tax, it roughly resembles a partnership for federal income tax purposes in that corporate income is divided pro rata among stockholders and taxed directly to them whether distributed or not. Stockholders also take their share of the corporation's net operating loss deduction and treat their share of the corporation's net capital gain as their own. However, in most other respects, a Subchapter S corporation is subject to the usual corporate tax provisions, e. g., §§ 302, 331, 351, 368.

Subchapter S corporations are referred to by the Code as electing "small business corporations." § 1371. This terminology is somewhat misleading. Qualification for Subchapter S status is not related to the volume of business or net worth of the corporation but instead to the number and identity of its stockholders and the corporation's capital structure.

§ 2. Eligibility

A domestic corporation may qualify as a Subchapter S corporation only if all the statutory requirements of § 1371 are met. There are four basic requirements, § 1371(a)(1)–(4):

(a) *Not More Than 15 Stockholders.* The corporation initially must have 15 or fewer stockholders. § 1371(a)(1). In determining the number of stockholders a joint tenant or a tenant in common is considered a separate stockholder. A limited exception exists if the co-owners are husband and wife; regardless of the form of their ownership, they are regarded as only one stockholder. § 1371(c).

(b) *Only Individuals, Estates, or Certain Trusts as Stockholders.* Stockholders must be individuals, estates, or certain trusts; a partnership, or typical trust or a corporation as a stockholder disqualifies the corporation. § 1371(a)(2). Furthermore, all individual stockholders must either be citizens or resident aliens of the United States. § 1371(a)(3). Under § 1371(e), a trust may qualify as a stockholder, but only if it is: (i) a grantor trust (if owned by a grantor who himself could have qualified as a stockholder) and all its assets are treated as being owned by the grantor (under §§ 671–677); this rule remains effective for a limited period (up to two years) after the death of the grantor, if the corpus of the trust is includible in the gross estate of the grantor for Federal estate tax purposes; (ii) a voting trust (but each beneficiary is counted as one stockholder); or (iii) a trust which obtains stock under a will (but only for a 60 day period after it obtains the stock). § 1371(a), (e).

An "estate" includes only the estate of a deceased stockholder. However, if stock is held by a guardian for an individual under a disability, other than bankruptcy, the corporation is not disqualified. The minor or other person for whom the stock is held by the guardian is considered as the individual stockholder. Rev.Rul. 66–266. The bankruptcy estate of a bankrupt stockholder is considered a new (and impermissible) stockholder; a Chapter XI receiver, however, does not displace a stockholder's ownership. CHM Co. (T.C.1977).

(c) *Only One Class of Stock.* The corporation may not have more than one class of stock. § 1371(a)(4). The Regulations state that only issued and outstanding stock is to be considered and that the outstanding shares must be identical with respect to the rights and interest which they convey in control, dividend rights and liquidation preferences. However, separate classes of stock (under state law) which differ only in that each class of stock has the right to elect members of the board of directors in a number proportionate to the number of shares in each class are not considered separate "classes" for purposes of Subchapter S. Regs. § 1.1371–1(g).

An issue frequently litigated in the past has been whether purported debt obligations issued by a thinly capitalized corporation were really stock of a separate class. The Service's original position, that purported debt obligations which were really an equity interest automatically resulted in a second class of stock, was, after some initial support, rejected by the courts. See e. g., Gamman (T.C.1966). Amended Regulations, § 1.1371–1(g), which provide that debt obligations which actually represent equity capital will "generally" constitute a second class of stock (unless owned in proportion to nominal stockholdings, in which case they could represent "contributions to capital") also have been rejected. See e. g., Amory Cotton Oil Co. (5th Cir. 1972). The Service announced in 1973 that pending the issuance of new regulations it will no longer litigate this issue. T.I.R. 1248. As of late 1980, new regulations had not been proposed.

(d) *No Ownership of Subsidiaries.* Another requirement is that the corporation not be a member of an affiliated group as defined by § 1504. § 1371(a) (introductory clause). Generally, this prevents an electing corporation from owning more than 80 percent of the voting and nonvoting stock of another corporation. (Having its own stock 80 percent owned by another corporation is already prevented by the requirement that stockholders be individuals, their estates, or certain trusts.) An exception exists if the subsidiary has never begun business and has no taxable income. This permits a corporation to reserve its corporate name in other states by establishing shell subsidiaries in those states. § 1371(d); Regs. § 1.1371–1(c)(2).

§ 3. Procedure for Making the Election

The method of making the election is described in § 1372 and the Regulations thereunder. The corporation must file a statement of election and consents thereto by its stockholders during the first 75 days of the taxable year for which the election is to be effective or at any time during the preceding taxable year. § 1372(c)(1). The Regulations provide that the taxable year of a new corporation begins when the corporation has stockholders or acquires assets or begins doing business, whichever first occurs. Regs. § 1.1372–2(b). Once made, the election need not be renewed annually since it remains effective for subsequent years. If an election is made for a taxable year after the 75th day of that year, it will not be valid for that year but will be treated as made for the following year.

§ 4. Termination

The election may be terminated by voluntary action of all the stockholders, by a new stockholder affirmatively refusing to consent to the election, or automatically by the corporation ceasing to be a small business corporation or having excessive foreign or passive investment income. § 1372(e). In the first case, the corporation under

§ 1372(e)(2) may "revoke" the election by filing a statement indicating its desire to revoke along with consents from all stockholders. If the statement is filed during the first month of the taxable year, it will normally be effective for the entire taxable year and for all subsequent years. A revocation cannot be effective, however, for the first taxable year during which the election is effective. Regs. § 1.1372–4(c).

Beginning in 1977, a new stockholder may terminate Subchapter S status by affirmatively refusing to consent to the election. The refusal must be filed within 60 days after the date on which he acquired the stock. In the case of an executor or administrator of a decedent the refusal must be filed within 60 days after the executor or administrator qualifies or within 60 days of the last day of the taxable year of the corporation during which the decedent died, whichever is earlier. Prior to 1977, the election was terminated unless the new stockholder affirmatively consented; the Tax Reform Act of 1976 shifted the burden of this requirement to prevent inadvertent disqualifications.

Automatic termination of the election occurs if (a) the electing corporation ceases to meet the "small business corporation" definition of § 1371 (a), or (b) the corporation derives more than 80 percent of its gross receipts from foreign sources,

§ 1372(e) (4), or more than 20 percent of its gross receipts in the form of "passive investment income," § 1372(e) (5). An exception from the passive investment income limitation exists for the electing corporation's first two years of operation if passive investment income is less than $3,000. § 1372(e) (5) (B).

These rules restrict gross receipts, as distinguished from gross income. The Regulations define gross receipts to be the total amount received or accrued by the corporation in computing taxable income without reduction for costs, deductions, etc. However, for purposes of the passive income limitation, gross receipts from the sale or exchange of stock or securities are taken into account only to the extent of gains therefrom. Amounts received under § 331 upon complete liquidation of a corporation are excluded from gross receipts if the corporation owned more than 50 percent of each class of the stock of the liquidating corporation. The Regulations also specify that amounts received as a loan, repayment of a loan, contributions to capital, issuance by a corporation of its own stock, or nontaxable sales or exchanges (other than one to which § 337 applies) will not be included in gross receipts. Regs. § 1.1372–4(b) (5) (iv).

The limitation on the amount of passive investment income requires that a Subchapter S corporation derive its income primarily from operating rather than investment activities. Passive investment income includes rents, royalties, dividends, interest, annuities, and profits from transfers of stock or securities. In the case of rental income, if "significant services" are rendered to the occupant by the corporation, payments received by it will not constitute "rents" for determining passive income. Regs. § 1.1372–4(b)(5)(vi). Thus, income from operation of a boarding house or hotel would not produce passive investment income. The IRS position is that the "significant services" exception exists only for rents. Thus, interest received by a loan company or gains on the sale of stock by a broker will be counted as "passive income." Valley Loan Ass'n (D.Colo. 1966); Zychinski (8th Cir. 1974).

The tax consequences of a voluntary revocation of the election differ significantly from the consequences resulting from an automatic termination. A voluntary revocation can be effective for a given taxable year only if made during the first month of that year; a revocation filed later in the year will be effective for the following year. On the other hand, the effect of an automatic termination (or affirmative refusal of a new stockholder to consent to the election) is retroactive and will disqualify the corporation for the entire year during which the termination occurred. Therefore if stockholders feel uncertain about the desirability of the election at the beginning of the year, they could maintain the election and if events prove that the election is disadvantageous, the stockholders could "trigger" termination by, for example, selling or giving a share of stock to a new stockholder who would thereafter affirmatively refuse to consent to the election; the transfer, of course, must have "economic reality", e. g., not be made with an understanding that the stock be returned on request, as in Hook (T.C.1972). It is generally believed that a "bona fide" gift of one share for the purpose of terminating the election will suffice, see 6 P–H Fed. Taxes 1980 ¶ 33,373; *Hook* specifically did not reach the question whether an economically real transfer for the sole purpose of terminating the election would be effective.

Because a minority shareholder could possibly break the election through a gift of one share to his child who would affirmatively refuse to consent, even though a majority of stockholders wanted the election to remain in effect, stockholder agreements aimed at preventing such transfers of stock, e. g., a right of first refusal, are normally adopted by electing corporations.

Both voluntary and automatic termination present the common disadvantage that a new election cannot normally be made for five years. § 1372(f). Disqualification extends to any "successor corporation," defined by the Regulations to be a corporation with substantially the same assets as the old corporation or one with 50 percent or more of the stock owned by the same persons who owned 50 percent of the stock of the old corporation. Consent to a new election before the end of the five year period may be given by the Commissioner, but the Regulations make it clear that obtaining it will be difficult unless 50 percent of the corporation's stock is owned by persons who were not stockholders during the termination year, or the event causing termination was outside the control of the corporation and its controlling stockholders (e. g., a minority stockholder's transfer of stock to a nonqualifying trust). Regs. § 1.1372–5.

§ 5. Treatment of the Electing Corporation

Generally, electing corporations are not subject to the corporate income tax. § 1372(b)(1). Although exemption from the tax of § 11 is the major benefit, Subchapter S corporations also are exempt from the accumulated earnings tax of § 531 and the personal holding company tax of § 541. A limited exception, discussed below, is made for certain capital gains realized by the corporation.

Prior to 1966, a corporation anticipating a large capital gain could elect under Subchapter S, realize and distribute the capital gain, then terminate its election in the following year. This procedure avoided a capital gains tax at the corporate level and substituted capital gains tax for ordinary income tax at the stockholder level. Section 1378 was added in 1966 to limit this abuse by imposing a corporate tax if the net capital gain exceeds $25,000 and also exceeds 50 percent of the corporation's taxable income and such taxable income itself exceeds $25,000. The tax imposed is the lower of (1) 28 percent (the § 1201 (a) rate) of the net capital gain over $25,000, or (2) an amount equal to the tax which would have been imposed by § 11 on the corporation's taxable income if the corporation had not elected under Subchapter S. (The tax therefore will never exceed the tax that would have been imposed in the absence of an election.) Since § 1378 is intended to limit "one-shot" elections, exceptions are provided for new businesses (during the first four years of existence provided that an election has been in effect for each of its taxable years, § 1378(c)(2)) and for corporations that have maintained Subchapter S status for the previous three years. § 1378(c)(1). An exception to the exceptions exists for certain property with a substituted basis received by the electing corporation from a nonelecting corporation. § 1378(c) (3).

The minimum tax, §§ 56–58, is generally not applicable to Subchapter S corporations; instead the corporation's items of tax preference are apportioned pro rata among the stockholders. However, in the case of capital gains, § 58(d)(2) provides that the minimum tax is imposed on a Subchapter S corporation to the extent the gains are subject to tax under § 1378.

The corporation's "taxable income," while not important to it except for determining tax under § 1378, is important to its stockholders whose income is determined by the character (in certain circumstances) and the amount of such income. The corporation's taxable income is computed in the normal way except that several deductions are disallowed. The intercorporate dividends received deduction, §§ 243–246, is disallowed, as is a deduction for net operating losses under § 172 (including carrybacks to nonelecting years and carryovers from nonelecting years). § 1373(d). Net capital losses may be carried forward 5 years under § 1212(a)(1)(B) to offset future capital gains, but may not be carried back, § 1212(a)(3). Subchapter S corporations are also subject to a number of restrictions on the timing or amount of certain deductions added by the Tax Reform Act of 1976 to limit the use of "tax shelters," e. g., § 465 which limits loss deductions from all business and investment activities other than real estate to the amount of the investment "at risk" and § 280 which requires capitalization of certain costs incurred in the production of films, records, books, and similar property.

The Service takes the position that election of Subchapter S status is a disposition of § 38 property and may trigger recapture of the investment credit. Regs. § 1.47–4(b) provides a relief procedure if the corporation and its stockholders agree to notify IRS of any disposition of the property and to be jointly liable for the payment of any tax due as a result of the disposition.

§ 6. Treatment of Stockholders

(a) *In General.* Actual distributions to stockholders out of an electing corporation's e & p receive dividend treatment as would a distribution by a nonelecting corporation (except that the dividend exclusion, § 116, does not apply to actual or constructive distributions out of current e & p, § 1375(b), for the policy reason that there is no "double taxation" of such earnings). The major difference resulting from the election is that stockholders of the electing corporation on the last day of the corporation's taxable year must include in their income the amount they would have received as a dividend if the electing corporation had made a pro rata distribution of all "undistributed taxable income" ("UTI") for that year. § 1373(b). UTI for the year is defined by 1373(c) as taxable income (with § 1373 (d) modifications) minus dividends paid in cash

(i. e., not in other property) out of current e & p
(and minus any corporate minimum tax or § 1378
(a) capital gain tax). (Taxable income is computed under § 1373(d) without the § 172 net
operating loss deduction and without special corporate deductions such as the § 243 dividends received deduction).

Stockholders increase their basis in their stock
by an amount equal to this constructive distribution. § 1376. This has an effect similar to an
actual dividend distribution followed by a reinvestment of the amount received. Once this income has been taxed, it is regarded as "previously taxed income" ("PTI") and may, in certain
limited circumstances, be distributed tax-free in
subsequent years. § 1375(d).

Example: A and B are the two equal stockholders of Z Corp., a Subchapter S corporation.
A and B each have a basis of $10,000 in their Z
Corp. stock. In 1979, Z Corp. has current e & p
of $50,000 but distributes only $10,000 to A and
$15,000 to B. A includes in income not only the
$10,000 actually distributed to him but also his
pro rata share of UTI, i. e., $15,000, and increases
his basis in his stock to $25,000. B likewise re-
ports income of $25,000 and increases his basis to
$20,000. On these facts, Z Corp. has $25,000 of
PTI, $15,000 of which is A's share and $10,000 of
which is B's share.

(b) *Pass-through of Net Capital Gains.* A stockholder's pro rata share of net capital gains, to the extent of the corporation's taxable income (or current e & p, whichever is lower) for the year, is treated by the stockholder as long term capital gain whether distributed or not. § 1375 (a).

Example: In 1979, A Corp., a Subchapter S corporation for the last five years, realizes a $100,000 long-term capital gain. A Corp. has $50,000 of accumulated e & p and $20,000 of taxable income (and current e & p) for the year. (Aside from the capital gain, A Corp. operated at a loss.) $50,000 is distributed to the stockholders of A. The stockholders of A treat only $20,000 of the distribution as capital gain, and $30,000 of the distribution is taxable as a dividend. See Regs. § 1.1375–1(f), *Example (2).*

(c) *Pass-through of Net Operating Losses.* One of the most important and attractive features of Subchapter S status is the pass-through of net operating losses to the stockholders. Stockholders may use these current losses as an ordinary loss deduction in computing their individual adjusted gross income. § 1374(a), (b). Any unused excess is carried back three years and the remainder carried forward for 7 years (or the stockholder may elect to forego the carryback) under the net operating loss provisions of § 172.

Just as the stockholder's share of UTI increases his basis in his stock, his share of operating losses reduces the basis of his stock. § 1376(b). If the basis of his stock is exhausted, losses then reduce the basis of any corporate indebtedness held by the stockholder. Once the basis of both is exhausted the stockholder can no longer deduct his share of losses; unless he is willing to make an additional stock or debt investment in the corporation before the end of its taxable year, the stockholder loses these deductions forever.

Unlike a stockholder's share of UTI, which passes through at the end of the corporation's taxable year, his share of losses is allocated on a daily basis. § 1374(c)(1). Thus, losses, unlike UTI, cannot be shifted at year's end by a transfer of stock.

(d) *Distribution of PTI*. As mentioned earlier, a stockholder's PTI may be distributed tax-free to him in later years. § 1375(d). However, the Regulations impose severe restrictions on such distributions. Only distributions in cash, in excess of current e & p, qualify. Also, the right to receive distributions of PTI is personal and cannot be transferred with the stock. Moreover, if the Subchapter S election terminates, PTI can no longer be withdrawn tax-free.

Because these restrictions tend to lock in PTI, many Subchapter S corporations distribute current earnings in cash each year to avoid creation of PTI. Since a small business may require reinvestment of earnings, stockholders may return the funds to the corporation in the form of loans. However, there is a danger that the Service may "collapse" the transaction to characterize it as a distribution of property (a debt obligation), which does not reduce UTI. See e. g., DeTreville (4th Cir. 1971) (an insufficient funds check which stockholder endorsed back to the corporation was not a cash distribution). An additional problem is that the amount of the distribution needed to prevent creation of UTI may not be known at the close of the year. Section 1375(f), for the most part, eliminates this problem by providing that all distributions made by the 15th day of the third month following the close of a taxable year (the due date for a corporate tax return) to persons who were stockholders during that year shall be treated as distributions during that year.

A distribution of PTI may take place only during a year in which a valid Subchapter S election is in effect. A stockholder receiving such a distribution treats it as a return of capital, first reducing his basis and any excess being taxed as a capital gain. Distributions of PTI do not reduce the corporation's e & p. Regs. § 1.1375–4(a).

For purposes of determining whether a distribution is out of PTI the corporation's current e &

p are computed without regard to § 312(k) (which requires the use of straight line depreciation in computing e & p). § 1377(d).

Example: Sub S Corp. has for the current year $10,000 of taxable income, $12,000 of current e & p (the $2,000 difference representing the excess of fast depreciation over straight line which, under § 312(k), is disregarded in computing e & p) and $1,000 of PTI, i. e., UTI previously taxed to A, Sub S Corp.'s sole stockholder. In the current year Sub S Corp. distributes $12,000 in cash to A. Solely for purposes of determining whether Sub S Corp. has distributed PTI, its current e & p are considered to be $10,000. Accordingly, $1,000 of the amount distributed is treated as a distribution of PTI (the lesser of PTI or the amount in excess of current e & p distributed) and $11,000 is treated as a distribution of current e & p and is taxed as a dividend. The remaining $1,000 of undistributed current e & p increases accumulated e & p. If no actual distribution takes place, A has $10,000 of ordinary income, his PTI account is increased by $10,000 and the accumulated e & p of Sub S Corp. are increased by $2,000. Cf. Senate Report on § 901 of the Tax Reform Act of 1976.

(e) *Allocation of Income Among Family Members.* Section 1375(c) gives the IRS authority to allocate the dividends (actual and constructive) of a Subchapter S corporation from one stockholder to another if the stockholders are members of the same family and the Service determines such allocation is necessary in order to reflect the value of services rendered to the corporation by such stockholders. For purposes of § 1375(c), the family of a stockholder includes only his spouse, ancestors, and lineal descendants. This limits the shifting of income within a family through the payment of inadequate salaries. It can be avoided, however, if the family member receiving the inadequate salary is not a stockholder.

INDEX

References are to Pages

INDEX

[*351*]

INDEX
References are to Pages

[*357*]

[*358*]

INDEX

INDEX

References are to Pages

INDEX

†